Retrieving Aristotle in an Age of Crisis

SUNY series in Ancient Greek Philosophy

Anthony Preus, editor

Retrieving Aristotle in an Age of Crisis

DAVID ROOCHNIK

SUNY PRESS

Cover image of the tree: © Olaru Radian-Alexandru/Bigstockphoto.com
Cover image of the DNA: © Scott R. Bowlin/Bigstockphoto.com

Published by State University of New York Press, Albany

Printed in the United States of America

For information, contact State University of New York Press, Albany, NY
www.sunypress.edu

Production by Diane Ganeles
Marketing by Fran Keneston

Library of Congress Cataloging-in-Publication Data

Roochnik, David.
Retrieving Aristotle in an age of crisis / David Roochnik.
p. cm. — (SUNY series in ancient Greek philosophy)
Includes bibliographical references (p.) and index.
ISBN 978-1-4384-4518-2 (pbk. : alk. paper)
ISBN 978-1-4384-4519-9 (hardcover : alk. paper)
1. Aristotle. I. Title.

B485.R565 2012
185—dc23 2012005001

10 9 8 7 6 5 4 3 2 1

Contents

Acknowledgments	vii
A Note to the Reader	ix
Prologue	xi
Introduction: Why Aristotle Matters.	1
Chapter One: The Stars Are Eternal.	17
I.1: There Are Only Three Dimensions.	17
I.2: Threeness Determines Wholeness.	21
I.3: There Are Four Elements.	30
I.4: Elements Naturally Move to Their Natural Place.	31
I.5: The Circle Is Perfect.	35
I.6: The Body Moving in Circular Orbit Is Eternal.	37
I.7: History Is More or Less Bunk.	38
I.8: Religion Bears Witness to the Truth.	42
Chapter Two: Nature is Purpose.	45
II.1: Teleology Is Good Science.	45
II.2: Intelligent Design Isn't All Stupid.	54
II.3: Some Beings Are Natural; Others Are Not.	57
II.4: Form Is Nature More than Matter.	60
II.5: Form Is More Divine than Matter.	63
II.6: Nature Is Hierarchical.	67
II.7: To Understand Nature, Study Its Best Examples.	69
II.8: The Finite Is Better than the Infinite.	71
II.9: Good Science Appreciates Things as They Are.	77

Chapter Three: Being Is Good. 81
III.1: Metaphysics Is Onto-Theology. 81
III.2: There Are Substances Out There. 84
III.3: We Know a Substance When We See One. 92
III.4: God Is Alive and Good. 98
III.5: To Stand Firmly on the Side of Life. 109

Chapter Four: Truth Is Easy. 115
IV.1: If the Eye Were an Animal, Vision Would Be Its Soul. 115
IV.2: The World Is Nourishing. 118
IV.3: Perceiving Is Like Eating. 119
IV.4: We Are Wrong More Often than Not. 131
IV.5: Thinking Is Like Perceiving (Which Is Like Eating). 136
IV.6: We Can Say What We Think. 142
IV.7: We "Truth" the World. 144

Chapter Five: The Theoretical Life Is Divine. 149
V.1: Life Is Meaningful. 150
V.2: Happiness Is Objective. 153
V.3: Good Life Comes from Good Habits. 158
V.4: Freedom Isn't All It's Cracked Up To Be. 162
V.5: Moral Evaluation Requires Stories. 165
V.6: Smart Moral People Are Better than Dumb Moral People. 167
V.7: Lack-of-Leisure Is for the Sake of Leisure. 173
V.8: *Theôria* Is Not "Contemplation." 178

Chapter Six: Enough Is Enough. 189
VI.1: The Best City Needs the Best Life. 191
VI.2: The Practical Life Is Not the Best. 193
VI.3: Natural Slavery Is Justified. 196
VI.4: A Woman's Place Is in the Home. 201
VI.5: Small, but Not Too Small, Is Beautiful. 207
VI.6: War Is for the Sake of Peace. 213
VI.7: Philosophy Cures. 213

Epilogue 217

Notes 219

Bibliography 233

Index 237

Acknowledgments

I am grateful to several generations of Boston University students who allowed me to think through Aristotle's writings with them. In particular, I would like to thank Nir Eisikovits, who, as a member of a seminar that took place more than a decade ago, helped me to understand better what it is I find so profoundly attractive in the Philosopher's thought.

I am grateful to the Humanities Center of Boston University for granting me a semester of research leave during which I wrote the first draft of this book. I am fortunate to have had two fine colleagues and friends who also doubled as chair of my department during the years of preparation it took to write this book: Charles Griswold and Dan Dahlstrom.

The University of Chicago Press generously allowed me to reprint a portion of my article "What is *Theoria? Nicomachean Ethics,* Book 10.7–8," which appeared in *Classical Philology* (©2009 by the University of Chicago), as did the *Review of Metaphysics* for "Aristotle's Defense of the Theoretical Life: Comments on *Politics* VII" (2008).

Mr. I-Kai Jeng provided me with valuable editorial assistance and prepared the index for this book. Any mistakes that remain are surely my own.

A Note to the Reader

Like Aristotle, I begin many a sentence with "we." This pronoun is meant to refer to the reader and myself. I use it on two occasions. First, I often discuss what I take to be experiences we all share. So, for example, we experience physical bodies as having three dimensions and time as being constituted by a past, present, and future. Second, sometimes "we" refers to us as residents of contemporary culture who hold certain views and general conceptions that have been taken for granted since the advent of the modern period (conceived as around 1600). So, for example, we know that the earth orbits the sun. My use of the pronoun may sometimes seem presumptuous. If so, the reader is invited to challenge it. Indeed, a goal of this book is precisely to make us wonder who "we" are.

The genius of Aristotle's thought is found in its comprehensiveness and its coherence. He thinks through the entire world from top (the stars) to bottom (the earth). As a result, no part of his work, no individual argument or theoretical bit, can be fully appreciated without an understanding of where it fits in the whole. For this reason, this book must, at least in summary fashion, address the entirety of his worldview. I urge readers to defer judgment on any particular item that is discussed until they are able to locate it within the context of the whole thought. As a guide to doing this, I will frequently point to later sections of the book by using the symbol (>). So, for example, to refer ahead to chapter 3, section 5, the reader will see (>III.5). To offer reminders of what has already been discussed, I will use the symbol (<).

As Aristotle scholars will quickly realize, I sometimes devote a short section to a topic that would require a long book to be fully addressed. To compensate for such brevity, in the endnotes I often cite scholarly works that offer accounts far more elaborate than my own. I also point the reader to background material and occasionally discuss textual points that are particularly controversial. It is not necessary, however, to turn to these endnotes in order to follow the book's argument. The body of the text can stand on its own, and a knowledge of Aristotelian scholarship is not required to understand it.

Unless otherwise noted, translations of Aristotle are my own. Included in the Bibliography are the Greek texts that were used as well as English translations that I have consulted. I have consistently rendered the titles of Aristotle's works into English, rather than into Latin. So, for example, instead of *De Caelo* I opt for *On the Heavens.* All spellings of Greek words are phonetical. The Greek η (êta) is rendered by "ê" and ω (omega) by "ô." All lexical information comes from the Liddell-Scott *Greek-English Lexicon.* Quotations are typically followed by a parenthesis containing the standard pagination and line numbering of the 1831 edition of Immanuel Bekker.

This book builds on and borrows its title from an earlier work, *Retrieving the Ancients: An Introduction to Greek Philosophy* (Blackwell, 2004). Even though its chapter on Aristotle was but one of four, it became clear to me in writing it that the entire book was Aristotelian in spirit. The present book substantially elaborates much of what was asserted in chapter 4 of that work. As a result, there are a few pages of overlap between them, all of which are noted.

Prologue

While it took years of study to prepare to write this book, its immediate inspiration came from attending a performance of Tom Stoppard's play *Arcadia*. One scene in particular, the fifth in Act 2, convinced me to write it as I have (namely, as a polemic). It features Bernard, a scholar of romantic poetry who is doing some research on Lord Byron. In the ferocious speech that follows, he is responding to a comment made by Valentine, a biologist who is mathematically analyzing the fluctuations in the grouse population at his home, Sidley Park in England. He has just described Bernard's own research as "trivial." Also on stage is Hannah, also a literary scholar but one with a greater commitment to historical accuracy than Bernard seems to have. They are antagonists throughout the play. Bernard wrote a scathing review of Hannah's best-selling biography of Lady Caroline Lamb and has just informed her that there was an error on the dust jacket of her book. (It contained a drawing of Byron and a woman falsely identified there as being Lamb.) In turn, Hannah sums up her views of Bernard's beloved romantic period by calling it a "sham":

"It's what happened to the Enlightenment, isn't it? A century of intellectual rigor turned in on itself. A mind in chaos suspected of genius" (I.2).

Finally, there is Chloë, Valentine's sister, who is enamored of Bernard.

> Bernard: Oh, you're going to zap me with penicillin and pesticides. Spare me that and I'll spare you the bomb and aerosols. But don't confuse progress with perfectibility. A great poet is always timely. A great philosopher is an urgent need. There's no rush for Isaac Newton. We were quite happy with Aristotle's cosmos. Personally, I preferred it. Fifty-five crystal spheres geared to God's crankshaft is my idea of a satisfying universe. I can't think of anything more trivial than the speed of light. Quarks, quasars—big bangs, black holes—who gives a shit? How did you people

con us out of all that status? All that money? And why are you pleased with yourselves?

Chloë: Are you against penicillin, Bernard?

Bernard: Don't feed the animals. (*Back* to Valentine) I'd push the lot of you over a cliff myself. Except the one in the wheelchair, I think I'd lose the sympathy vote before people had time to think it through.

Hannah: (*Loudly*) What the hell do you mean, the dust-jacket?

Bernard: (*Ignoring her*) If knowledge isn't self-knowledge it isn't doing much, mate. Is the universe expanding? It is contracting? Is it standing on one leg and singing 'When Father Painted the Parlour?' Leave me out. I can expand my universe without you. 'She walks in beauty, like the night of cloudless climes and starry skies, and all that's best of dark and bright meet in her aspect and her eyes.' There you are, he wrote it after coming home from a party. (*With offensive politeness.*) What is it that you're doing with grouse, Valentine, I'd love to know?

(*Valentine stands up and it is suddenly apparent that he is shaking and close to tears.*)

Bernard "preferred" Aristotle's cosmos to the expanding universe of contemporary physics for, he says, "we were quite happy" with it. Of course, he is wrong, at least if his "we" refers to his companions, for neither Valentine nor Hannah shares his affection for the old philosopher's "fifty-five crystal spheres."[1] Nonetheless, he explains his preference to them when he declares, "If knowledge isn't self-knowledge it isn't doing much, mate." Apparently, Aristotle's cosmology somehow can teach us about ourselves, something the quarks and quasars of mathematical physics, which conned "us out of all that status," cannot do.

Although Stoppard surely has sympathy for Bernard's views, it would be a mistake simply to attribute them to the playwright. For he makes it abundantly clear that Bernard is a foolish man. He has convinced himself that one Ezra Chater, a minor literary figure, was killed by Byron in a duel after the poet had seduced his wife, and this was why Byron left England for Lisbon in 1810. There is a bit of circumstantial evidence for this hypothesis, but Bernard leaps to his conclusion far too fast. After he publishes the results of his research and receives accolades for what he himself describes as "the most sensational literary discovery of the century," Hannah calmly informs him that in fact Chater died in Martinique, the victim of a monkey bite. As a result, Bernard is, as he puts it, "fucked" (II.7). Stoppard has thus put this bitingly angry, revelatory, and spellbinding speech, and in particular his praise of Aristotle, into the mouth of a man whom Hannah accurately describes as "arrogant, greedy and reckless" (II.5). And, as his dead-wrong hypothesis about Byron and Chater shows, he is foolish as well.[2]

The title and setting of *Arcadia* disclose an analogous sort of foolishness. As Hannah explains, until 1740 Sidley Park contained a formal Italian garden, which means it was a masterpiece of geometrically precise design. It was transformed by Capability Brown, who imposed on it the form of an English landscape garden whose serpentine lines and asymmetrical arrangements of trees were designed above all else to embody a pastoral ideal and thereby to look "natural." In 1810 Sidley Park was changed again, this time into a picturesque garden, with its carefully crafted evocation of the wildness of nature and its deliberately constructed ruins. Hannah explains the first two steps of this progression.

> Hannah: There's an engraving of Sidley Park in 1730 that makes you want to weep. Paradise in the age of reason. By 1760 everything had everything had gone—the topiary, pools and terraces, fountains, an avenue of limes—the whole sublime geometry was ploughed under by Capability Brown. The grass went from the doorstep to the horizon and the best box hedge in Derbyshire was dug up for the ha-ha so that the fools could pretend they were living in God's countryside (I.2).

Walking the paths of Sidley Park in 1800, or Central Park in New York City today, "fools" may think they are looking at nature. Indeed, for centuries the pastoral ideal championed by Capability Brown has shaped our notion of how a natural setting should look. In fact, however, the design of the English landscape garden was based on conventions borrowed from painting. As Hannah again explains, "English landscape was invented by gardeners imitating foreign painters who were invoking classical authors" (I.2). The classical author she has in mind is Virgil, who in his *Eclogues* gave voice to the pastoral fantasy of Arcadia.[3]

Just as "fools" think Central Park is more natural than the buildings that flank it, so too is Bernard foolish in willfully preferring Aristotle's worldview, at the heart of which is the philosopher's supreme confidence that with his naked eye and his power of reason he can objectively study nature itself. The scientific revolution dismantled that confidence, and ever since Aristotelian cosmology has been dead as a doornail. And yet, at least in the performance I attended, Bernard's speech was the showstopper.

Tom Stoppard's *Arcadia* convinced me to try to defend Aristotle's view of the world, even though it requires running the risk of becoming foolish. For, as we all know, the Philosopher was wrong about much. He was a geocentrist who thought that the stars, weightless and eternal, orbited the earth in perfect circles and constituted the outermost sphere of a finite cosmos. He was a biologist who, like a child, thought that nature was purposive and so did nothing in vain. He argued on behalf of a living "god" that was no more than "thought thinking itself" yet also was the motionless mover of the entire world. Unlike those of us who know how the brain and nervous system actually work, he believed that objects in the world were quite like what our senses tell us they are: really red or blue, really hot or cold or wet or dry. He was an ethicist who believed that human life was meaningful and happiness attainable, and a political theorist who argued in defense of natural slavery and the subordination of women. Thus we are confident that on most counts he was as dead wrong as Bernard was about Ezra Chater.

Nonetheless, this book defends Aristotle, and I would be delighted if I have invested it with even a fraction of the vulgar ferocity that Bernard brings to the stage. It argues that even today, in fact especially today, mired as we are in a crisis of our own making—one in which, to quote again from *Arcadia*, "[w]e have found all the mysteries and lost all the meaning" (II.7)—it is both possible and reasonable to prefer Aristotle's world. For it is truly "satisfying" and full of meaning and so it passes the test that Bernard insists modern physics fails: "if knowledge isn't self-knowledge it isn't doing much, mate." Aristotle gives a rational account, a theory, of the world from top to bottom and it does much: it teaches us about the world in which *we* actually live. Compared to that, the speed of light really is "trivial."

The task ahead may now seem absurd: what we take to be the palpably false convictions of the philosopher will be defended. But at least consider the following, thoroughly non-Aristotelian, justification of it. In the second of his *Meditations on First Philosophy* Descartes engages in what today would be called a "thought experiment."

> Thus I will suppose not a supremely good God, the source of truth, but rather an evil genius, as clever and deceitful as he is

> powerful, who has directed his entire efforts to misleading me. I will regard the heavens, the air, the earth, colors, shapes, sounds, and all external things as nothing but the deceptive games of my dreams, with which he lays snares for my credulity. I will regard myself as having no hands, no eyes, no flesh, no blood, no senses, but as nevertheless falsely believing that I possess all these things.[4]

Descartes conjures up this wild fantasy as an epistemic tool, for his goal is to discover an indubitable truth-claim that can withstand all skeptical doubts and any machination of the "evil genius." He believes he has succeeded.

> But there is a deceiver (I know not who he is) powerful and sly in the highest degree, who is always purposely deceiving me. Then there is no doubt that I exist, if he deceives me. And deceive me as he will, he can never bring it about that I am nothing so long as I shall think that I am something. Thus it must be granted that, after weighing everything carefully and sufficiently, one must come to the considered judgment that the statement "I am, I exist" is necessarily true every time it is uttered by me or conceived in my mind.

Such thought experiments are now familiar. Philosophers have imagined a "twin-earth," which is exactly like our own with the one exception of having no water, and a universe that contains only two iron spheres each with a diameter of a mile.[5] If they are allowed to do this, then surely it is fair to indulge in the following scenario. Suppose that there were a humane "genius" as powerful as the biblical God, who directs his entire efforts to assuring the veracity of our ordinary perceptions of the world. So, for example, when we see (and say) that the sun rises in the East and sets in the West, we could be confident that it actually does traverse the sky. When we feel the air cooling our skin, it would be reasonable to infer that the air itself is cool. Because we regularly observe that the fires we light move upward, which is why we always place the match under the cigarette, we would be justified in asserting that it is in the nature of fire to move upward. We look down to see the earth and up to gaze at the stars, and that's exactly where they actually are: for the earth is the center of the world. All the "external things" of the world, then, would be explicable by us in the same terms in which we ordinarily encounter them. Thus does the genius instill within us the confidence to trust our ordinary perceptions and the language we use to describe and understand them.

In the grip of such a fantasy, the world, from top to bottom, would be comprehensible in human terms. In it we would be at home. This, what might be called the world of ordinary experience, is what Aristotle studies and about it he is consistently illuminating.

Let me be clear: Aristotle does not endorse this fantasy. He thinks of himself as straightforwardly studying and articulating the world itself, and not as performing any sort of thought experiment. Many readers, however, will not have this luxury, for we have lived too long in the grip of the Copernican revolution, the Lockean distinction between primary and secondary qualities, the rejection of teleological biology and its replacement with Darwin's theory of natural selection, the discovery that stars have histories and that the universe extends indefinitely beyond what we can see with our naked eye. For them, it is perhaps only as a thought experiment that the Aristotelian worldview can gain any traction. But if they let it sink in, and especially if they compare it to the thoroughly dehumanized universe of the Higgs boson, of big bangs and black holes, of geological time, neurons firing, and selfish genes hard at work—and to those many contemporary philosophers who are sure that the scientists know far more than they—they may come to sympathize with Bernard's advice: "don't confuse progress with perfectibility." For better or worse, we are human beings, and laying claim to the world as our own is a fundamental feature of our ordinary lives. In the name of self-knowledge this too deserves to be studied, and before it is too late.

An analogous thought experiment: imagine that we are scientists who must abide by the following rules. We are not permitted to use observational tools, such as microscopes or telescopes, or to perform experiments in the artificial environment of a laboratory. Instead, we are required to use only our naked eyes and our capacity to reason to make sense of the world. The results of our efforts would, I propose, approximate what Aristotle accomplishes in his work. He offers a full articulation and explanation of what we actually see.

Introduction

Why Aristotle Matters.

Ours is a time of crisis. The future is pregnant with catastrophic possibility. If the bombs go off, human culture as we know it will be wiped out. And if the bombs don't go off, this will be a first: a tool invented and mass produced, but never used. (Or rather, used but once and then put away for safekeeping). Even if the nuclear weapons remain quiet, the warming of the earth, caused by the relentless burning of carbon-based fuels, may do enough damage by itself. Cities could be swamped.

Bill McKibben, as alarmed by this latter possibility as anyone writing today, thinks that because so much carbon has already been spewed into our atmosphere, we no longer live on the earth, a planet whose unique and delicate balance of climatic conditions has allowed human life to flourish on its generous surface. We now live on EAARTH, the title of his recent book, which is a new, warmer place far less congenial to the civilization we call our own.[1] McKibben argues that the crisis is now: very quickly we must change our ways, before it is too late.

Skeptics will complain that McKibben's predictions are too dire. Even so, no rational person can deny the possibility that climate change will inflict enormous damage. And if it's not that, it could well be the poisoning of our oceans. We watched in horror when the Deepwater Horizon oil rig blew up and the earth began its copious bleed into the Gulf of Mexico. We are fearful that the fish on which human beings have fed for centuries are rapidly disappearing. Or, back on land, we worry that in the not too distant future more than half of the species of plants and animals could vanish and that the rainforests could go up in smoke.[2]

These are only the most blatant versions of the fear we have of a technological society devouring itself, of a Doctor Frankenstein who cannot control his monster. There are more subtle ones as well. The ubiquitous cells and miniaturized screens, the vast array of earphones, threaten to destroy the possibility of face-to-face communication and perhaps of friendship itself. Cybersex may supplant the friction of bodies in contact. The global economy, interconnected by fiber-optic cables and organized around airports, renders the notion of the local, of a place of our own, nearly obsolete. Few people live in a place anymore. If they do, they or their children will leave soon or watch their communities get swallowed by sprawl.

Then there is the gradual replacement of the soul by a brain understood to be a stew of chemicals energized by electrical impulses. Every day we learn more about how it works. And every day some aspect of what we used to think of as the "self" disappears.

Our mechanical ingenuity is fantastic. Our drugs allow us to remake bodies and reconfigure consciousness. At the end of the day, however, no one understands for what purpose we are reconfiguring. Some of us dread the time when we can choose our children's physical and mental attributes just as easily as we now choose the color of our socks.

We live in an age of crisis, with only a generation or two left to extricate us from the morass into which we are rapidly falling; only a generation or two left to save the world. And yet hordes of the well-heeled sleepwalk through their lives, dreaming only of real estate, exotic vacations, old wine, losing weight, and staying young. They visit their gyms daily, strap themselves onto machines, and peddle resolutely . . . to nowhere.

On the one hand, a tirade such as mine can be chalked up as the rant of a non-scientist who doesn't really understand how the brain works or what a computer model of the atmosphere actually entails. It can be dismissed as the soppy cliché of gray-haired nostalgia. On the other hand, anyone who doesn't take it seriously is irresponsible and just not paying attention.

My tirade is hardly original. Like a shadow, versions of it have trailed modern Western science and technology since its inception. Alexandre Koyré cites John Donne's "Anatomy of the World," written in 1611:

> . . . new Philosophy calls all in doubt,
> The element of fire is quite put out;
> The Sun is lost, and th'earth, and no mans wit
> Can well direct him where to looke for it.
> And freely men confesses that this world's spent,
> When in the Planets, and the Firmament
> They seeke so many new; then see that this
> Is crumbled out againe to his Atomies.
> 'Tis all in pieces, all coherence gone.[3]

Nor is the word "crisis" especially novel. In 1935 Edmund Husserl wrote "Philosophy and the Crisis of European Humanity," a lecture in which he expressed sentiments not too different from the ones animating this book. "The European nations are sick," he wrote. "Europe itself, it is said, is in crisis." Husserl offered a diagnosis: "I am certain that the European crisis has its roots in a misguided rationalism" that gave rise, beginning around 1600 in the work of Galileo, to mathematical physics and the technology it spawned. Commenting on a later scientific achievement, namely Einstein's theory of relativity, Husserl pinpointed what is misguided about European rationalism.[4] "Einstein's revolutionary innovations concern the formulae through which the idealized and naively objectified *physis* [nature] is dealt with. But how formulae in general, how mathematical objectification in general, receive meaning on the foundation of life and the intuitively given surrounding world—of this we learn nothing; and thus Einstein does not reform the space and time in which our vital life runs its course."[5]

The universe studied by mathematical physics tells us nothing about the "meaning" of our lives, about the space and time, the world, in which we live. It leaves no special room for ordinary human experience, for it is a science thoroughly purged of anthropomorphism. Indeed, liberation from a merely human perspective is the source of the enormous success, and the pride, of modern science. Consider what Spinoza, writing around 1670, had to say: "Men commonly suppose that all natural things act like themselves." Thus, to take the prime example, because men "do all things with an end [or purpose] in view; that is, they seek what is useful," they (falsely) believe that there are "final causes"—purposes, goals, ends—built into nature itself. For Spinoza this "teleological" conception of nature, which was basic to premodern or Aristotelian science, was no more than anthropomorphism run amok. Human beings project themselves onto the screen of a nonhuman universe, which in reality operates mechanically rather than purposively. They delude themselves into seeing what they want to see, namely a natural order that operates like themselves. But nature doesn't work that way. Teleology, according to Spinoza, was no more than a "misconception" that had hardened into "a superstition." The centuries spent looking for final causes had inhibited the search for real or "efficient" ones and so had stopped the progress of science dead in its tracks. In defiance of what was then traditional wisdom, Spinoza proudly declared that "nature has no fixed aim in view, and that all final causes are merely fabrications of men."[6] Freed from its pathetic search for purposes, scientific research was poised to penetrate into the workings of nature itself.

Consider another instance of anthropocentrism that modern science systematically debunked: geocentrism. For millennia before Copernicus, scientists and philosophers, as well as ordinary people, located the earth at the center of the world. Even if such a view today seems laughable, it actually makes good sense . . . if, that is, the world is viewed from a strictly human perspective and observed by means of sense perception. After all, from down here on what seems to be a stationary earth, with but the naked eye as our tool, we see the stars above. We watch the sun move across the sky from East to West each day and we speak of its rising and setting. From such a limited vantage point, it surely looks as if the earth is the center of the world. But geocentrism is, of course, silly from the non-anthropocentric perspective of modern astronomy. We know that, far from being the center of the universe, the earth is no more than one among untold many particle clusters moving through space.

The Darwinian revolution in biology also de-centered the human. No longer were the various species of animals conceived as Aristotle understood them, namely, as permanently distinct from one another and forming a hierarchy, a *scala naturae*, with humans, the only animals that think, located squarely at the top. Now we know that higher mammals and birds have brains that work in complicated ways that may approach thinking and that no species has an enduring ontological integrity of its own. Instead, the species are in gradual, chemical development, one from the other. With the genetic basis of evolution now better understood than Darwin could have dreamed, we know that the difference between a man and a mollusk is not as great as people had thought for many millennia. As Richard Dawkins puts it, "[a]n octopus is nothing like a mouse, and both are quite different from an oak tree. Yet in their fundamental chemistry they are rather uniform, and in particular the replicators that they bear, the genes, are basically the same kind of molecule in all of us—from bacteria to elephants."[7] Furthermore, we are today entirely confident that the biological world operates through the principles of natural selection, which is described by Dawkins as "the blind, unconscious, automatic process which Darwin discovered, and which we now know is the explanation for the existence and the *apparently* [my emphasis] purposeful form of all life." Appearances, the way the natural world seems to an ordinary human glance, are deceptive and tell us nothing about reality, for in fact nature "has no purpose in mind."[8]

The stripping away of teleology and all other anthropomorphic vestiges of Aristotelian philosophy by modern science, the de-centering of the human, is what provokes Tom Stoppard's character Bernard, just discussed in the Preface, to complain to a scientist in the room, "How did you people con us out of all that status?" In angry response, he opts for Aristotle: "We were quite happy with Aristotle's cosmos. Personally," he says, "I preferred it."

Bernard uses a key word. A "cosmos," Koyré tell us, is a "conception of the world as a finite, closed, and hierarchically ordered whole."[9] It is a conception fundamental to Aristotle's philosophy. In his "world"—which I henceforth take to be synonymous with "cosmos"—beings have their proper place. Chunky ones like rocks belong down here on earth; fire belongs up there in the heavens. Some beings are better than, ontologically superior to, others. The stars, for example, are made of a material not found here on earth. They are eternal and thus superior to everything located in the sub-lunar sphere. Here on earth, animals are "higher" than plants, which are higher than rocks and wood. And the human animal, the only one that strives to understand the world, is best of all. The world is a closed and "differentiated set of innerworldy places" populated by different kinds of beings that naturally fit in these places. It is an intelligible, orderly, and thus beautiful whole, and within its confines human beings find their home. By contrast, the universe studied by modern physics is, to cite Koyré again, "indefinite and even infinite . . . no longer united by natural subordination, but unified only by the identity of its ultimate and basic components and laws." The "scientific revolution" of the seventeenth century, which was a revolt against Aristotle and the scholastics who employed him in the service of their religion, is precisely "the story of the destruction of the Cosmos and the infinitization of the universe."

Modern science has discovered how natural things actually work instead of how they merely look to self-absorbed human beings who project their own earthly preoccupations onto a nonhuman screen. As a result, it has learned how to intervene into natural processes and unleash the energy latent within them. The result is power. Francis Bacon, writing in 1620, famously expressed the point: "Human knowledge and human power meet in one; for where the cause is not known, the effect cannot be produced. Nature to be commanded must be obeyed."[10] Descartes, writing in 1637 with the optimistic spirit intrinsic to the modern scientific project, elaborated and in so doing predicted the extraordinary ascent of what today we call neuroscience.

> It is possible to reach knowledge that will be of much utility in this life; and that instead of the speculative philosophy now taught in the schools [instead of a curriculum decisively shaped by Aristotle] we can find a practical one, by which, knowing the nature and behavior of fire, water, air, stars and the heavens, and all the other bodies which surround us, as well as we now understand the different skills of our workers, we can employ these entities for all the purposes for which they are suited, and

> so make ourselves master and possessors of nature. This would not only be desirable in bringing about the invention of an infinity of devices to enable us to enjoy the fruits of agriculture and all the wealth of the earth without labor, but even more so in conserving health, the principal good and the basis of all other goods in this life. For the mind is so dependent upon the humours and the condition of the organs of the body that if it is possible to find some way to make men in general wiser and more clever than they have been so far, I believe that it is in medicine that it should be sought. It is true that medicine at present contains little of such great value; but without intending to belittle it, I am sure that everyone, even among those who follow the profession, will admit that everything we know is almost nothing compared with what remains to be discovered, and that we might rid ourselves of an infinity of maladies of body as well as of mind, and perhaps also of the enfeeblement of old age, if we have sufficient understanding of the causes and of all the remedies which nature has provided.[11]

Becoming "masters and possessors of nature" requires power. But power is one thing, while "meaning" is quite another. Husserl complains that modern science, despite its technical advances, tells us nothing about how it "receives meaning." Even if today we know how to "rid ourselves of an infinity of maladies of body as well as of mind," even if molecular biology in tandem with the pharmaceutical industry has produced a vast number of effective medications, we do not know what it "means" to be healthy or sick. We don't really know what to do with ourselves.

Before going forward, this word "meaning" must be clarified. It has two senses. The first is linguistic and refers to "signification," as in "the meaning of the word 'hat' is a covering for the head." The second is "purpose" or "intent," as in "I meant to turn off the lights, but forgot to do so." In the common phrase "the meaning of life," these two senses are combined, for with it we are speaking about the purpose of life that can be signified. "Meaning" is intelligible purpose that can be explained and made sense of through language.

If the "book of nature," as Galileo famously put it, is written in "the characters of mathematics," then modern physics lacks the vocabulary to address the meaning of life.

This did not bother Spinoza. The truth, he said, "might have lain hidden from the human race through all eternity, had not mathematics, which deals not in the final causes, but the essence and properties of things, offered to men another standard of truth." Descartes is even more enthusiastic. "I was especially pleased with mathematics, because of the certainty and self-evidence of its proofs; but I did not yet see its true usefulness and, thinking it was good only for the mechanical arts, I was astonished that nothing more noble had been built on so firm and solid a foundation. On the other hand, I compared the ethical writings of the ancient pagans [principally Aristotle] to very superb and magnificent palaces built only on mud and sand."[12]

However useful the language of mathematics is for predicting the motions of material clumps, it can tell us nothing about the meaning of what Husserl calls the "space and time in which our vital life runs its course." By contrast, this is precisely what the "ethical writings" of ancient philosophers like Aristotle attempted to do.

Technology applies the results of the sciences. The physicists study the internal structure of the atom, and then the engineers design the machine to unleash its energy. The properties of petroleum become well understood, the geologists learn how to locate it underground, and the internal combustion engine gets its fuel. The geneticists determine the structure of the genome, and the pharmaceutical companies line up to manufacture drugs that can alter the workings of the human body. The science informing our technology is garnered through a study of the universe. From its perspective, the earth itself is no more than a speck. The crisis addressed in this book emerges because the scientific understanding of how things work at the level of the universe unleashes forces that can overwhelm the world. Nuclear power is the clearest example. We know how to tap into it, but there is not enough room down here on earth to use it safely. Modern science may be purged of the blinkers of anthropocentrism, but it is we *anthropoi* who will use and suffer from its technological applications down here on earth, which for better or worse is where we live.

From the beginning modern science has been attacked by what today is called the "religious right." The Bible tells a story in which God gave humanity a special place in His creation. Such a conception, from which human life gains its meaning, is jeopardized by the indefinitely extended, center-less universe of modern physics and, probably even more so, by the indifference of natural selection to the uniqueness of our species. This book also goes on the attack but it steers clear of religion. This is a philosophical work. But it is not a modern one. Instead, I turn back to Aristotle, once called "the Philosopher" by the scholars of the Middle Ages. It was Aristotle who shaped the curriculum of the first European universities and held a firm grip on the philosophical imagination of the West until roughly 1600. The dawn of modernity, as ushered in by thinkers like Galileo, Descartes,

Spinoza, Bacon, and Locke, was a frontal and successful assault on Aristotelianism. Hobbes (writing in 1651) sharply summarizes: "The natural philosophy of [the Greeks] was rather a dream than science, and set forth in senseless and insignificant language, which cannot be avoided by those that will teach philosophy without having first attained great knowledge in geometry. . . . Their moral philosophy is but a description of their own passions. . . . And I believe that scarce anything can be more absurdly said in natural philosophy than that which is now called *Aristotle's Metaphysics*; nor more repugnant to government, than much of that he hath said in his *Politics*; more ignorantly, than a great part of his *Ethics*."[13]

For Hobbes, Aristotelian philosophy is no more than a cosmic pipe dream of purposes. His language is "senseless" because it is ordinary Greek rather than a technical language modeled on mathematical formulae. His moral philosophy is no more than "a description of [our] own passions"; in other words, anthropomorphic claptrap. And his teaching on politics is "repugnant to government." For Hobbes and his mates, a new conception of European philosophy was sorely needed.

The revolutionaries won. With the possible exception of his ethics, Aristotle is dead as a doornail. Nonetheless, to paraphrase Bernard, personally I prefer Aristotle's cosmos. This book explains why. It defends Aristotle's natural science, metaphysics, politics, and ethics (all of which can summarily be termed his "philosophy"), and it does so in the hope of "saving the world."

I use this last phrase playfully and with an eye on two of its senses. The first is vaguely embarrassing. "Saving the world" is what the crusader, the Don Quixote, the moral fanatic, sets out to do. Nonetheless, I do not entirely disavow this intention. This book is polemical and argues for a thorough revision of the status quo. The second is more serious. Aristotle's philosophy is guided by the methodological principle of "saving the phenomena." "Phenomenon" is derived from the Greek word *phainomenon,* which means "that which appears or shows itself." Although Aristotle himself does not use this exact phrase, he is guided by the principle it expresses.[14] To explain by means of an example, consider Book VII of the *Nicomachean Ethics,* whose topic is "moral weakness" (*akrasia*).

The morally weak person falls victim to desires or passions that overturn the dictates of reason. As a result, he does something wrong even though he knows it to be wrong. Before providing his own analysis of moral weakness, Aristotle examines the views of his predecessor, Socrates, who held an extreme position on this issue: he denied that moral weakness even existed. For Socrates, all wrongdoing was caused by ignorance, not by weakness or a failure to act in ways the agent knows to be right. Aristotle immediately objects to this position because it "plainly conflicts with the phenomena" (1145b28). It certainly *seems* that people who know what they should do regularly fail to do it because they are too weak to resist the passion or desire that inclines them to act badly. Common sense tells us that some people will eat a third piece of cake even though they know it is detrimental to their health because they cannot resist doing so. Others cannot keep their hands off their neighbor's spouse even though they know adultery is wrong. And others yet, when they lose their temper, hit much harder than they know they should. All of them regret what they have done when the desire or passion has cooled and their heads have cleared.

Because the phenomena, our ordinary experience of the world, speak so loudly on behalf of the existence of moral weakness, Aristotle is inclined to affirm it. By his lights, a theory such as Socrates' that is so radically at odds with the phenomena is, for this reason alone, flawed. It is paradoxical, for it deviates from, stands "to the side of" (*para*), *doxa*, "opinion," "judgment," "belief," or more generally "the way things seem to be." In other words, the goal of Aristotelian theory is to save the world of ordinary experience, not destroy it. On the basis of the confidence he has in the epistemic value and evidentiary force of the phenomena, Aristotle objects to Socrates.

On the other hand, Socrates was a famously smart guy, and so the opinion he expressed on this issue was not a run-of-the-mill *doxa*. Instead, it was one of what Aristotle calls *ta endoxa*, "the reputable opinions." These are beliefs or opinions (*doxa*) that "seem true to everyone or to most people or to the wise, either to all of the wise or to most of the wise or to the best known and most reputable of the wise" (*Topics* 100b21–22).[15]

A reputable belief is actually a phenomenon in its own right, a constitutive element of ordinary human experience. What "everyone" or the "wise" say and believe about the world is part of the world.[16] For example, the vast majority of us would say that the many objects we see moving about from place to place are real. Thus, the argument of a philosopher like Parmenides, who altogether denied the reality of motion, and instead offered his version of ontological monism, is automatically suspect because it conflicts with the phenomena. If Parmenides were right, then the world that the vast majority of people take for granted would be a self-delusion.[17] On the basis of this sort of reasoning, Aristotle is convinced that the pronouncements of Socrates, well known as someone "wise," cannot simply be wrong. If he were, his *doxa* would have no epistemic value or evidentiary force. At the same time, in denying the reality of moral weakness, Socrates could not be entirely right. If he were, the phenomena would be contradicted.

So, Aristotle steers a middle course: Socrates was both right and wrong.

Aristotle's solution conceives of two modalities of knowledge. One is present when we have knowledge but are not actually using it. A reader of this book, for example, knows arithmetic, but she is not now performing a computation. When, however, she is asked to answer the question "Fifty-nine times 290 is what?," her knowledge of arithmetic will kick into gear and she will calculate the sum. In doing so she will have used the knowledge that, until faced with the problem, she merely possessed.

Equipped with these two senses of knowledge, Aristotle can maintain that Socrates was both right and wrong in stating that moral weakness was impossible. He was right when it comes to knowledge in the fully activated sense of being used but wrong when it comes to knowing in the sense of having knowledge but not using it. Only in the latter case is moral weakness possible.

By steering this middle way, Aristotle saves the phenomena. His theory of moral weakness pays heed to what appears obvious: people regularly know what they should do but fail to do it because they are overcome by desire or passion. It also incorporates the opinion of Socrates. The philosopher was not all wrong; his *doxa* remains intact.

Aristotle describes his own "phenomenological method" as follows: "It is necessary, just as in the other studies, to set down the phenomena (*tithentas ta phainomena*) and first of all to review the puzzles. In this way, the reputable beliefs (*ta endoxa*) about these affections will be shown; if not all the reputable beliefs then most and the most authoritative of them. For if the difficulties are dissolved and the reputable beliefs are left intact, then the showing will have been adequate" (*Nicomachean Ethics* 1145b2–7).[18]

The goal of Aristotelian "theorizing"—a word that derives from the Greek *theôrein*, "to look at," and is a crucial term in his vocabulary (>II.3, V.8)—is to make manifest, to bring to light, what shows itself in ordinary, linguistically saturated experience. Such an enterprise is anthropocentric only in taking its bearings from the perspective of, and in this sense being centered upon, the human being. This version of anthropocentrism must be distinguished from two others. Aristotle does not, for example, maintain that "everything has a value or is good only in relation to human beings."[19] Nor is Aristotle a relativist like Protagoras, who believed that because "human being is the measure of all things" it is impossible to attain knowledge of anything beyond the human.[20] Even if his theorizing is centered in the human, it always looks outward to the world that exists beyond ourselves. Indeed, Aristotle is best characterized as a "realist" who has "extraordinary confidence" in the adequacy of the human cognitive capacity "to tell us, fairly directly, about the most important causes in the world."[21] To explain, consider the following: "One should start from things that are 'known.' But this term has two meanings. First, there is what is known to us; second, there is what is known simply. Perhaps it is necessary for us to begin with what is known to us" (*Nicomachean Ethics* 1095b2–4).

The process of knowing begins with what is most readily known "to us." So, for example, the initial mode of our contact with the external world is through sense-perception. We sense that the flame is hot. Even if this perception tells us little about the nature of either fire or heat, and so as an epistemic beginning is "slight" (*Metaphysics* 1029b8) and "unclear" (*Physics* 184a19), in general perception is the proper beginning of inquiry. Furthermore, even when great advances in knowing have been made, the beginning is preserved rather than discarded or overturned. In other words, the progression from what is known to us to what is knowable simply or "by nature" is continuous. At its end, regardless of how sophisticated our theories have become, the testimony of our senses remains intact. The flame really is hot.

Aristotle summarizes: "learning comes to be for all of us through what is less known by nature and proceeds to what is more known by nature. . . . One must strive to know what is in general knowable by beginning with what is poorly known but is nonetheless known to oneself" (*Metaphysics* 1029b3–11).

To clarify the above by means of a sharp contrast, consider two of Aristotle's most trenchant critics. First is Descartes. His goal was to attain knowledge that was entirely certain and free from all doubt. In order to achieve this, he began by questioning all of his beliefs, especially those based upon his sense-perceptions. As discussed in the *Preface*, he imagined that there was an "evil genius" who devoted all his energies to deceiving human beings. By means of such an extreme thought experiment, Descartes could doubt even whether he had a body or whether there was a world outside of himself. He finally concluded that only one proposition could withstand such "hyperbolic" doubt: " 'I am, I exist' is necessarily true every time I utter it or conceive it in my mind." I cannot doubt that I exist, he argued, because in so doubting I am thinking that perhaps I do not exist. But it is "I" who is doing the doubting. Doubting is a kind of thinking, and thinking always has to have a "subject"; a thinker who thinks. Thus, even in doubting whether I exist I prove to myself that I do.[22]

Even if this argument is sound, it shows that "I" exist only as a "thinking thing," a being that thinks, for example, about its own existence. Whether "I" have a body or the external world also exists or any information gained through my senses is accurate remains unknown. As a result, reconnecting the "I"—the subject or the mind—and the world becomes Descartes's most pressing philosophical task.

Cartesian skepticism and his sort of "evil genius" thought experiment have long been used by modern philosophers as tools to call into question ordinary claims to knowledge. Even today they are obsessed with the mind–body or subject–world relationship, which for them remains the most intractable of problems. By contrast, Aristotle begins in trust. He faces no mind–body problem, and it does not occur to him to worry about the existence of an external world. The process of knowing, of theorizing, begins with what is known to us, and this is largely supplied to us by our senses. I know the flame is hot, that I have a body and that I live in the world.

Second, consider Francis Bacon (who wrote in 1620). He borrowed the biblical injunction against worshipping false idols in order to challenge Aristotle's "extraordinary confidence" in the ordinary human capacity to know the world as it really is. An idol for Bacon is a false notion that "so besets men's minds that truth can hardly find entrance."[23] The first idol, which lays the groundwork for the rest, is "of the tribe." It has its "foundation in human nature itself. For it is a false assertion that the sense of man is the measure of things." Instead, Bacon claims, "the human understanding is like a false mirror which . . . distorts and discolors the nature of things by mingling its own nature with it." Differently stated, the main obstacle to gaining the truth is anthropomorphism. When human beings think that the universe has a "shape" (*morphê*) similar to their own, they distort reality. Spinoza's critique of teleology is again apt. Human beings act with goals or purposes in mind and try to achieve what they think is good. Deluded by the idol of the tribe, one might think that the natural world is purposive or even good. But it is not. Access to the truth thus requires the rigorous application of a method that forces the scientist to repress her uniquely human concerns and to protect her inquiry from being infected by them. She must study the universe as it really is rather than as a projection of her own hopes, needs, and desires. She must resist the temptation of the idol of the tribe.

A more specific version of this idea is found in Bacon's "idol of the marketplace," which refers to the way people talk among themselves in ordinary life. "For it is by discourse [language] that men associate; and words are imposed according to the apprehension of the vulgar [the common people]. . . . words plainly force and overrule the understanding and throw all into confusion." Ordinary language (English or Greek, and so on) is used in the conduct of daily life. But it is useless as a tool for understanding the truth about the universe. For example, English uses nouns like "tree" and "dog." Such words might suggest that the basic units of reality are beings of some sort that are named by them (which Aristotle called "substances"). One might mistakenly go even further and think that entities like "dogness" or "treeness," which might be called "essences," are constitutive of reality. But this is false, for a tree is no more than a bunch of atoms and molecules moving through space. To think an essence like "treeness" is fundamentally real is to be seduced by the idol of ordinary language.

Bacon sums up: "The human understanding is of its own nature prone to suppose the existence of more order and regularity in the world than it finds." Our daily lives make sense to us. We divide our world into patterns, kinds, strata of reality. Trees are not dogs, dogs are not cats. Humans are more worthy than ants, which is why we feel no guilt in crushing them, and living beings are essentially different from inanimate ones. The sky is above, the earth below, and we are lucky to be here, for it is beautiful and good. But all this is no more than an anthropomorphic dream.

To reiterate, Bacon's notion of the idol is similar to Spinoza's statement that "men commonly suppose that all natural things act like themselves with an end in view." Men are, Bacon continues, "by nature . . . prone to embrace" such teleological "misunderstandings." In other words, it is in our "nature" to think of the world as like ourselves. Therefore, to "find entrance" into the truth, the scientist must ruthlessly suppress her own nature. Eschewing ordinary language, despising the "apparently"—but not really—"purposeful form of all life," she must purge her research of all vestiges of the human.

In this vein, consider Dawkins's description of natural selection: it is a process "that takes between thousands and millions of decades to complete." But "our brains are built to deal with events on radically different timescales from those that characterize evolutionary change. We are equipped to appreciate processes that take seconds, minutes, years, or, at most, decades to complete."[24] As a result, in order to grasp the truth about biological nature, one must cease to think within a human timescale. Modern science thus requires, quite literally, dehumanization.

By contrast, Aristotle is, to use Martha Nussbaum's phrase, a "professional human being."[25] He operates strictly within "the space and time in which our vital life runs its course." Whether we care to admit it or not, at the end of the day, when we leave our laboratories and turn off the computers and then finally go home we are *anthropoi*. And so Bernard is not off the mark in reminding us with his characteristic bluntness, "If knowledge isn't self-knowledge it isn't doing much, mate."

Husserl helped initiate the twentieth-century philosophical movement known as "phenomenology," which was developed and revised significantly by his even more famous student Martin Heidegger. The word derives from the Greek *phainomena* and *logos*; the latter is itself derived from *legein*, "to speak, tell, say," and means "rational account, speech, explanation." Heidegger describes the task of phenomenology as "to let that which shows itself be seen from itself in the very way in which it shows itself from itself."[26] In other words, phenomenology is a *logos*, a rational account, which aims for a kind of transparency. Through it the phenomena, the world or that which appears in ordinary human experience, come through and are sighted. The phenomenological *logos* brings the world in which we live into light.

To a significant degree, this book belongs, at least in spirit, in the camp of the twentieth-century phenomenologists and their many successors (such as Hans Jonas and Hannah Arendt), for these thinkers were convinced that modern European rationalism is "misguided" and that an alternative conception of rationality had to be forged. Nonetheless, it concentrates exclusively on the Philosopher. Doing so is not as drastically at odds with the phenomenological movement as it might seem. This is because of the influence Aristotle wielded over its development. Husserl's teacher, for example, was Franz Brentano, himself an Aristotle scholar, and Heidegger's early work was characterized by a deep and fertile preoccupation with Aristotle.[27] Turning back to Aristotle, then, could even serve as an introduction to German phenomenology. This is not, however, the intention of this book.

The reason that this book distances itself from twentieth-century phenomenology can only be crudely asserted: Aristotle does a better job than the Germans in giving a *logos* of the phenomena, in bringing the world of ordinary experience to light. He is a genius at the study and articulation of what stands before our eyes. And the language he uses is well suited to this task: it is, by and large, ordinary rather than technical or artificial. By contrast, Husserl's terminology is thickly and irremediably technical, whereas Heidegger is dense to the point of occlusion. Not Aristotle. His work is "like a running commentary to the [world]," which he illuminates "chapter by chapter."[28] We read his writings and then we must look carefully at the world, the one in which we actually inhabit, to see if he is right. The demand placed upon the Philosopher's reader is never to lose sight of where and how we conduct our lives, how we speak to one another and what it is we share.

Twentieth-century German philosophers would seem to have a decisive advantage over Aristotle. As modern thinkers, they would seem to be in a better position to comment on a culture so decisively shaped by modern science and technology. But Aristotle is not as disadvantaged by his having lived 2,400 years ago as he might seem for two reasons. First, he was intensely engaged in dialogue with his own predecessors, two of whom, Democritus and Empedocles (who both wrote approximately one hundred years before him), held views that were stunningly modern. Democritean atoms, for example, are more akin to the "corpuscles" of Galileo and Boyle than to Aristotelian substances.[29] And Darwin himself, citing an Empedoclean account of the development of human teeth, acknowledged that "we here see the principle of natural selection shadowed forth."[30] In other words, by arguing against thinkers like Democritus and Empedocles, Aristotle confronted some of the most basic principles of modern science.

Second, precisely because he is not writing under the enormous shadow of modern mathematical physics, Aristotle may be in an even better position to offer comment than twentieth-century philosophers. Husserl, for example, was resolved to make his own phenomenology as "hard" as any of the contemporary natural sciences. Stanley Rosen has argued that this very commitment distances Husserl from the ordinary world to which he claimed fidelity. "The question is therefore how a rigorously scientific philosophy can restore to science its meaning for life. In other words, is not the rigor of science the cause of its loss of meaning for life?" Rather than letting the phenomena use their own idiom to speak for themselves, Husserl employed a technical apparatus that transformed the object of his inquiry. As a result, like the "misguided" rationalism he hoped to overcome, his phenomenology was locked into a method that disfigured the ordinary world of human experience. "The pure formalism of the mathematical physicist," Rosen says, "leaves no room for the affirmation of the value or sense for human existence of the structures he or she studies. This affirmation must come from outside science. And it must also come from outside phenomenology."[31] The phenomena must speak for themselves, and this Aristotle, better than twentieth-century thinkers, enables them to do.

The paragraphs above are neither a responsible nor adequate retort to the work of those twentieth-century thinkers who, like me, were inspired by Aristotle. The writings of Hannah Arendt, for example, are by themselves worthy of a serious study. My remarks may ultimately express no more than a personal preference and my own sense of urgency to return to the source of so much important philosophical thought of the past century.

In any case, back to Aristotle. He was wrong in thinking that the earth is the center of the universe. But whether we care to admit it or not, the earth is where we live and so remains even today the center of our world. The utter disregard for this fact, this truth, has plunged us into an age of crisis. If the bombs don't get us, global warming might. For these reasons, then, retrieving Aristotle is not entirely foolish. Nonetheless, due diligence must be paid to the fact that he was, more than once, wrong. My cognizance of Aristotle's errors is represented by the titles of this book's chapters and subsections. Almost every one is a short declarative sentence that expresses an Aristotelian proposition that we know to be false. Chapter One is thus titled "The Stars Are Eternal."

Minimally, this book is a good exercise and a lesson in cultural history. The scientific revolution, in whose shadow we still stand, made Aristotle its foremost target. As a result, in order to understand the nature of modern science, and therefore our own culture, we must have some knowledge of the enemy in opposition to whom it originally defined itself. By studying the ways in which Aristotle's philosophical argumentation differ so decisively from modern European rationalism, we will learn much about modernity itself. Most important, by understanding how humane his arguments are, we will appreciate how thoroughly inhumane our science has become.[32]

My hope, however, is that this book will do more than provide a bit of self-diagnosis or historical information or an interesting thought experiment. My real goal, of course, is to save the world by attempting, even at this late date, to retrieve Aristotle.

Chapter One

The Stars Are Eternal.

In *On the Heavens*, his cosmological treatise, Aristotle argues that the heavenly bodies (moon, planets, sun, and stars) revolve around the earth on fixed circular paths. They are made of stuff not found here on earth and are more "honorable" than, ontologically superior to, bodies found in the sub-lunar sphere. They are weightless and eternal. They are divine.

We take Aristotle's claims to be not merely wrong but laughably so. The sun, not the earth, is the center of our solar system, the planets do not move in circular orbits, matter is homogeneous, and stars have both weight and a history.

This chapter analyzes Aristotle's arguments on behalf of these claims. Not only that: it defends them.

I.1: There Are Only Three Dimensions.

Aristotle begins his study of the heavenly bodies by asserting that bodies, or physical entities in general, have three dimensions. A "continuous magnitude," or an infinitely divisible measure of quantity, that is divisible in one way only is a line. A magnitude divisible in two ways, namely length and width, is a plane; in three ways—length, width, depth—a body. "There is no other magnitude or dimension besides these" (*On the Heavens* 268a9). Three-dimensional bodies are, therefore, the complete magnitude.

Proponents of today's "string theory" would disagree. For them there are as many as twenty-six dimensions. Others would count time as a fourth dimension. Contemporary topologists are free to work (algebraically) with as many dimensions as they like. But for Aristotle, there are only three. Of course, three-dimensionality is the way in which we experience bodies in everyday life. But Aristotle does more than simply rely on this commonsensical fact as support for his position. Instead, he offers the following argument defending it.

> There is no dimension other than these [the three dimensions] since three are all and "in three ways" is the same as "in all ways." For[#1] just as the Pythagoreans say, the all and all things have been determined by the three. For[#2] end (*teleutê*), middle (*meson*) and beginning (*archê*) hold the number of the all, and their number is three. Thus it is that we have taken this number from nature as one of her laws. Furthermore[#3] we use this number in the rituals performed in worship of the gods. And[#4] the way we name objects reveals this same point as well. For of two things or two people we say "both" and we do not say "all." We first use this term when it comes to three. As has been said, we follow these practices because nature itself leads us in this way. (268a9–20)

Aristotle summons four reasons, flagged by my underlining and numeration, to demonstrate that "three are all," a proposition that in turn is used to support the claim that physical bodies have three dimensions. The first (#1) summons a reputable belief (one that is *endoxos*) passed down by the Pythagoreans.[1] On its own, such a reference would hardly prove that "three are all" or even explain what this phrase means. Nonetheless, as discussed in the Introduction, a reputable belief is that which "seems true to everyone or to most people or to the wise, either to all of the wise or to most of the wise or to the best known and most reputable of the wise" (*Topics,* 100b21–22) and by itself carries some evidentiary force. Even if it is neither entirely right nor maximally clear, it will never be all wrong. It can thus be counted as some sort of epistemic clue (>IV).

Aristotle next supplies an independent conceptual argument on behalf of the claim that "three are all." He asserts in #2 that a whole must have an end, middle, and beginning, and thus is triadic in structure. This is the key to understanding and appreciating Aristotle's argument and it is discussed in detail shortly (>I.2).

In #3 Aristotle alludes to religious practices in which the triad figures prominently. He may be referring to the pouring of one libation to the gods, a second to the heroes, and a third to Zeus the savior. Whether he is or not cannot be determined because so many Greek religious rituals were triadically structured.[2] This prominence of the triad may be derived from a primitive division of the cosmos into sky above, earth below, and some in between that mediates or connects the two. Hesiod, for example, has the god Sky descend upon the goddess Earth in order to begin the process of generating the rest of the cosmos. In this case, nightfall could be construed as a connective tissue (as could rainfall). Many a myth, including one found in Plato's *Symposium*, treats human being as in between the immortal, found above, and the mortal, found below.[3]

Reason #4 refers to the fact that ordinary language, both Greek and English at least, testifies to the exceptional status of the three. If there are two apples on the table, and I tell you that I want them, you might ask, "Do you really want both?" You wouldn't ask, "Do you want all of them?" If my eyes hurt, and you ask me, "Which one hurts?" I will answer, "Both of them" rather than "All of them." The word "all" is first used when I have at least three items to count. (That Greek verbs have, in addition to the singular and the plural, the dual further reinforces this point.) For Aristotle, this linguistic observation counts as another piece of evidence for, a reason to believe that, threeness determines allness.[4]

Differently stated, in a (nontechnical) sense three is the first "real" number. If there is but a single item clearly visible on the table, say a book, no one would ask the question, "How many books are on the table?" Instead, someone might ask, "What's that on the table?" One item is not counted, but recognized for what it is. Only when there are at least two items does the question "How many?" become relevant. This fact is reflected in the Greek word *arithmos*, which means "number" as well as "a count." A count requires a plurality, a number of items or units. This is also why, in standard Greek arithmetic, two was taken to be the first number. (See *Physics* 220a27.) However, in order to determine that there are two books on the table, there must be some way of differentiating them. Either they are not by the same author, or even if they are two virtually identical copies of the same book, they are made from different pieces of paper and located in different places on the table. In short, if there is to be a two there must be a third; a differentiating principle. In this sense, three is the first "real" number.

Because reasons #3 and #4 seem to do no more than report bits of anthropological data, it is easy to formulate objections to them. Why, for example, should the fact that many religious rituals and practices are triadically structured play any role whatsoever in an argument about the nature of the nonhuman cosmos? This question resurfaces later in *On the Heavens* when Aristotle deploys a similar argumentative strategy. After having argued that the "first body," the fifth element of which the stars and planets are made, is eternal and divine, and so more "honorable" than any found here on earth, he asserts that "all human beings have a conception of the gods and all, both barbarian and Greek, assign the highest place to the divine" (270b5–7). He cites this putative fact as a supplementary piece of evidence to confirm his theoretical analysis of the nature of the "first body." Exactly as in #3, Aristotle marshals an anthropological datum—namely, that human beings regularly locate god upstairs—in the service of his scientific claim that the heavenly bodies above us are eternal. (Also see *Metaphysics* 1074b1–15.)

Aristotle seems to invest these sorts of anthropological data with the same sort of evidentiary value he finds in empirical observations. "By appealing to perception, this conclusion [that the heavenly bodies are eternal] follows in a manner sufficient in order to generate human conviction. For in all time past, according to the memory that has been passed down, no change has appeared (*phainetai*) to have taken place either in the whole of the outermost heaven or in any one of its proper parts" (270b13–15).[5]

In other words, according to the best record of empirical observations made by astronomers available at the time, nothing has changed in the heavens. Therefore, Aristotle reasons, the heavenly bodies must eternally move in the same orbit.

Aristotle's conjunction of these two strands of evidence—one citing the phenomena of religious belief and ordinary language and the other empirical observations of the heavens—tells much about how he argues, how he thinks, in general. As discussed in the Introduction, his theory aims to do justice to the phenomena, the way the world shows itself to us in ordinary experience. It is, in other words, "phenomenological." The "phenomena," however, must be construed broadly, for they include both empirical observations and the "reputable beliefs" (*ta endoxa*). They include, as Owen put it in a famous essay, the *legomena*, "the things said" or "linguistic usage" or "the conceptual structure revealed by language." Or to cite Nussbaum, in addition to empirical observations, "Aristotle's *phainomena* must be understood to be our beliefs and interpretations, often as revealed in linguistic usage."[6] The world shows itself to us not only through our senses, but also in the way we talk and how we conduct ourselves in daily life.

Because his theorizing is characterized by this sort of hybrid argumentation, Aristotle seems subject to the charge of anthropocentrism—or, even worse, anthropomorphism—of exactly the sort Bacon and Spinoza criticized so harshly. Regardless of whether this charge is fair or not, Aristotle himself certainly would deny that he is projecting a human perspective onto a nonhuman screen. Instead, he claims quite the opposite: "we follow these practices because nature itself leads us in this way" (268a19–20). So, for example, the number three is privileged in human practices and language not because human beings favor it, but because we "have taken it from nature" (268a13). The ways in which we speak and perform our religious rituals are guided by the way things really are. In turn, such phenomena can provide evidence about the world as it really is.

Of course, it is necessary to explain why phenomena like ordinary language and religious practices have epistemic value. To prefigure the discussion whose elaboration constitutes a major chunk of Chapter Four, Aristotle believes that human beings by nature tend to get things right. As he puts it, "human beings are naturally and sufficiently disposed towards seeking the truth, and in most cases attain the truth" (*Rhetoric* 1355a15). We are "truthing" animals whose perceptual, cognitive, and linguistic apparatus are well suited to know the world. As such, it is entirely reasonable to pay attention to how we talk and act in order to figure out how things, including things like the planets and stars, really are.[7]

I.2: Threeness Determines Wholeness.

Back to the argument in *On the Heavens*: bodies have only three dimensions because "end, middle and beginning hold the number of the all, and their number is three." To begin elaboration, consider the following definitions Aristotle offers of the "all" and the "whole":

1. " 'Whole' (*holon*) means 'that from which no part of that which is said to be by nature a whole is missing" (*Metaphysics* 1023b26).
2. "That of which nothing is outside is complete (*teleion*) and whole. For we define a 'whole' thus: as that from which nothing is absent" (*Physics* 207a9–11).
3. " 'All' (*pan*) means 'a quantity that has a beginning, middle and termination point (*eschaton*) but whose positions make no difference.' If position does make a difference, then it is a whole" (*Metaphysics* 1024a1–3).

A "whole" is an ordered unity of parts, whereas an "all" is an unordered collection or sum of parts. Aristotle's terminology vacillates between these three texts and *On the Heavens.* In the latter, *pan*, translated as "all," actually means "whole" in the sense given in the *Metaphysics* and *Physics* (and which is the only concern of this section).[8]

These definitions illuminate what Aristotle means when he says, to paraphrase, that the number of the whole is three; or that threeness determines wholeness; or that wholes are by nature triadic. Because it is an ordered unity of parts, a whole has a beginning and an end, and something in between. So, for example, the word "BAT" is a whole. It is not an "all" because the position of the elements does matter. The word "BAT" cannot be captured by a simple list of its letters, for the letters B, A, and T can be combined in more than one way. "TAB" is not the same as "BAT." For "BAT" to be what it is, its three letters must be in their proper order. A whole is more than "all" of its parts because it has a formal structure, an intelligible ordering of its parts. The spelling of "BAT" begins with the letter B and continues in proper sequence until T. Then the end has been reached, and the word is complete. "BAT" stands available for inspection as a whole.[9]

To approach this same point from a different angle: in the *Physics*, Aristotle says, "The whole and the complete (*teleion*) are either entirely the same or of kindred nature." The whole is "complete" because its *telos,* its end, goal, or purpose, has been achieved and "nothing is complete that does not have a *telos*." This implies, as Aristotle next states, that "the *telos* is a limit (*peras*)" (207a13–15). For if something can be completed then it is limited; after beginning and traversing what is in-between, an end is reached. Recall that in *On the Heavens* Aristotle says that the three-dimensional body is the "complete" (*teleion*: 268a22) magnitude. With it the counting of the dimensions reaches its end.

Another sense of *teleion* requires brief mention. In the *Metaphysics*, Aristotle assigns it two meanings. The first is essentially the same as that of the "whole:" it is that "outside of which it is impossible to find one of its parts" (1021b12–13). The second is "that which is in accord with excellence and the good cannot be exceeded in its kind. For example, a perfect doctor or a perfect flutist are those who, according to the form of the excellence that belongs to them, lack nothing" (1021b15–17). Here *teleion* is translated as "perfect," which in English has the same ambiguity as the Greek; it means both "complete" or "without omission" and "most excellent" (>II.8). In some sense, then, three-dimensional bodies, as the complete or *teleion* magnitude, are better than lines or planes.

Aristotle argues that because "three are all and 'in three ways' is the same as 'in all ways' "—in other words, because threeness determines the wholeness—there are only three dimensions. Three, in other words, is privileged, for it is the number of completeness. On the one hand, this is a just silly bit of numerology. Three is not special. It's just another number. To glorify it as Aristotle (following the Pythagoreans) does is to invest it with qualities that belong not to it, but to a prejudice held by (some) human beings. On the other hand, if Aristotelian cosmology is construed as phenomenological and is thus required to remain faithful to ordinary experience, a possible line of defense is opened up. For our experience is indeed constituted by the triadic nature of wholeness. Consider the following examples.

1. *The topological whole.* When we open our eyes and walk forward, what is in front of us appears as a triangulated whole. There is what is to the left of us, the right of us, and in front of us. When we stop walking and remain in one place, we can look upward to what is above, downward to what is below, and straight ahead to what is level with ourselves. Finally, there is front, back, and center. In sum, our experience of occupying a place in the physical world is triangulated, and is so in three different ways. In Aristotelian terms, there are six "parts and forms," six "divisions" or "directions," of place: up, down, left, right, front, back (*Physics* 208b12).

It is reasonably easy to explain why we experience the world this way. Like other animals, we are bilaterally symmetrical, and vision is thus bifocal. We have left and right eyes, as well as hands, legs, and so forth, and we divide our visual field directionally as a result. Left and right are defined by means of a center. There is that which is to the left of the center, that is, me, and that which is to the right, and so the horizontal directionality of the visual field is triangulated. So too is it divided vertically. There is the above me, accessible visually when I tilt my head and look upward, the below me, and the place I occupy right here. Because I look forward, but remember and so am aware that there is something behind, so too are these directions bifurcated.

Aristotle is thus quite right. Our experience of the world, of the way we occupy a place, is as a triangulated whole. But Aristotle does not rest content with this. For the next move he makes is to insist that the six directions are not relative to us.

> Up and down, right and left [front and back] are not only relative to us. For they are not always the same in relation to us, but instead depend on our position so that when we turn they change. . . . In nature, however, each is distinct and exists independently. For that which is up is not a matter of chance but instead is to where fire or a light body moves. Similarly, what is down is not a matter of chance but is to where heavy or earthy bodies move. They differ not only in position but also in power. (*Physics* 208b14–22)

Up and down, left and right, are objective features of the world. As Aristotle puts it in *On the Heavens*, "it is clear that the heavens have up and down and right and left" (285a30). Furthermore, "the beginning of the rotation of the heavens is the side from which the stars rise, so that would be its right, and where they set would be its left" (285b20). Such assertions seem to be a clear, even a pathetic, case of anthropocentricism. This at least was the verdict of one of Aristotle's first modern critics. Giordano Bruno, an early (around 1600) advocate for an infinite universe, argued against Aristotle that "doubtlessly the inhabitants of the moon believe themselves at the centre [of a great horizon] that embraces the earth, the sun, and the other stars, and is the boundary of the radii of their own horizon."[10] In other words, for the man in the moon, the earth is above and not below. In Bruno's infinite universe, up and down are relative, and Aristotle's argument that they are objective is faulty at best.

Nonetheless, Aristotle's argument can be defended if we construe it as operating, to cite Nussbaum again, "inside the circle of appearances."[11] We experience an orderly world divided into up and down and right here; we witness the sun rising in the East (to the right) and setting in the West. In this sense, *On the Heavens* is a "phenomenological cosmology," a theoretical account of the way the heavenly bodies show themselves to us. Even so, Aristotle insists that his theory is objectively true of the world. We have, for example, privileged the number three as the source of wholeness not because of any uniquely human inclination, but because we have learned this lesson "from nature itself." A comment by Helen Lang helps to explain.

> Unlike later physics (and much philosophy) Aristotle's arguments respond immediately and directly to experience. We experience objects as heavy and as always going down when they are left to "do their own thing"; the stars appear to move while we feel ourselves to be stationary and in the center. Indeed, the range of Aristotle's examples, consistently appealing to everyday experience and common sense, may be unequaled in the history of science or philosophy. . . . By answering to experience, these arguments speak and have always spoken to their readers. And so they speak also to us.[12]

2. *The temporal triad.* Like our experience of a triangulated topological whole, by whose directions we orient ourselves as we propel ourselves through it, so too is our experience of time divided triadically. Aristotle defines time as "the counting of motion with respect to the before and after" (*Physics* 219b2). As he later formulates, "the now is a mid-point (*mesotês*)

serving as both beginning and end—the beginning of the future time, and the end of past time" (251b20–22).

3. *The syllogistic whole.* Logical reasoning, which for Aristotle is paradigmatically found in the "syllogism," is the making of connections, and thus is structurally triadic. He explains: "a syllogism is a form of words (*logos*) in which, when some certain assumptions are made, something other than what has been assumed necessarily follows from the fact that the assumptions are such" (*Prior Analytics* 24b20). A syllogism is an argument, a logically connected whole, and it "is effected by means of three terms" (*Posterior Analytics* 81b10): the major, the minor, and the middle. (See *Prior Analytics* 26a22.) To illustrate, consider the first example Aristotle offers in the *Prior Analytics*: "if A is predicated of all B, and B of all C, A must necessarily be predicated of all C" (25b36–38). To diagram this in such a way as to make its structure visible:

All B is A.
All C is B.
Therefore, All C is A.

If all human beings (B) have hearts (A), and if all women (C) are human beings (B), then all women (C) have hearts (A). The major term is A; it is that "in which the middle is contained." The minor term is C; it is that "which falls under the middle term" (26a3). The middle term (*to meson*) is B, and as the diagram above clearly shows provides the connective link that drives the logical inference forward. Syllogistic reasoning is a mode of logical connecting and as such is both holistic—it is a self-contained logical package—as well as triadic.[13]

4. *The practical whole.* "Excellence," Aristotle writes in the *Nicomachean Ethics*, is a midpoint (*mestotês*) that aims at the mean (*to meson*) (1106b26–28). In other words, our practical or ethical lives are structured triadically. To explain by way of an example: you have a friend who is struggling financially. You have some money, and because you strive to be a generous person you want to help. But you are not quite sure how. On the one hand, if you give your friend too much money, you run the risk of demeaning and thus alienating her. A substantial gift can be construed as a kind of domination. On the other hand, you do not want to give too little, either. If you give your friend but a dollar, which provides no substantial assistance, you run the risk of being, and being thought of as, cheap. In order to be generous, and to retain the friendship, you must give just the

right amount: not too much, not too little. This is what Aristotle calls *to meson*, "the mean" or what can also be translated as "the middle" or "the center." (See *Nicomachean Ethics* 1106b18 and >V.6.)

Our practical lives are triangulated as we aim to steer a middle path between too much and too little. If, in debating how much money to give your friend, you hit upon what is just right, you have achieved your goal, your *telos*, and completed the transaction well. Our actions, if successful, have a kind of wholeness to them that is determined by the three.

5. *A Whole Life*. A complete human life has three basic stages: being young, in the prime, and old. (See *Rhetoric* II.12–14.) Generally speaking, young people tend to be impetuous, passionate, trusting, hopeful, and eager for companions. At the other extreme, the very old are bad-tempered, mistrustful, small-minded, cowardly, miserly, and bereft of strong desire and hope. They talk repetitively about the past and have no sense of humor. Best of all are those in the prime of life, who are "in between" (*metaxu*: 1390a25) the two extremes. They aim for both what is fine and what is advantageous, are neither frugal nor extravagant, combine prudence with courage.

6. *Tripartite psychology*. When describing themselves, human beings have a natural tendency to bifurcate. So, for example, we often rebuke ourselves. If you eat the third piece of cake, knowing that the excess calories will do you no good, you may then get angry with yourself and even say aloud, "You idiot!" Who's talking to whom here? Somehow the self speaks to itself. But this bifurcation invites, as always, a tripartition. For there must be some sort of bridge between the rebuker, which Plato in Book IV of the *Republic* called "reason"—in this case, the rational capacity to determine that a third piece of cake is unhealthy—and the rebuked, which he called "desire." The bridge between the two is the emotional energy, in this case anger, that fuels the rebuke. Reason may determine that three pieces of cake are too many, even while desire craves them. But only by becoming angry at itself can the *psyche* rebuke itself. (The Greek word *psuchê* is usually but inadequately translated as "soul." Throughout this book *psyche* is used: >IV.1. Thus, Aristotle's book whose traditional title is *De Anima* is rendered as *On the Psyche.*)

In the *Nicomachean Ethics* Aristotle offers a similar psychological bifurcation: one aspect of the human *psyche* is rational or "has *logos*," whereas the other is bereft of reason (*alogon:* 1102a28). The latter can be subdivided: one is "responsible for nurture and growth"—in other words is entirely irrational—whereas the other does "partake of reason" (1102b14). It can somehow listen to rational commands, and as such provides the bridge between the fully rational and the irrational aspects or parts of the *psyche.*

(Chapter Four below shows just how fully Aristotle deploys the notion of a tripartite *psyche.*)

7. *Motion (or change) is triadic.* In Book I of the *Physics,* Aristotle, as he customarily does, reviews the theories of his predecessors who did notable work in the study of nature (*phusis*). All were, in one way or another, concerned with articulating the principles that would explain the observable fact that natural beings move or change. Aristotle notes that in attempting to do this, his predecessors, the first physicists, "made their first principles opposites" (188a19). So, for example, Democritus believed that the world of physical change could ultimately be explained by reference to "the full," his solid and indivisible atoms, and "the empty," the void through which his atoms moved (188a22). Other thinkers invoked pairs of opposites, such as the hot and cold, wet and dry, odd and even, love and hate (188b33). First principles must come in pairs, Aristotle argues, because, since they are primary, they cannot be derived either from each other or from anything else. If a first principle could be explained as coming from something else, then it would not be first. Furthermore, there cannot be but one first principle since it must be "of something" (184a4); hence, the very notion of a principle implies that there must be at least two. Finally, there cannot be an unlimited number of principles because Nature itself is intelligible, and the unlimited is not knowable (189a15). (See >II.8.)

For the study of nature, there must be at least two opposed first principles because change is a kind of "becoming," and when something changes it becomes other than it is. So, for example, my hair, formerly brown, became gray. As such, it became not-brown. An animal, now alive, will die and thus cease to be alive. An object here on my desk will fall to the floor. It is here now, but upon completing its fall will no longer be here. Change understood as something becoming other-than-what-it-was is thus a transition between opposites, and so it was that "the truth itself forced" (188b30) the first physicists to think in terms of opposites. But two principles by themselves are not enough to explain change. If my hair, once brown, is now gray and thus not-brown, it nonetheless remains my hair. Brown does not become not-brown; this is what happened to my hair. Brownness was once present in my hair; now it is gone. But the hair remains. Similarly, if the animal shifts from being alive to being not-alive, its body remains as a pile of inanimate material stuff. An animal is an organically intact and animated material clump rather than an inert and decomposing pile. Living cannot simply become dead; only animals suffer that change. In general, then, an opposite cannot simply leap over into its opposite. Instead, a third principle must somehow underlie or suffer the change. As

Aristotle puts it, "It is clear something must underlie the opposites, and that the opposites are always two" (191a4–5). Here today, gone tomorrow. What is? Something. Hence, the principles are three.[14]

Another opponent Aristotle takes up in Book I is Parmenides, who maintained that, appearances to the contrary, change is not really real. His argument was roughly this: If something changes, it comes to be other than it was. If something comes to be, it comes to be from either being or from non-being. If it comes to be from being, it does not really come to be at all. And nothing can come from non-being. Therefore, change itself is conceptually impossible.

To derail this argument, and to save the phenomena, Aristotle invokes three principles: matter, privation, and form. The privation is what is absent from something before it suffers a change. The form is what the substance gains, what becomes present in it, after the change has occurred. The remaining principle is the matter, what underlies and persists through the transition from absence to presence. This triad allows Aristotle to avoid the Parmenidean dilemma. When something changes or comes into being—when, say, my hair becomes gray—it comes into being both from what is, namely my hair, and from what is not; from the privation, the non-being, of gray.

This complicated train of thought is discussed below (>II.4). For the moment, let this suffice: change over time is experienced as a transition between opposites undergirded by a substratum underlying or suffering the change. When something changes, the process is a unified, because triadic, whole.

To put this point more simply: change proceeds from opposites. What is brown becomes gray or not-brown. "But there must be something underlying which changes to contraries, for it is not the contraries that change. Matter, this underlying object, remains during the change. [This, in addition to the two contraries, is the] the third besides the contraries" (*Metaphysics* 1069b8). Such is, at least, the experience of ordinary motion.

8. *The narrative whole*. In the *Poetics,* Aristotle says that a tragedy is an "imitation of an action that is serious, complete (*teleias*) and of a certain magnitude" (1449b25). Later he reformulates: "Tragedy is an imitation of an action that is complete and whole (*holês*: 1450b25)," and he defines a "whole" in the same terms he uses in *On the Heavens*: "that which has a beginning, middle and an end" (1450b27).

A good tragedy must have a unified plot. Plot, "the arrangement of the incidents" (1450a5), is defined as an "imitation of the action" (1450a4), and so it becomes the central element, or as Aristotle calls it, the animating principle or "soul" (1450a37), of tragedy as such. Without a unified narrative or plot, a drama is no more than a string of episodes. It is not only a bad piece of work, but also a lifeless one.

A good tragedy requires narrative unity because it is an imitation of an "action" or a *praxis*. Like many of Aristotle's critical terms, this one is equivocal. In the broadest sense, it can refer to any kind of "doing" whatsoever. In the *Historia Animalium*, for example, "the behaviors (*praxeis*)" of animals are said to be a way of differentiating them (487a11), while in the *Nicomachean Ethics* neither children nor animals are said to "act" (*praxei*: 1111a26). One sense of the word is of a human life conceived neither as an isolated action nor as a sequence of merely biological activities, but as the consistent and characteristic pattern of activity a human being engages in over a long period of time. This is what Aristotle has in mind when he says in the *Politics* (1325a32) that "happiness is a *praxis*." Happiness does not occur in an isolated or single moment. It is the work of a lifetime. This sense of *praxis* comes close to what Aristotle calls "actuality" (*energeia)* in his definition of happiness in the *Ethics* as "actuality in conformity with virtue" (1098b31), and is discussed in some detail below (>II.4, III.5, V.2).

A tragedy imitates a *praxis* in this last sense. It must have a unified plot structure because *praxis* conceived as a significant chunk of a human life is a meaningful whole.[15] To be intelligible one must be able to tell a story about it; it must have a beginning, a middle, and an end. We begin in childhood, and if we are lucky we mature and then die in our old age. In order for our lives, or any portion of our lives, to be meaningfully discussed or shared with another, there must be a coherent structuring of these parts. Human life, in other words, must have a narrative structure in order to make sense. We must be able to tell our stories. For example, when two people begin the process of getting to know each other, and perhaps of becoming friends, they exchange their stories. Where do you come from? Where did you go to school? Who are your parents, where do you live now? Indeed, as poets as old as Homer and neurologists as contemporary as Oliver Sacks have understood, stories are essential in the formation of human identity.[16]

That Aristotle offers the same definition of the "whole" in both *On the Heavens* and the *Poetics* sharply raises the question of whether he is anthropomorphizing. The subject of his cosmology is the heavenly bodies, which are surely not human, but it begins with a discussion of what seems to be a distinctly human notion, or experience, of wholeness. He says that all bodies must have three dimensions because "three is all." Threeness determines wholeness because it is constituted by a "beginning, middle and end." This may be true about stories we tell each other in order to make sense of our lives, and words like "BAT." But Aristotle goes much further.

He says that "we have taken this number from nature itself" (268a14). To reiterate the objection that Hobbes, Bacon, and Spinoza would fire at him: this is anthropomorphic claptrap. We may like the number three down here in our little earthly village. We may use it in our religious practices and give it a special place in our language. Our perceptual, temporal, ethical, and linguistic lives may be organized around it. None of this, however, tells us much about "nature itself."

Yes, it does. Aristotle articulates the contours of a world seen by the naked eyes of people who speak languages like Greek or English, who look upward to the sky and downward to the earth, who organize their spatial experience by means of left, right, and center. We are people who, in trying to be a decent friend, care about whether our gifts are too much or too little. And in making a friend, we share our stories. Our experience of the world comes in wholes, which are indeed constituted triadically. *On the Heavens* extends this basic conception to the uppermost spheres of the world. As such, his treatise is a work of "commonsense" or "phenomenological" cosmology. It articulates the structure of a world that in its entirety makes sense, and does so in thoroughly human terms.

I.3: There Are Four Elements.

Back to the main argument of *On the Heavens*, in which Aristotle supports the contention that the stars are eternal. After establishing the three-dimensionality of bodies, he next asserts that there are four simple elements in the sub-lunar world; earth, air, water, and fire. This was the traditional view of Greek science—that is, a reputable belief—dating back at least two hundred years. The Greeks were off by ninety-nine, but the notion of a finite number of primitive elements that compose the larger conglomerates of the material world has long retained its grip on the scientific imagination.

One might wonder, however, why, if threeness determines allness, there are four elements. This is not an inconsistency because Aristotle nowhere insists that all fundamental principles must come in threes. If he were to slavishly follow the principle of threeness by claiming that there are only three elements, he would blind himself to the phenomena. Instead, he bases his enumeration of the elements on the *endoxa*, the prevailing conceptions of ancient "chemistry," which itself was based on naked-eye observation of what is given to us on a bulky scale in ordinary experience. We take fire and water to be fundamentally unlike each other because we use one to make the other disappear. Earth resists and air surrounds. But the best way to defend the Aristotelian quartet is to try to challenge his thesis on the same level on which he offers it: what would be a reasonable candidate for a fifth, readily observable element that would be on a par with earth, air, fire, and water? No answer. There are only four.

I.4: Elements Naturally Move to Their Natural Place.

On the Heavens continues: "We say that all natural bodies and magnitudes are capable in themselves of locomotion [movement in place]. For we say that nature is the origin of motion in them" (268b17). A similar statement is found in the *Physics*: a being that is by nature "has in itself the origin of motion and rest" (192b13–14).

Natural bodies move from place to place. That the origin of their doing so is "in themselves" does not mean that things like rocks move themselves. Self-movement is reserved for living beings, while rocks need to be moved by something else. Still, that they are capable of being moved is a fundamental aspect of what they are, and in this sense movability is "in" them.

On the other hand, there is a sense in which the principle of motion of natural bodies is "in themselves." If I throw a rock up in the air, it will return to earth. It will do so on its own unless it is impeded by some countervailing object. As a natural being, a rock has its own "natural motion." Because it is an earthy thing, its natural direction or inclination is downward, or "toward the center." When the rock hits ground, it stays there. It is at rest and will remain so unless moved by another object because it has reached its natural resting place. The same pattern holds for fire and air. They naturally move upward, away from the center, whereas water flows downward. As Lang puts it, "inclination is an intrinsic ability in each element to be moved toward its proper place as found in nature."[17]

Aristotle's conception of place (*topos*) is fundamental not only to his physics but, as Chapters Five and Six of this book show, to his ethical and political thinking as well. In fact, his entire view of the world is deeply "topological." He begins discussing place in *Physics* Book IV by saying that "everyone assumes that beings (*ta onta*) are somewhere. For what is not is nowhere. For where is the goat-stag or the sphinx?" (*Physics* 208a29–31).[18] We regularly, perhaps even naturally, ask where something is. The goal of *Physics* Book IV is thus to provide an answer to the question "What is the where of things?" (Lang 1998, 68).[19]

There are at least two reasonable candidates for a general answer: in a place or in the void. Aristotle rejects the latter because for him it is no more than "a special case of place, i.e., a place with nothing in it" (Lang

1998, 68). Because his conception of the void is similar to the indeterminate space of the modern universe, his rejection of it sheds light on how radically his physics differs from our own. Most important, Aristotelian place, unlike space, has a kind of "power" (208b11), which is intimately linked to the notion of the objectivity of direction. Each of the four elements, unless obstructed, is carried to its own place. Fire is always carried up and earth down. As mentioned above (<I.2), the six distinctions within, or the six forms of, place—up, down, left, right, front, and back—are not just relative to us, but are objective features of the natural world. Places do not differ merely by position. Instead, they have a kind of causal power insofar as the elements naturally move toward them. An earthy, heavy body naturally moves downward. By contrast, the void is no more than a neutral or indeterminate space through which all bodies move by following the same laws of motion. Most important, space of this sort "is internally undifferentiated—two spaces are identical, if they are of equal dimensions" (Lang 1998, 69). Aristotle sees it differently. The heavens above us are different from the earth below. Fire goes up, water down. Right, where the sun rises, is different from left where it sets. The world is heterogeneous, differentiated, stratified into different places.

Aristotle's theory of place may seem easily debunked by means of Newtonian mechanics and its concept of empty space. It is not, for Aristotle's theory conforms to the patterns of everyday interaction with the material world. When we perceive a body, say a tree, it is located somewhere. We do not experience it as being in the midst of an indeterminate space whose many locations can only be determined by means of a coordinate system, for we never actually experience the indeterminate or the void. This is why "most people" assign such significance to place. Things belong somewhere. When we build a campfire, we put the newspaper on the bottom, the kindling on top of that, and the heavier pieces of wood on top of the kindling. We do so because we know that fire moves upward. When we buy a house, we examine the basement carefully to see if there has been water damage, because that is where water goes. The world makes sense. It is orderly. Things have a place.

Not surprisingly, Aristotle cites a reputable opinion as confirmation of his topologically based physics. He refers to the poet Hesiod, whose *Theogony* is the story of how the world and all its objects came into being. First of all, says Hesiod, there was *chaos,* which even if etymologically the same as our "chaos" (which means an unordered mess of parts) is better translated as "chasm" or even emptiness. Immediately after the chasm came earth. Aristotle interprets this line as revealing Hesiod's understanding of the fact that there needs to be a place for all the many things—trees, mountains, people, rivers, nymphs—his poem describes as coming into being. For they cannot exist nowhere or in the chasm.

> That there is place and that it is independent of bodies and that every body is perceptible as being in a place is a reasonable belief. Thus it would seem that Hesiod spoke correctly when he made "the chasm" the first of all things. For he wrote, at any rate, that "first of all the chasm came to be, and then next broad bosomed earth." He did so because he understood that it was necessary first of all for there to be room for things. Just like most people, he understood that every thing has to be somewhere and in a place. (*Physics* 208b27–33)[20]

Aristotle defines *topos* as the limit "of the containing body" (211b14). As such, place is not itself a material part of a thing. Instead it is more like the form or the shape of a thing. My computer has three dimensions and is sitting on my desk. It is made of stuff like plastic and silicon; in Aristotle's lingo, some bits of earth, air, water, or fire. The stuff has been molded into a shape or form by the computer maker. Its shape is visible, which is why the Greek word for form, *eidos*, is derived from the verb "to see" and could be translated as "the look" of a thing. Rather than being a separate part, the form is the entirety of the way the computer, shaped by its outermost edge or limit, looks.

Even though it too is a limit, a place is not a form. A form "is the limit of the thing contained whereas place is the limit of the containing body" (Lang 1998, 86). A place is like a "vessel" (210a24). A vessel, like a bottle, is that which things, which have a form, are *in*. Like an immovable vessel, a place "holds" change.

Problems aplenty arise. For example, place seems close to being a body because it is three-dimensional, but the phenomenon of "replacement" shows that it is not. There may now be water in a bottle. When the water is poured out it is replaced by air. Where the water was is now where the air is, and the air also could be replaced by another body. Because the same place can be occupied by different bodies, place is not body. (See *Physics* 208b1–7.) Nor, as argued above, is it a form. Instead, place "is the first unmoved limit of that which contains" (212a20).

To do more than scratch the surface of this issue would require a much longer book. For present purposes the key point is only this: place has "power." It causes the "order of nature" itself. Lang explains that "place is the formal constitutive principle that renders the cosmos directional . . . and so constitutes all place within the cosmos as 'up,' 'down,' and so forth" (Lang 1998, 69). It is precisely such directionality that renders the cosmos itself orderly. To cite Koyré's definition again, a cosmos is "a conception of the world as a finite, closed, and hierarchically ordered whole." To say it is "hierarchical" means that things have their place. They fit somewhere in the cosmos. Stars are above us, earth below, and animals like us are in between.

By contrast, in a universe of indefinite space nothing belongs anywhere or is objectively above or below, to the right or the left. Such directions are entirely relative, for there is no stable center. Perhaps this is the view from the perspective of the Hubble telescope, but it defies the logic of human experience and activity. We do belong. We are higher than mosquitoes, which is why we do not clutch in guilt when we kill one, and we are lower than the sun, on which all life on earth depends. Aristotle's physics is topological. It articulates a finite, determinate cosmos, not an indefinite universe. While the notion of a cosmos is entirely outdated in the twenty-first century, it is so only in the hands of the practicing astrophysicists. For daily life is lived in order, in a place, on earth, at home.

Koyré reveals much when he offers the following eulogy of Copernicus. "It is very difficult," he tells us, "at the present time to comprehend and appreciate the magnitude of intellectual effort, boldness and moral courage involved in the work of Copernicus." The heliocentric system he championed forced him to challenge and then dismiss "what common sense accepts with naive, confident certitude"; namely the apparently observable facts that the earth stands still and the heavens above move, facts that were enshrined not only in the cosmology of ancient and medieval physics, but in philosophy and theology as well. Copernicus was "incomparably daring" because his thought "tore the Earth from its foundations and launched it into the heavens."[21] He forced the scientist to think himself outside of himself, into a world of mathematical physics in which human beings have no special place. His physics was a vast improvement over Aristotle's in terms of actually understanding how the solar system works. It fulfilled the Baconian dream of forging a new knowledge that actually bequeaths to its possessor genuine power. For only in the light of the Copernican revolution has it become possible to create machines that can actually take us to the moon, launch the Hubble telescope, and let us glimpse the universe for what it really is.

The problem is that we still do live on earth and so, as long as we are here, the stars are above us, the earth under our feet.

The background assumptions Aristotle needs to complete his argument that the stars are eternal are now available, and so he can continue.

> Every motion from place to place [locomotion] is either straight or circular or a mixture of the two. For these two are the only simple motions. The reason for this is that straight and circular lines are the only simple magnitudes. Circular motion is that around the center; straight is up and down. By "up" I mean away from the center; by "down" I mean toward the center. Thus, every simple motion is either away from the center, towards the center, or around the center. This seems to follow the argument put forth at the beginning: for body was completed by the number three and so too is the motion of body. (*On the Heavens* 268b17–27)

Here Aristotle does invoke the principle that threeness determines allness but not in order to clinch his argument that there are only three simple motions. Instead, his conclusion "seems to follow" his earlier argument that, like all else, body is completed by the three, and so has only three dimensions. His actual argument is independent. There are only two simple lines—the straight and the circle—and thus only two simple motions that correspond: rectilinear and circular. There are, therefore, only three primary, directed motions: straight up, or away from the center; straight down, or toward the center; and circular motion around the center. As just discussed, each of four simple bodies has a natural motion. Earth and water move straight down, fire and water move straight up. But what moves around in a circle? This is a slot that has to be filled, and by a simple body. None is available, at least down here on earth. Therefore, Aristotle concludes, the simple body that moves in a circle must be composed of a fifth element unlike the four sub-lunar ones, all of which naturally move in a rectilinear fashion. That this "first body" moves in a circle has extraordinary consequences.

I.5: The Circle Is Perfect.

Circular motion is "primary" because the circle, unlike any other figure, is "complete" or "perfect" (*teleion*: 269a20; <I.2, >II.8). An infinite line cannot be complete for the obvious reason that it has no end, and a finite line segment can always be extended (269a23). A circle is complete, intact, wholly itself, because its radius cannot be extended or shortened without an entirely new circle being drawn. It simply is what it is, for it lacks nothing.

Regardless of whether the circle is "perfect" within the field of geometry, it can be verified phenomenologically. For the circle maintains a very strong hold on our imaginations. Perhaps this is because we are conscious of living diurnally; our days revolve from dawn to dawn. Our seasons too move cyclically, beginning in spring, moving through the harvest of fall, dying in the winter only to begin again. If we are lucky we give birth to our children, who give birth to theirs, and we thereby become, however metaphorically, immortal. In these senses, the circle represents completion.

As every teacher knows, a classroom whose seats are arranged in a circle has an entirely different feel than one whose seats are arranged in straight lines that direct the student's attention to the front. In the latter, there is a single authority figure to whom the students defer. In the former, every seat is equal. Each point on a circle is both beginning and end, and equidistant from the center. There is no way of adding a seat without changing the circle. Because of its completeness, each individual is an equal participant, and conversation is more likely to occur. Any number of traditions, from religious conceptions of sacred geometry to artistic ones that feature the circle and sphere, could be summoned to reinforce this privileging of the circle. Such reasoning sounds like anthropomorphizing at its worst. Hume certainly thought so.

> Euclid has fully explained all the qualities of the circle; but has not, in any proposition, said a word of its beauty. The reason is evident. The beauty is not a quality of the circle. It lies not in any part of the line, whose parts are equally distant from a common center. It is only the effect, which that figure produces upon the mind, whose peculiar fabric or structure renders it susceptible of such sentiments."[22]

For Hume, the aesthetic experience of the beautiful circle is explicable solely on the basis of the "peculiar fabric or structure" of the human mind. In his view, to attribute beauty to the circle is to impose or project human inclinations upon it. Even if this were so, it still would not be necessary to junk Aristotle. If the goal of his theory is to save the phenomena, and these include a wide variety of human experiences and practices, then his argument too can be saved. As he says, "for they say that human affairs (*ta anthropina pragmata*) are circular" (*Physics* 223b24–25). The circle does appear to us as perfect, complete, and, as even Hume admits, beautiful.

I.6: The Body Moving in Circular Orbit Is Eternal.

Aristotle continues: "Thus if someone syllogizes (*sullogizomenos*) from all our premises he would be convinced that there is some other body separate from those around us here, and that it has a more honorable nature to the extent that it is removed from things here" (269b15). The stars are above us, made of different stuff, ontologically superior to and thus more "honorable" than what is found on earth.[23] Such, at least, is the result of the syllogism in *On the Heavens,* which roughly is this: there are three simple motions: straight up, straight down, and circular. Every simple body moves in a simple motion, and every simple motion must be performed by a simple body. The four sub-lunar elements move either straight up or straight down. Therefore, there must be a fifth element, not found in the sub-lunar sphere, that moves in a circle.

Furthermore, because the heavy is "that whose nature it is to move towards the center, the light that whose nature it is to move away from the center" (269b25), because all simple bodies have only one natural motion, the heavenly bodies moving in a circular orbit are neither heavy nor light. That is why they simply stay up at the outermost sphere of the heavens, orbiting around the earth in a perfect circular path.

The final straw comes with this argument: the opposite of up is down, and of down up. But the circle has no opposite. Because "everything that is generated comes into being out of an opposite" (<I.2) and "opposites have opposite motions" (270a15), the heavenly bodies moving in circular orbits are neither generated nor perish. "It looks then as if nature correctly exempted from the class of opposites that which was to be ungenerated and indestructible" (270a20). The stars are eternal. Because their circular motion is "one and continuous" and, unlike a rectilinear motion, never comes to an end (*Physics.* 265a27), they orbit the earth forever. Furthermore, "we must conceive of the stars as partaking in life" (*On the Heavens* 292a18).

Bacon would be disgusted by this sort of "syllogizing," for it seems driven not by the sort of ruthlessly methodical observation required by good science, but by a demand for a clean and comforting logical pattern. In other words, the Aristotelian syllogism is really a form of anthropomorphizing rather than a ruthless scrutinizing of nature. About it Bacon complains that it is "no match for the subtlety of nature." Employment of the syllogism amounts to seduction by the "idol of the tribe": "The human understanding is of its own nature prone to suppose the existence of more order and regularity in the world than it finds. And though there may be things in nature which are singular and unmatched, yet it devises for them parallels and conjugates relatives which do not exist. Hence the fiction that all the celestial bodies move in perfect circles."[24]

On the one hand, Bacon gets it exactly right: Aristotle does suppose the existence of regularity. "In all things," he says, "nature is the cause of order" (*Physics* 252a12). On the other hand, from Bacon's critical perspective, this conviction is really no more than a kind of self-absorption. In Aristotle's defense: the world does make sense. We walk through doors rather than walls, wear light clothing in the summer, put umbrellas above ourselves when it starts to rain, and, except when we are in strangely anxious moods, rarely doubt that the sidewalk will still be there when we leave the building. The world makes sense and the syllogism is one way we make sense of it, for it is a means by which we move conceptually beyond a given proposition that we take to be true. It is a way of extending reason's reach and the principal tool by which Aristotle "projects" the order he finds in nature onto the farthest reaches of the heavens.

"Projects" is ambiguous. As in the phrase "wish projection," it can mean that Aristotle imposes his own concerns and prejudices onto a nonhuman screen and thereby distorts his observation of the world. We wish the nonhuman cosmos looked like us and so we attribute to it features familiar to us. More in keeping with Aristotle's own understanding of his philosophical enterprise is the sense available through the example of an overhead projector. It projects by enlarging an image onto a screen that retains the same proportions and shape of the original. The syllogism operates in this sense. It allows human reason to reach the heavens by logically projecting features of the world that have been discovered by the naked eye down here on earth. Differently stated, Aristotle's cosmology works from the bottom up. Beginning down here, and in this sense being resolutely geo- and anthropocentric, it syllogizes its way upward to the heavens. It is meticulous and careful and the result is a coherent and beautiful conception of a cosmos in which human beings can find a place.

I.7: History Is More or Less Bunk.

Using the syllogism and relying on what he takes to be decent empirical observations, Aristotle argues that because they are made of stuff not found on earth and are carried in a circular orbit around the earth, the stars are everlasting and thus divine. Strikingly, because most at odds with a modern philosophical sensibility, his argument has relied upon the phenomenon of ordinary language. Recall, for example, that he cited a feature of Greek—that the word "all" is not used to name two objects, but only three or more—to reinforce his claim that bodies have three dimensions. He makes a similar move when he invokes a possibly "fanciful" etymology of "aither" in order to corroborate his scientific argument about the nature of the stars. The word is, he says, derived from the Greek words for "always" and "run."[25]

> It seems too that the name of this first body has been passed down to the present time by the ancients, who thought of it in the way as we discuss it. For it is necessary to consider that the same beliefs arrive to us not just once or twice but an unlimited number of times. Thus the ancients, believing that the primary body was something different from earth and fire and air and water, gave the name *aither* to the highest place, bestowing upon it this name from the fact that for eternity it "always" (*aei*) "runs" (*thein*). (*On the Heavens* 270b15–25)

Ordinary people have long called the stuff up there "aither," that which "always runs," and they have coined this word precisely because they take it to last forever. An anthropological datum is again used to reinforce a cosmological claim.

Note this statement found in the quotation above: "the same beliefs arrive to us not just once or twice, but an unlimited number of times." Aristotle repeats it, while offering much the same argument, in his treatise *Meteorology*. Aristotle states that it is not "just we who happen to believe" that the first body is eternal. Instead, this is an ancient belief. He explains: "For what is called 'aither' has been a common term since antiquity. . . . For the ancients seemed to believe that the body that is always 'running' (*theon*) is at the same time divine (*theion*) in nature. They determined to call it 'aither' because such a body was the same as nothing that is in our midst. For we assert that not once or twice nor just a few times do the same beliefs circulate among human beings, but an infinite number of times" (339b20–30).

"This curious doctrine" that the same beliefs circulate among human beings for an infinite number of times "results," Leggatt argues, "from Aristotle's belief that the universe is everlasting and that the earth, or at least parts of it, undergoes periodic destructive flooding."[26] Where, for example, once there was dry now there is wet and where once there was wet, such as the banks of the Nile, there is now dry, as the great river has deposited its silt (351b30). These sorts of reversals have occurred throughout the indefinite stretch of geological time. Furthermore, "it is necessary to think that these changes occur in an orderly cycle." There were, Aristotle reasons, periodic floods in which whole civilizations were destroyed. When the land became dry again, a new civilization replaced the old one. But the same beliefs held by the prior group cropped up once again. He thinks this for at least four reasons: (1) Despite the changes undergone on its surface, the essential structure of the earth—indeed, of the world in general—remains unchanged forever. (2) Time itself is everlasting. (3) The human species, like all species, is everlasting. (4) Throughout history, the human *psyche*, in particular its perceptual and cognitive apparatus, has undergone no essential change. (These first three claims are discussed later in Chapter Three and the fourth in Chapter Four.) As a result, human beings think the same basic thoughts over and over again, even as great civilizations (like ours) come and go.

This notion is reinforced by a passage from the *Politics.* Here Aristotle notes the antiquity of certain features of political life. For example, his own recommendation that the agricultural and military classes of a well-organized city should be kept separate can, he thinks, be traced as far back as the Egyptians. This is emblematic of the fact that essential political structures continually reappear throughout history.

> It is almost necessary to think that other political structures have been discovered many, more likely an infinite number of, times throughout the immense reach of time. For it is probable that need itself taught men about those aspects of political life that address what is necessary [to sustain human life], while it is reasonable to think that what contributes to luxury and abundance should also find their development. A clue that [such political structures] are ancient is that they can be found in Egypt. For they seem to be the most ancient of peoples and yet they had laws and a political system. (1329b25–33)

The need for food, shelter, security, and community remains constant throughout history, and so basic political institutions that respond to such needs, such as laws, will reappear an unlimited number of times.

To generalize again: while Aristotle is aware that geological time is vast and far beyond human comprehension (see *Meterology* 351b8), he nonetheless maintains that there is no essential change, no progress, in history. Although he would have his own reasons for thinking so, he would thus not shy away from Henry Ford's notorious statement that "history is more or less bunk."[27]

The great contrast and break with Aristotle's (with the ancient) view of history came with the advent of Christianity, which at least in some of its iterations holds that there is an essential difference between human lives lived before and after the birth of Jesus Christ. In Dante's *Inferno*, for example, even the most worthy of ancient philosophers and poets, especially his beloved Virgil, are consigned to Limbo, the first circle of Hell.[28] Simply because of the historical period into which they were born, the possibility of salvation, available only to those born in the "Common Era," is irrevocably closed to them. On this view, then, with the passage of millennia there has been progress of incalculable significance.

The Christian view, itself dependent upon the equally linear story of revelation told in the Hebrew Bible, helped shape the modern scientific one, at least insofar as the latter also was convinced of the reality of historical progress. The many revolutionaries of the period hoped to usher in a new age in which human life would be transformed by the advances in technology. Recall Descartes's enthusiastic outburst, cited in the Introduction, concerning the future developments that awaited medical science: "It is true that medicine at present contains little of such great value; but without intending to belittle it, I am sure that everyone, even among those who follow the profession, will admit that everything we know is almost nothing compared with what remains to be discovered, and that we might rid ourselves of an infinity of maladies of body as well as of mind, and perhaps also of the enfeeblement of old age, if we have sufficient understanding of the causes and of all the remedies which nature has provided."

While Descartes may or may not have invested much hope in the salvation of his Christian soul, the passage above, so remarkably prophetic of our own medically obsessed culture, clearly shows him anticipating technological salvation: the "enfeeblement" of old age can be defeated by those properly in the know.

A singular figure in this discussion is Hegel, whose notion of the unfolding of "spirit" throughout history shaped so much of the nineteenth century historically based scholarship whose shadow still looms large. On his view, history imposes essential constraints on human achievement. It was simply impossible, for example, for the fullness of truth to have been discovered in Ancient Greece, for it had not yet been made present. Even today we take a Hegelian conception of history for granted by simply assuming that periods of the past differ in some essential way from the present. To dismiss the relevance of history and instead to join Aristotle in believing that a human being can in any period simply behold the truth will provoke the ire of a thinker like Richard Rorty, who, paraphrasing Hegel's remark that "no one can escape the substance of his time any more than he can jump out of his own skin," characterized classical philosophy, and thus Aristotle's own work, as "the impossible attempt to step outside of our skins."[29]

For Aristotle, we can transcend the particulars of our historical circumstances. Despite the changes the surface of the earth undergoes, the world is constant and available for inspection by anyone who thinks about it hard and well enough. Truth is available no matter when the philosopher lives.

I.8: Religion Bears Witness to the Truth.

A perennial view and one Aristotle takes to be both compatible with and supportive of the results of his cosmological theorizing is that there is a God who forever lives upstairs. Most people express this idea in the form of stories and images rather than in the sort of syllogized or conceptual language Aristotle deploys in his own writings. Nonetheless, when an ordinary person worships a God above, she, however non-philosophical she may be, touches upon the truth. Aristotle explains:

> It has been transmitted from the ancients and the earliest of thinkers and bequeathed to modern thinkers in the form of myths that the heavenly bodies are divine and that the divine encompasses the entirety of nature. The mythical formulation of this view has been added with an eye towards persuading the majority of people and is for their benefit when it comes to the establishment of laws. For it is told to the many that these [divine beings] are in the form of human beings and are like other animals. . . . But if someone were to isolate the primary belief in these traditional views—namely, that the first beings are divine—he would consider them to have been spoken divinely and that while it is likely that every science and philosophy has been discovered many times, and then has perished again, these beliefs about the divine have been saved to this day like a relic. The ancient belief and what has come down to us from the first thinkers is only to this extent apparent (*phanera*) to us. (*Metaphysics* 1074b1–14)

Aristotle distinguishes between the "many," those ordinary folk incapable of understanding complex arguments about the nature of the cosmos (and in need of religious institutions to keep them in line), and the philosophical few. The latter make arguments like those found in *On the Heavens*. The former go to church. In so doing they bear witness, however inarticulately, to the truth of the world.

Consider this passage from *On the Heavens*: "If one trusts in the principles that have been laid down, it is apparent from what has been said that the first body is eternal and admitting neither of growth nor of decay it is ageless and does not suffer any alteration. Thus it seems that the *logos* bears witness (*marturein*) to the phenomena and the phenomena to the *logos*. For all human beings have a conception about the gods and all, both barbarian and Greek, assign the highest place to the divine" (270b1–7).

A witness, a "martyr," offers testimony or provides evidence. A carefully argued *logos* gives evidence about, articulates, illuminates, and preserves the phenomena, the way the world shows itself in ordinary experience. Unlike all objects found on earth, Aristotle has argued, the heavenly bodies are made of a weightless, eternal stuff. He supports this contention by referring to empirical observations: the orbits of the heavenly bodies do not appear to change, nor do stars fall down. His *logos* explains why. Conversely, the phenomena provide testimony to the *logos*. Aristotle summons an ordinary religious conviction or reputable belief, that god lives eternally on high, as witness for the truth of the *logos* offered in *On the Heavens*.

Far from the irreconcilable antagonists they are now taken to be, religion and science are allies. The fact that "all" human beings worship a god above, a statement surely exaggerated, coupled with Aristotle's conviction that human beings regularly and naturally attain the truth—a conviction as central to his thinking as it is foreign to ours—testifies to the scientific truth that the heavenly bodies are eternal.

Imagine that Aristotle is correct in believing that human beings regularly attain something of the truth. Imagine further that the world from top (the stars) to bottom (the earth) is comprehensible in the same familiar terms we use to navigate through the contours of our own daily lives. If so, there would be good reason to think that the heavenly bodies above us are just that: above us. According to the nontechnical observations of the naked eye, they don't fall down, their paths are constant, and they do not change. This is consistent with the religious belief that above us there is an everlasting being ontologically superior to the fire, earth, water, and air of which we and all other earthly beings are made.

Such a thinking will seem pathetically naïve to contemporary deflationists like Richard Dawkins and Daniel Dennett. The titles of their recent books tell much: *The God Delusion* and *Breaking The Spell: Religion as a Natural Phenomenon.*[30] Both follow the path blazed by Spinoza and think they know why ignorant human beings continue to worship a God that does not exist. In Dennett's view, the human animal may well have evolved in such a manner as to dispose it to think, quite falsely, that God in various forms exists. In fact, this tendency, which is perhaps even a consequence of our neuronal architecture, may have actually enhanced the survival prospects of our species in the distant past. Consider the following description of his position.

It begins with the elementary assertion that "everything that moves needs something like a mind, to keep it out of harm's way and help it find the good things." To this end, there arose in very ancient times the evolutionary adaptation that one researcher has called a "hyperactive agent detection device, or HADD." This cognitive skill taught us, or a very early version of us, that we live in a world of other minds—and taught us too well, because it instilled "the urge to treat things—especially frustrating things—as agents with beliefs and desires." This urge is "deeply rooted in human biology," and it results in a "fantasy-generation process" that left us "finding agency wherever anything puzzles or frightens us." Eventually this animism issued in deities, who were simply the "agents who had access to all the strategic information" that we desperately lacked.[31]

The disposition of the modern philosopher is to distrust the testimony of common sense, "folk psychology," the senses unaided by powerful observational tools, natural language, and certainly the intuitions that animate religious conviction. In other words, he or she assumes that except in the extraordinary environment of the laboratory or in the process of mathematical analysis we tend to get things all wrong. Believing this modern science has ushered in an age of spectacular scientific and technological progress. As each day passes we seem to be getting closer to the Cartesian dream of becoming "masters and possessors of nature."

But to recall the caveat offered by Tom Stoppard's character Bernard, "don't confuse progress with perfectibility." The former is potentially infinite, whereas the latter, expressed in the Greek word *teleion* (>II.8), requires some conception of a *telos,* an end, goal, or purpose. No matter how powerful our machines become, it is far from clear that we will consistently be able to put them to good use.

Chapter Two

Nature Is Purpose.

"Nature is purpose (*telos*)"

—*Physics* 194a28

"Nature does everything for the sake of something"

—On Respiration 471b25

"Nature does nothing in vain"

—*Politics* 1253a9[1]

"In seeking to show that Nature does nothing in vain . . . [men] seem to have shown only this, that Nature and the gods are as crazy as mankind"

—Spinoza, *Ethics*, Appendix to Part I

II.1: Teleology Is Good Science.

An Aristotelian science—or better yet, an Aristotelian theory—articulates the "causes" of things. As he puts it, "we say that to know what something is and to know the cause (*to aition*) of what it is are the same" (*Posterior Analytics* 93a5).

Book I.1 of the *Metaphysics* explains what a "cause" is by offering a developmental account of knowledge in general. To summarize: all animals have some kind of sense perception (*aisthesis*) that affords them awareness of the external world. While plants also have the capacity to nourish and reproduce themselves, animals are distinguished by their ability to perceive at least some aspect of the external world. From such perceptions some animals develop a memory. Other more highly developed animals can somehow collect their memories into what Aristotle calls "experience," the translation of *empeiria,* the root of our word "empirical." It is not clear how this occurs, but "many memories of the same thing result in the capacity for having a single experience" (980a27). Experience, then, is like a "coagulation of memories."[2] Some human beings are limited to this sort of cognitive apprehension of the world. Take, for example, an amateur car mechanic. He has been around cars his entire life and so he can fix his own and others like his own. He can hear when a piston isn't firing properly and see when a belt is worn, and then fix them both. But he cannot explain why his work succeeds, or on the basis of what physical principles an engine operates. What he lacks, therefore, is what Aristotle here calls *techne,* which in this context connotes knowledge in a broad sense (and is at the root of the English "technical").

"Knowledge comes to be whenever from many thoughts that have emerged from experience one universal conception emerges about these similar things" (981a5–7). Someone who has experienced the pain of many headaches and then the relief that comes by taking aspirin will recommend aspirin to a friend suffering a headache, and it may help. But he cannot say much beyond "Aspirin usually works, at least for me." He cannot explain what aspirin is or what a headache is or why the former helps to alleviate the latter. By contrast, the person trained in medical science has studied physiology, knows how aspirin interacts with the blood, and can do exactly this. In medical school she has studied the human body as such; that is, the form (*eidos*) of the human body. Because all human beings belong to the same species (*eidos*), they are structurally similar to one another and so aspirin works in roughly the same fashion in all their bodies. The physician knows this and so can do more than recommend aspirin. She has a *logos* (981a15), a rational account of the cause, and so can explain why the aspirin works. The person of experience, by contrast, only "knows" that it works. An answer to the "why question" constitutes knowledge of the cause.[3]

Differently stated, unlike a merely experienced person, one with knowledge can teach. In fact, "in general, a sign of one who knows is the ability to teach" (981b7); that is, to explain and articulate the cause to someone else.

As he shows in the *Physics,* a salient feature of an Aristotelian science is that it requires knowledge of four different causes; four kinds of answers to different sorts of questions. Each has a traditional title, ones Aristotle himself does not use but are helpful nonetheless.

1. The *material cause* answers the question "What is its stuff?" or "What is it made of?" Bronze, for example, is the material cause of the statue.

2. The *formal cause* answers the question "What is it?" This is the *logos* of the "essence" or, more literally, the "what it is to be" (>III.2).
3. The *efficient cause* is the "first origin of a change or rest." For example, the person who has deliberated is the cause (of an action) and the father is the cause of the child. In general, the efficient cause is the producer (*to poion*) of an effect (194b30–32). As such, it corresponds most closely to the modern conception of a cause.
4. The *final cause* is something's goal, purpose, or end (*telos*). It answers the question "What is it for?" or "For the sake of what is it?" Aristotle's example is health, which is understood as the "end" of walking (when one walks in order to get salubrious exercise) (194b33).

In summing up this section, Aristotle says, "causes are spoken of in this many ways" (195a4). This statement, as well as the comments offered above, might suggest that causes are somehow linguistic entities. There are four sorts of questions that human beings frequently ask, and the answers to them become the four causes. Aristotle says as much in the *Posterior Analytics*: "there are four kinds of question that we ask, and they correspond to the kinds of things that we know" (89b23–24). Such remarks provoke the standard challenge: why should a good scientist, striving to understand the causal structure of reality, care about what sorts of questions people typically ask? More generally, the critic might object, the way people ordinarily talk is never scientifically relevant (unless one is studying psychology or linguistics). While people often do ask questions like "Why do trees have roots?" and mean by it "What is the purpose of the root system of a tree?" a rigorous study of nature does not concern itself with purposes. To think it should is to be badly seduced by ordinary language.

The serious scientist working in the contemporary laboratory is interested in only one kind of cause: that which produces an effect or the "efficient" cause. Unlike today's scientist—whose goal is to attain power over nature by learning how effects are produced—how, in other words, things work—Aristotle himself attributes the most significance to the formal cause. In order to fully understand a being, one must understand what it is. The world is composed of a multitude of different sorts of beings, each with its own "ontological integrity," a phrase to be explained shortly. And to know the world, we must know and be able to explain what they are (>III.2).

As Aristotle himself well understood, the final cause is controversial. In fact, in *Physics* II.8 he articulates, in order to refute, the position of a potential critic:

> There is a question: what stops nature from acting neither purposively nor because it is better, but instead like rain? Rain does not fall in order that grain may grow but from necessity. For that which has been drawn up must be cooled and that which has been cooled and has become water must come down. That grains grows when this happens is a coincidence. In a similar fashion, if some grain on the threshing floor is destroyed by rain, it did not rain for the sake of destroying that grain. This was a coincidence. What stops us from thinking that the same is true of the parts of natural organisms? For example, why isn't it from necessity that the front teeth come up sharp and fit for tearing while the back ones are useful for chewing food? Isn't it the case that the back teeth didn't come into being for the sake of this but that it merely happened that way? More generally, isn't this true of all the other parts of animals in which the "for sake of which" seems to belong? Whenever they happened to come into being in a fashion as if they were for the sake of something, the organism, having been favorably constituted by chance, happened to survive. Those animals that were not favorably constituted, just as Empedocles said about the man-faced oxen, perished. (198b17–33)

Aristotle's opponent—in the passage above it is the fifth-century thinker Empedocles—takes his bearings from a process like the falling of rain.[4] This is, as Aristotle seems to grant, a purposeless or mechanical event that occurs only because of the contact-actions between various elements. When water is heated it evaporates and is drawn upward in the atmosphere, where it is then cooled. Becoming more "earth-like" or heavier, it falls to the ground. As he puts it in the *Meteorology*, "moisture always rises on account of the power of heat and is carried downward towards the earth on account of cold" (347a8–10).

While rain is necessary for grain to grow, and in this sense causes it, it does not fall for the purpose of growing grain. (Nor is it the result of a benevolent deity who arranged for rain to fall just where and when we need it to.) Instead, agriculture is just a coincidental, a lucky (for us) by-product of an otherwise mechanical (efficient) set of events. As such, Aristotle is not an "anthropocentrist" of the sort who believes that "the entire contents of the natural world, including not only plants and animals but perhaps even seasons and weather, exist and function primarily for the benefit of man."[5] Instead, his anthropocentrism maintains that the earth is the center of the world and that as a result theoretical inquiry takes it bearings from how the world looks from an earthbound, naked-eye, human perspective.

When Aristotle criticizes his opponent, it is not because of the way he analyzes how rain works, but for conceiving of all nature as modeled on this sort of causal event. A thinker like Empedocles would, for example, explain the sharpness of our front teeth as the result of a chance event—we would say a genetic mutation—that occurred in our ancestors of millennia ago. Because it enhanced their survival prospects, it was passed on to future generations. There was no purposiveness at work in the front teeth becoming sharp, only random events that happened to work out well for the human animals, who then passed on this trait to their offspring. Aristotle objects:

> It is impossible for things to be like this. For [the front and back teeth] and everything that is by nature either always or for the most part comes to be in this fashion, while nothing that occurs because of luck or chance happens this way. For it does not seem to be either from luck or from coincidence that it often rains in the winter. If, by contrast, it rains during the dog days of summer it would be counted as a chance occurrence. Similarly, it does not seem to be from chance that it is hot in the summer but only if it is hot in the winter. So, if it seems to be either a matter of chance or a matter of the "for the sake of which," and if these things are not a matter of chance or coincidence, they must be a matter of the "for the sake of which." Even those [like Empedocles] holding these views would say that all these things are by nature. Therefore, the "for the sake of which" is present within those things that come to be or are by nature. (198b33–199a7)

If something happens "always or for the most part" it cannot be because of chance. If it were to rain in Greece during the summer, this would be recognized as a fluke, for normally, or naturally, it is hot in the summer.[6] Because generation after generation of human beings have sharp front teeth chance is eliminated as a causal factor, and Empedocles was thus quite wrong. Worse than that, thinkers like Empedocles who deny teleology "destroy what is by nature and indeed nature itself. For those things that are by nature, being moved continuously by some principle in themselves, arrive at some *telos*" (199b15). Destroy teleology, destroy nature.

Clearly, another name must be added to the list of Aristotle's opponents: Darwin. The notions of adaptation and survival that Aristotle attributes to Empedocles prefigured, however dimly, the theory of natural selection. Darwin himself says as much when he comments on this very passage from the *Physics:*

> Aristotle . . . after remarking that rain does not fall in order to make the corn grow, any more than it falls to spoil the farmer's corn when threshed out of doors, applies the same argument to organisation: and adds . . . so what hinders the different parts [of the body] from having this merely accidental relation in nature? as the teeth, for example, grow by necessity, the front ones sharp, adapted for dividing, and the grinders flat, and serviceable for masticating the food; since they were not made for the sake of this, but it was the result of accident. And in like manner as to the other parts in which there appears to exist an adaptation to an end. Wheresoever, therefore, all things together (that is all the parts of one whole) happened like as if they were made for the sake of something, these were preserved, having been appropriately constituted by an internal spontaneity; and whatsoever things were not thus constituted perished, and still perish. We here see the principle of natural selection shadowed forth, but how little Aristotle fully comprehended this principle, is shown by his remarks on the formation of the teeth.[7]

For Darwin, had Aristotle but followed Empedocles' lead in accounting for the sharpness of the front teeth, he would not have fallen into the abyss of teleology. Unfortunately, by insisting that efficient causality and chance, coupled with the drive to survive, are not sufficient to explain organic structure of animals and the regularity of biological reproduction, he wrongly attributed purposiveness to nature itself.

Aristotle understands that efficient causality and chance can produce effects that seem to be, but are not, purposive.

> What is for the sake of something could come about from chance. For example, we say that it was by chance that the stranger came and ransomed the prisoner whenever he came and did this just as if he had come in order to do this even when he

> did not come in order to do this. And in this case the result is by accident [even if it was beneficial]. For luck is an accidental cause, just as we said earlier. But whenever this [sort of beneficial result] occurs always or for the most part it cannot come to be by accident or by luck. In natural beings, the result always does come about in this way [for the most part or always], unless there is some impediment. (*Physics* 199b18–26)

Aristotle's example here (which might be a literary allusion) is the rich stranger who stumbles upon a prisoner, whom he then ransoms. He did not arrive at the prisoner's location on purpose; he just happened to be in the right place at the right time in order to save him.[8] By contrast, the regularity of the reproduction and the consistent organization of living beings cannot be explained in this manner. In generation after generation of human beings the teeth do good work as they tear food and prepare it for digestion. They fulfill a purpose that contributes to the well-being of the entire animal. Chance cannot account for organisms that regularly reproduce themselves such that their parts do a good job in maintaining their integrity as living beings. Teleology is required to explain this stable and nonrandom character of nature, especially the recurrence of the parts of animals.

Of course, we know Aristotle is wrong. Indeed, showing that any sort of teleology is misguided precisely because it misunderstands the role of chance is the purpose of Richard Dawkins's book *The Blind Watchmaker*.[9]

Dawkins begins by acknowledging, as of course he must, "the nonrandomness that we see in living systems" (44). In other words, no reasonable observer can deny the fantastically consistent patterns and structures repeated in the generation of animals. Such reiterated order can best be explained, he thinks, by the theory of natural selection.

> Evolution basically consists of endless repetition of reproduction. In every generation, reproduction takes the genes that are supplied to it by the previous generation, and hands them on to the next generation but with minor random errors—mutations. A mutation simply consists in +1 or −1 being added to the value of a randomly chosen gene. This means that, as the generations go by, the total amount of genetic difference from the original ancestor can become very large, cumulatively, one small step at a time. But although the mutations are random, the cumulative change over the generations is not random. The progeny of any one generation are different from their parents

in random directions. But which of those progeny is selected to go forward into the next generation is not random. (56)

Chance is only a "minor ingredient" (49) in this process, for through "cumulative selection" organisms become "quintessentially *non*random" (49). In other words, biological reproduction regularizes the generations of organisms to a high degree, even if random mutations have occurred in past generations. As a result, Dawkins is every bit as impressed as Aristotle by the marvelous order and complexity of animal life. Indeed, he is every bit as impressed by this as was William Paley, the eighteenth-century theologian who famously deployed an analogy to argue on behalf of what is now called "intelligent design." If he were to find a stone in a heath, Paley argued, and were asked how it had come to be there, "I might possibly answer that, for any thing I knew to the contrary, it had lain there forever." But such an answer would fail were one to find a watch, for it is a mechanism of such complicated design, whose "several parts are framed and put together for a purpose," that an "inference is inevitable: that the watch must have had a maker; that there must have existed, at some time and at some place or other, an artificer who formed it." Because "the contrivances of nature surpass the contrivances of art . . . in a degree which exceeds all computation"—in other words, because a living organism is vastly more complex than a watch—there must, Paley concluded, be an intelligent Creator, a grand designer of nature. The subtitle of his book *Natural Theology* (originally published in 1802) states its thesis: *Evidences of the Existence and Attributes of the Deity; Collected from the Appearances of Nature.*[10]

Dawkins, the title of whose book is inspired by Paley's analogy, assaults it with a vengeance. "The analogy between telescope and eye, between watch and living organism, is false. All appearances to the contrary, the only watchmaker in nature is the blind forces of physics, albeit deployed in a very special way. . . . Natural selection, the blind, unconscious, automatic process which Darwin discovered, and which we now know is the explanation for the existence and apparently purposeful form of all life, has no purpose in mind" (5)

By using the phrases "all *appearances* to the contrary" and "*apparently* purposeful form of all life" (my emphasis), Dawkins reiterates a sentiment familiar since the time of Bacon and Spinoza. Although nature itself has no purpose in mind—indeed, it has no mind—human beings are naturally but mistakenly seduced by appearances, by how the world shows itself to them in ordinary, naked-eye experience. As a result, many people foolishly take the natural world to be teleologically ordered. A more specific reason for this common—in fact, this natural—error is that we are almost entirely surrounded by the products of human artifice. Most of the objects with which we interact on a daily basis have been produced and put where they are by other human beings who had a specific purpose in mind when they did so. Remaining pegged to the immediacy of the human environment could thus easily seduce one into thinking that the nonhuman world, nature itself, is teleologically ordered in an analogous fashion.

Dawkins has another explanation for why people believe that nature is purpose. "It is," he suggests, "almost as if [the human brain] were specifically designed to misunderstand Darwinism" (xv). He elaborates with an example: "Our brains are built to deal with events on radically different timescales from those that characterize evolutionary change." We think in terms of events or processes that take hours, days, years or decades. The outer limits of our ordinary timescale reach roughly from our grandparents to our grandchildren, and our ability to operate within this frame clearly enhances our ability to effectively manage our lives, and thus increases our prospect of survival. By contrast, "Darwinism is a theory of cumulative processes so slow that they take between thousands and millions of decades to complete." Therefore, to think through the world in the terms that constitute the theory of natural selection requires a monumental "effort of the imagination," for the scientist must "escape from the prison of familiar timescale" (xvi). In order for the Darwinian scientist to understand nature as it is in itself, and not as human beings wish it to be, she must assume a vantage point vastly beyond that of ordinary experience. Only from there will natural beings be understood as having emerged through the "blind forces of physics."

For Dawkins, thinking in terms of hours, days, and years—and in terms of purposes—is like being in "prison," from which the serious scientist escapes by conceiving the biological world in evolutionary terms and invoking a time scale whose units are in the millions of years. Entering the laboratory, therefore, the biologist must put on her scientist's hat and strive to leave her familiar human assumptions at the door. If her research is successful, then she will have learned something about how organisms actually work on the molecular level, and her results can then be usefully applied. But what exactly will be done with this knowledge she has discovered? Will it be used to create supermeds to heal us of our woes or weapons-grade germs to wipe us out? Even if some evolutionary changes have taken millions of years, in a single generation the fruits of modern biology have already greatly altered the way we actually live here on earth. And these changes are moving us to where? In other words, to what ends or purposes will biological research be put? Will anti-depressants be available in vending machines for those moments when we feel blue? Will sleeping pills be cleansed of their side effects so that insomnia will plague us no more? To reiterate the key point, today's biologist hasn't a clue. For in order to enter her lab properly, she had to check her humanity, which includes her disposition to think purposively, at the door. As a result, she has no knowledge to turn to for guidance on these thoroughly human questions. What she needs in order to bring the results of her research down to earth, to apply it technically in a decent and humane manner, is an understanding of what Dawkins calls our "prison."

It is precisely such a "prisonology" that Aristotle provides. His teleology fits the world in which we actually live our lives. By contrast, by suppressing teleology and methodically testing for and measuring efficient causality, Dawkins can explain, far better than Aristotle, how bats, whose eyes are tiny, nonetheless can find their prey at night. They have a complex sonar system that allows them to detect echoes of things, and Dawkins explains how it works. But where he goes deadly wrong is in this statement: "Darwinism encompasses all of life—human, animal, plant, bacterial . . . extraterrestrial. It provides the only satisfying explanation for why we all exist, why we are the way that we are. It is the bedrock on which rest all the disciplines known as the humanities" (x).

This pronouncement would be worth taking seriously only if explaining how things work were the single task of legitimate knowledge. But what if the goal of a theory aims to do more than that? What if, for example, someone seeks to know what things mean? This question may seem entirely out of place when studying the mechanics of the bat's sonar system. But when Dawkins asserts that Darwinism can tell us "why we all exist," he is far out of his depth. For, to reiterate, his "why" refers only to the efficient cause. But a normal human being asking, "Why do I exist?" is not and should not be satisfied by a lecture on genetics or a catalog of fossil evidence. We want to know purpose, and on this Darwinism can tell us nothing. Insofar as good science, good theorizing, must respect and take account of human experience, natural selection, for all it succeeds in telling us how the biological world works, fails the test.

II.2: Intelligent Design Isn't All Stupid.

With predecessors like Paley, a movement called "Intelligent Design" (ID) is afoot (especially in America), and people like Dawkins think it is both stupid and dangerous. Its proponents have gained visibility by fighting to revise the biology curricula of school systems around the country. Like Paley, Intelligent Designers hold that living organisms are so complex that they must have been created by some kind of higher force. They occasionally claim to be neutral as to what this higher force might be. In other words, they try to keep their specific religious convictions backstage and instead advance their position by appealing to what they take to be the high ground of intellectual honesty. On their view, Darwinian evolution, in which physical and chemical laws plus chance are adequate to explain all natural phenomena, is only a theory and so should be subjected to criticism and competition. The alternative it recommends is that some form of intelligence was actively at work in the coming into being, in the design, of the natural world. (See, for example, the Web site http://www.intelligentdesign.org/.)

The proponents of ID rightly emphasize that the consequences of both their own view and evolutionary theory go far beyond the scientific. The latter, which they describe as purely naturalistic, has profound implications for ethics, religion, and government and can be used to support non-theistic religions and beliefs systems, while ID supports traditional theistic beliefs. Included among such traditional beliefs would be the view that the biblical God was the intelligent creator of the extraordinarily complex world of animals.

Dawkins accuses the proponents of ID of trying to smuggle religious dogma into the school system under the guise of science. As he puts it, "the anti-evolution propagandists are always religiously motivated" (xi). Dawkins says this because he is convinced that there is no rational evidence for ID. He would be right about this if the only measure of rationality were that supplied by modern biology. Fortunately, this is not true.

A recent court ruling sided with Dawkins. In December 2005, in a case reminiscent of the 1925 Scopes Trial, a federal judge prohibited a Pennsylvania public school district from teaching Intelligent Design in biology classes, arguing that the concept is really but creationism in disguise. Still, as a cultural force, ID is far from dead, for its adherents have a firm hold on the imagination of many. This is not simply the result of ignorance and religious propagandizing, for ID isn't all stupid. Indeed, its plea for intellectual honesty has some merit, for there is surely a need for theories to compete against Darwinism. The best candidate would be Aristotelian teleology.

Intelligent Design is not stupid insofar as it is construed as a response to the "crisis" described in the Introduction to this book. A universe structured only by the blind forces of physics and whose relevant units of time span millions of years is one in which human beings have no place. It is meaningless and can offer no answer to the "why question" of human life. In the long run, it is uninhabitable. Because we actually do inhabit the earth it is not stupid to try to think through an alternative.

Consider the following remark by Michael Behe, a spokesman for Intelligent Design. "The strong appearance of design allows a disarmingly simple argument: if it looks, walks, and quacks like a duck, then absent compelling evidence to the contrary, we have warrant to conclude it's a duck. Design should not be overlooked simply because it's so obvious."[11]

This passage begins with an Aristotelian sentiment: a duck shows itself to be a duck; it is neither a goose nor a snail. It is an organic being characterized by its own ontological integrity; it is what it is and is not another thing. Precisely such "integrity" (which derives from the Latin *integer*, meaning "entire," "whole," or "complete") is challenged by the Darwinian model. No being simply is what it is; it has a history and is in the process of development. On a molecular level the duck is not really a duck at all and in fact is not too different from the snail.

The ontological integrity of a natural being (especially an animal), its form, goes hand in glove with teleology (>III.3). An animal is complete and organically unified, for all its parts contribute to the well-being or maintenance of the whole. As such, every part has a purpose, and this relationship between an animal and its parts is the paradigm of final causality.

Like Aristotle, and unlike Dawkins, Behe insists that good science must take cognizance of the appearances, especially the show of purposiveness characteristic of animals. But he draws a non-Aristotelian conclusion from his reckoning of the appearances, for with Paley he takes them as evidence of Design and hence of a Designer. By contrast, Aristotle takes it as evidence of the stable and orderly character of the natural world. Like Dawkins, his view of the world is "purely naturalistic." Furthermore, even though he himself regularly invokes an analogy between craft and nature (see, for example, *Physics* 199a12–20), Aristotle also would join Dawkins in thinking that ID pushes the analogy much too far. Even though he insists that teleology is good science, and natural beings, particularly living ones, can only be explained through some sort of purposiveness, his is a world with no Designer. As Allan Gotthelf puts it, even if Aristotle's conception of "organic development is actually directive," it is not "directed."[12] The world is purposively organized but not designed.

Although his thinking is also "purely naturalistic," Aristotle would criticize Darwinian natural selection for the same reason he criticizes Empedocles. The order, stability, regularity, and directiveness of the world cannot be explained by the blind forces of physics. There are purposes; there is meaning. Destroy teleology, destroy nature.

In short, Aristotelian teleology is a middle way between ID and evolutionary biology. Teleology affirms the purposiveness of nature without succumbing to the temptation of a Grand Designer. It is a naturalistic mode of thinking that does not strip the world bare of its goodness or beauty. Most important, Aristotelian theory, infused as it is with formal and final causality, bespeaks ordinary human life as it is actually experienced here on earth. For us, who see the world with naked eyes and say what we see, the front teeth *are* for the purpose of tearing food apart. Animals *are* identified by means of their visible species, the natural kinds to which they belong and which appear to be stable. They are macroscopic beings with ontological integrity, and some of them can even become our friends. A burning match is held underneath a cigar: fire *does* move upward toward the heavens. For us, as members of families and as citizens, the earth *is* the center of the world, at least the one in which we live and bury our dead. Unless we are in a laboratory, or examining the latest transmissions from the Hubble telescope, for us the world *is* a meaningful cosmos, not an infinite and hence meaningless universe. While over the millions of years of earth's history the climate in Greece has changed, in human memory it has "always or usually" been hot there in the summer. Even from the perspective of geological time, of which Aristotle was quite aware (<I.7), the world is orderly, stable, and purposively directive.

II.3: Some Beings Are Natural; Others Are Not.

Before going forward, a step back to the beginning, to the bedrock conception of nature that Aristotle articulates in the *Physics*.

> Some beings are natural; others are on account of different causes. Animals and their parts, plants and the simple bodies (like earth, fire, air and water) are natural. For we say that these beings and ones like them are natural. All of the beings that have been mentioned appear to differ from those that are not composed by nature. For all natural beings have in themselves an origin of motion and rest: some with respect to place, some with respect to growth and decay, some with respect to qualitative change. But to the extent that a bed or a cloak or any other similar sort of being is the result of human artifice

> (*techne*) it has no innate impulse of change. . . . For nature is the origin and cause of being moved and rest in those beings in which it belongs primarily and in virtue of itself, rather than accidentally. (192b8–24)

The beings of Aristotle's world are neatly divided into those that are natural, which have their origin of motion and rest within themselves, and those that are artificial, whose origin is in human artifice.[13] An unambiguous example of a natural being is a heavenly body like the moon or the sun, for human beings can have no effect on them or their movements in any way. These bodies just are what they are, as they move simply by virtue of a nonhuman principle at work within themselves. The best example of a natural being, however, and the first on Aristotle's list is an animal. It nourishes, reproduces, and moves itself and can perceive at least some aspect of the external world. While it is alive it maintains its ontological integrity, as its parts contribute to the functioning of the whole organism through metabolic activity. By contrast, a watch would not exist without the productive effort of a watchmaker who formed various materials into a working whole, and it would not keep time without an external source of energy.

The choice of animals as the first example of a natural being may seem odd. After all, it appears in a book called *Physics*, and in contemporary science animals seem to be the subject of a different discipline entirely, namely biology or zoology. Not for Aristotle. Physics is the study of nature in its broadest sense and so includes cosmology, meterology, zoology, psychology, geology, and botany. That animals are first on his list suggests that this is the best example not only of a natural being, but more generally, of being itself (>III.3).

Aristotle's confidence in making the distinction between what is natural and what is not should be challenged. Think of a dog. Because it is an animal, it seems to be a natural being. But a dog also is the product of some fifteen thousand years of domestication, the end result of which is a former wolf intentionally bred and thus well suited to interacting beneficially and enjoyably with human beings. Is such a being natural? What about agricultural items like the grape and the olive? At the farthest end of this spectrum lie genetically modified microbes, crops, insects, or even animals that have been cloned. Such gray-zone entities suggest that Aristotle may be overconfident in sharply dividing beings in the world into two categories: the artificial whose origin is in the human artificer and the natural, which stands on its own.

Another challenge: perhaps the human mind can never determine with certainty whether an entity is genuinely natural. The essential feature of a natural item (call it X) is its independence from human artifice; it has its origin of motion and rest within itself. However, thinking, seeing, or saying something about X automatically implicates the human agent who does the thinking, seeing, or saying something about X, and these activities might compromise any attempt to determine the independence of X from the agent. For in thinking about it, X becomes an object of thought. How, then, could its ability to exist not merely as an object of thought, but independently from thought, ever be proven? After all, proving is a kind of thinking.

A key word in explaining why Aristotle disagrees is *theoria*, the root of our "theory" and "theoretical." It derives from *theôrein*, whose original meaning is "to look at," and is one of Aristotle's favorite and most expressive words to describe the activity of thinking (>V.8).[14] Like ordinary looking, *theoria* does not alter the object being theorized. It does not, to extend the sensual metaphor, touch them and thus is able to apprehend an object without moving or changing it. If *theoria,* theoretical or intellectual activity in general, is like looking or seeing, then it is innocent, able to see things for what they really are without imposing itself upon them. The following is a prime example of Aristotle's "theoretical optimism."[15]

> It would be ridiculous to try to prove that nature exists. For it is apparent (*phaneron*) that there are many of these sorts of beings. And to prove what is apparent (*ta phanera*) through what is not apparent is characteristic of someone not able to distinguish between what is knowable through itself and what is not knowable through itself. It is clear, however, that it is possible to suffer this defect. For someone who has been blind from birth could argue about colors. In such cases, the argument (*logos*) would be merely about words rather than an instance of real thinking (*noein*). (*Physics* 193a3–9)

It is "apparent" to us that natural beings, whose origin of motion and rest are within themselves and not in us, exist. (Note that "apparent" translates *phaneron,* which like *phainomenon* derives from *phainesthai*, "to appear.") These beings show themselves to us in ordinary experience, and so it would be ridiculous to try to prove that this is so. A proof begins with something like an axiom, a primitive statement that must be taken as true and cannot itself be proven. "Axiom" derives from the Greek *axios* and thus refers to what is "worthy" of being counted as true. In other words, it is self-evident or somehow knowable through itself. The self-showing of natural beings to us is axiomatic. It would thus be as foolish to try to prove nature exists as it would be to prove that the principle of noncontradiction, which is the fundamental axiom required in all proof procedures, is true (>III.4).

Another way to approach this idea was suggested above: it would be ridiculous to try to prove that nature exists because a proof is a human activity and a natural being is one whose origin is independent of human activity. Trying to prove the natural exists would thus be like trying to prove that there is something that exists beyond consciousness. Once the proof has begun, the item in question has entered human consciousness.[16] Therefore, the best Aristotle can do to support his assertion is recommend that the reader look for herself. It is the world out there, rather than an argument, that secures the truth of Aristotle's assertion. A clever debater, who for example conjures up an "evil genius," can make sophisticated arguments purporting to show that nature does not exist, or that motion is not real, or that the ideas in our minds have no resemblance to real objects in the world. But serious thought, genuinely theoretical activity, is more than clever talk. It requires a careful looking at and an appreciative thinking about what is seen, and then a meticulous articulation in language or *logos*. If successful, the result is a truthful account or theory of the way things really are.

II.4: Form Is Nature More than Matter.

Back to the four causes: assume for a moment that Aristotle is right and that we can identify as natural those beings with the source of motion and rest within themselves rather than in a human technician. But more needs to be said about what these sorts of beings really are.

The core of Aristotle's view about natural beings is that they consist of form and matter. Matter is the stuff of which things are composed. Recall that Aristotle thinks there are four basic elements—earth, air, water, fire—as well as other primitive constituents of the material world, such as the hot and cold, and the dry and the wet. All natural things found on earth have these as their parts, and so matter makes an obvious and powerful claim to being "natural."

But there is a better candidate: form, the unifying shape of the whole being. Like *theoria,* which is derived from the verb "to look at," the Greek for "form" also has its roots in the visual: *eidos* is derived from the verb "to see." Literally, then, a form is the way a being looks (<I.4). Equally important, it is what is referred to by the name of a thing. I look at the animal on my couch, see what it is, and then say, "It's a cat." I do so because that's what it looks like and "cat" names the kind of animal it is. (The Latin translation of *eidos* is *species.*) The thing on my couch is com-

posed of elements such as calcium and carbon, but "cat" names the whole, the singular being seen by the person who speaks about it. A form, then, is what stands behind the word "cat" (>III.2).

Aristotle's conception of nature, and by extension the world itself, is captured in a single statement: "form is nature more than matter." To elaborate, imagine a pile of lumber in a woodworker's shop. It is potentially a bed, a chair, or a desk. Before it is made into a piece of furniture, it is no specific thing, just the stuff from which various pieces can be made. In a similar fashion, imagine a "pile" of carbon or calcium atoms, and contrast them with flesh or bone. "For potential flesh or bone does not yet have the nature of itself until it receives the form that is according to what we say flesh or bone is when we're talking about flesh or bone" (193b1). The pile of stuff is potentially this or that but what it is cannot be said. But a bone is what it is: actually a bone.

The above invokes what is perhaps the single most important distinction in Aristotle's thought: "actuality" or "actualization" standardly translates either *energeia* (more literally, "being-in-a-state-of-work") or *entelecheia* (being-in-the-state-of-having-reached-the-*telos*). "Potentiality" is the translation of *dunamis* (the root of "dynamite"). The two can be pegged analogically to form and matter: form is to actuality as matter is to potentiality. These terms are required to explain the concept of "motion" or "change," two ways of translating *kinesis*, which in turn is required to define nature (which is "a principle of motion or of change" [200b12]). Natural things are in motion. Therefore, because "our present study is about nature, we must not ignore the question, what is motion (*kinesis*)?" (200b12). And for this task the conceptual pair, actuality–potentiality, is required for a motion is "the actualization of what is potentially, insofar as it is potentially" (201a12).

A child is born. The father's semen, before being located in the mother's womb, was potentially that child. A beard changes from brown to gray; it was once potentially but is now actually gray. A woman learns how to play the guitar and thus makes the transition from being potentially to being actually musical. And the ball located now right here may, upon being kicked, soon be over there. We would call this last form of change "movement"; for Aristotle the more precise term would be "locomotion" or "change-of-place."

Kinesis, the actualization of what is potentially, requires the "having-of-an-end." In other words, in order for a change to occur and to be recognizable as it is occurring or when it has been completed, it must be directed at or have come to an end. The ball moved from there to here. I know this because I saw it before over there but now it has rolled over here. Its changing of place has come to an end. I know my beard has changed because it is now gray when once it was brown. We know when things are changing or have changed only because a *telos,* an end point of some sort, has rendered the change visible.

Differently stated: change or motion is an actualization but "an incomplete (*ateles*) one" (201b32). Something is changing if it hasn't reached its terminus yet. To explain that the changing is over, I would use the perfect tense—and recall that one translation of *teleion* is "perfect"—and say, "It has changed." I watch the pot of water on the stove as it nears the boiling point. The surface of the water begins to ripple and tiny bubbles appear. I know the water, which is potentially at the boiling point, is changing, is headed toward the boiling point because it is rolling but not boiling yet. Motion is visible to us as motion, and for this to be so it must have a *telos* toward which it is directed. If there were no *telos,* if the change were infinite or indeterminate, it would not be recognizable for what it is. For the rolling ball, if there were no "there" or never a time when the motion had ended or will end, the motion itself would become intelligible only through a geometrical representation. But motion is more concretely apprehensible than that. We see and recognize it and as such is a constitutive of our experience. We know to where the ball has rolled.

Considerations like those above make it clear that Aristotle's "final" is intimately related to his "formal" cause. *Telos* and *eidos* go hand in glove. "And since nature is two-fold, nature as matter and as form, and the form is the end, and since everything else is for the sake of the end, this cause [the formal] must be what things are for the sake of" (199a30–32).

Things move naturally and are directed to their form, their end. A ball is thrown upward but will be carried downward, its natural direction, back to the earth, which is its natural place (<I.4). A child is born and begins to grow toward being the fully mature animal. Its growth is teleological and headed toward an end; indeed, every part of its body contributes to the well-being of the whole body. The parts of the animal get their *telos* from the form of the animal, which in turn is where the animal's motions are directed.

To summarize: Aristotle thinks form is nature more than matter because (1) form and *telos* go hand in glove; (2) form or *telos* is required to understand motion, which is the "*entelecheia* of the potential insofar as it is potential"; (3) form is to actuality as matter is to potentiality and "each thing is said to be what it is when it is in a state of actuality, more so than when it is in a state of potentiality" (193b7).

Recall a statement by Richard Dawkins: "An octopus is nothing like a mouse, and both are quite different from an oak tree. Yet in their fundamental chemistry they are rather uniform." Despite his ignorance of molecular biology, Aristotle would agree. For him all living beings are composed of earth, air, water, and fire, just as, in the language of the nucleotides, all DNA is composed of A, T, C, and G. Where Aristotle disagrees is that for Dawkins, "chemistry" is the same as reality. For Aristotle, the ontological crux is in form not matter. On a "fundamental" level the world is not "uniform." Instead, it is heterogeneous, filled with beings that are what they are and not something else. An octopus differs essentially from a mouse. The world is replete with such beings that can be given names. When asked, "What's that on the couch?," we answer, "a cat." We do not answer, "a bunch of carbon atoms" or "an animal" or "a mammal." And we certainly don't answer, "an animal that has evolved over the course of thousands of years from the great cats of Africa." None of these responses would be sufficiently informative. Instead, to ask, "What is it?" is to express the desire to know what distinct being it is: it is a cat. This, for Aristotle, is where the investigation both begins and ends: with a single, intelligible, actual being. Form is nature more than matter.

For Dawkins and his like-minded ilk, saying, "I see the animal on the couch and it's a cat" and then making the leap to the notion that "form is nature more than matter" does no more than project the way we see and talk about objects encountered in our ordinary experience of the world onto an inhuman screen, namely nature itself. And this is no more than the talk of a man who lives contentedly in a prison of his own making. It is, short, it is the anthropomorphic fallacy par excellence.

II.5: Form Is More Divine than Matter.

Aristotle's study of nature, his physics, takes its bearings from life. On his roster of natural beings, animals come first. The best example of his teleology is the relationship between the parts of an animal and the whole in which they organically function. The paradigmatic case of motion, understood as the "*entelecheia*, the being-in-a-state-of-having-a-*telos*, of what is potential," is an animal's growing into its mature or final form. To clinch the argument that there is a distinction between a natural and an artificial object and that only the former has the principle of motion within itself, he reminds us that "from a human being a human being comes to be, but a bed does not come to be from a bed" (193b8). Finally, the word *phusis* itself is derived from *phuein*, "to make to grow" or to "generate." Nature finds its most illuminating expression in life not in inert objects moving through indeterminate, homogeneous space. In sum, Aristotle is a biocentrist and so, in an important sense, his worldview is entirely "pro-life."

Beyond his contention that form is nature more than matter, Aristotle veers toward views we might find absurd. Consider the following argument from the *Generation of Animals*, where Aristotle discusses why the animal world is divided into the male and the female. Teleology demands that the division must have a purpose. It does: it is for the sake of generation.

Aristotle commences his defense of this proposition by stating that there are two kinds of beings. Some, like the stars, are eternal and divine. Their being does not change (even as they move around the earth); they simply and always are what they are. Other beings, by contrast, are temporary and contingent; they come into being and pass out of being, and their existence is not secured by necessity. Such beings, Aristotle argues, can be better and worse. So, to cite the best example, "*psuchê* ["soul" or "life"; >IV.1] is better than body, and an animate (*empsuchon*) being is better than an inanimate (*apsuchon*) one" (731b).

The argument continues. A contingent being, which comes-into-being and passes-away, cannot be eternal. And yet even such beings, or at least living ones, can gain a foothold in eternity. This is through their form or species. The individual passes away, but through sexual reproduction the species lives on.

The biological world is divided into male and female for the purpose of sexual reproduction. In turn, the purpose of reproductive activity, which along with self-nourishment is the most natural of all life functions, is to allow the temporal to participate in the eternal. Living beings "produce another like itself; an animal produces an animal, a plant a plant, in order that they, as far as possible, can have a share in the eternal and the divine. For every living being strives for that" (*On the Psyche* 415a28–b1).

Another angle on the same point: the species are themselves permanent or eternal.

As Aristotle puts it, "there is always a class of human beings and of animals and of plants" (*Generation of Animals* 732a1). Species-forms, the natural divisions into kinds that constitute the biological realm, are permanent features of the world. Because all animals are divided into male and female, and these are for the sake of reproduction, they also are for the sake of eternity.

Yet another formulation: the form "is better and more divine" (732a5) than matter.

A first objection: species evolve and so are anything but permanent. To think they are is to remain trapped in the "prison" of the ordinary human time frame in which a turtle today was a turtle yesterday and will be again tomorrow. A second: the very notion of the eternal is nonsense.

Even if an eternal object did exist it would be absurd to think of oak trees as "striving" for it. Trees are "replicators that survived [and] built survival machines for themselves to live in," as Dawkins puts it.[17] They have no truck with the eternal. To think they do seems anachronistically romantic or vitalistic. It also reeks of anthropomorphism, for we human beings, so painfully aware of lacking it, might well long or strive or hope for the eternal. And yet even Dawkins indulges in a metaphor when he describes the DNA molecule, the "set of instructions for how to make a body written in the A, T, C, G alphabet of nucleotides." He calls it, with proper scare quotes, "the immortal coil."[18] For how else can one speak about the phenomenon of life reproducing itself?

There are good reasons why human beings, to speak only of our own species, might "strive" to have "a share in the eternal and the divine." Recall the temporal triad discussed in Chapter One (<I.2). Our experience of time is of a whole divided into a past and a future that are separated by the midpoint of the present or the "now." The "now" is the beginning of the future and the end of the past. As such, it has no duration of its own but instead is only "the limit of time" (222a12); it is the gateway between future and past. As a result, time is experienced as a flow from future to past with nothing but the present, which has no duration, to stand in between. And so nothing in our immediate experience, nothing that we touch with our hands or see with our eyes, lasts. As Aristotle puts it, time "wastes things away, and things get old by time, and forgetfulness rather than learning occurs because of time, and nothing young or beautiful comes to be because of time. For time in itself is the cause of destruction" (221a31–b2).

The future, which is not yet here, becomes the past, which is gone. Both are absent and so it is only in the "now" that we can look and hope for real being, genuine presence. But the "now" does not abide for, as nothing but a division between future and past, it has no duration. Time, the cause of destruction, is a ceaseless flow of future to past.

Regardless of what a contemporary physicist might say about the nature of time, the human experience of temporality is like this. We are aware that what is in the future will zip through the present and become the past. And there is much to lament in this being so. Aware that time is the cause of destruction, we long for presence and that which is impervious to the ravages of time, and this we call "eternal." "It is apparent (*phaneron*) that beings that always are, insofar as they always are, are not in time. For neither are they contained by time nor is their being measured by time. And a sign of this is that they do not suffer at the hands of time since they are not in time" (221b3–7).

Even if an eternal object does not exist, we know this: because we consciously and often quite reflectively experience the triadic nature of time we can conceive the eternal as pure presence immune from the destructive flow of time, even if we only do so by negation. Insofar as we are aware of and often pained by the "destruction" of which time is the cause we may well long for something, anything, that does not suffer at its hands. This phenomenon of human longing proves nothing about the existence of the longed-for object. Nonetheless, it is useful in explaining a variety of human activities. First and most obvious is religious activity. Equally basic, if not as immediately apparent, are two others. Consider, for example, intoxication. Human beings regularly drink and take drugs in order to achieve it and there are any number of reasons as to why. Intoxicated states are pleasurable. More specifically, people regularly tank up before a party in order to have more fun. This state of enhanced enjoyment, usually accompanied by music, comes about through the lifting of inhibitions that constrain ordinary life. A woman who would never willfully touch a stranger may, after the drinks, enjoy dancing with several. A man so shy that he cannot speak to women may become loquacious when stoned. An inhibition is a concern with future consequences shaped by memories of the past. In destroying inhibitions, then, intoxication serves to obliterate the hold of time and catapult the intoxicated into a state approximating simple presence.

Intoxication is often deliberately induced in order to provide a welcome contrast to the tedium and burdensome responsibilities of daily life. A serious person waits until the weekend, the Sabbath, the day of rest. Intoxication obliterates the past and mutes the call of the future; it gives us a taste of eternity, of presence.

An even more basic response to time as "the cause of destruction" is play (>V.7).[19] Play is what people do in their "free time," or leisure, when the player has no external demands to meet or expectations to fulfill, and there is no need to keep an eye on the clock. Play absorbs the player, for she is fully concentrated on the action, entirely self-chosen, at hand. In an athletic competition, for example, she is oblivious to anything going on beyond the limits of the play space, the field, or the court. The court becomes a sacred space where she is untroubled by the past and is free from the pressing responsibilities that would drive her toward any future other than the most immediate. As a result, as far as is humanly possible she is immersed in the present. She is thus separated from the ordinary flow of passing time and daily life. Play thereby affords a taste of eternity, understood as pure presence, and so a touch of the divine.

These brief examples do no more than suggest that human activities undertaken during times of leisure when the quotidian routine is temporarily suspended can best be interpreted as responses to the consciousness of the triadic nature of time and the resultant longing for eternity it generates. Most important: leisure is of enormous significance in Aristotle's practical philosophy and so is extensively discussed in later sections of this book (>II.9, V.7, VI.6).

II.6: Nature Is Hierarchical.

Because nature is teleologically structured, it also is ontologically hierarchical. Some things just *are* better than others. For example:

> Actuality is prior to potentiality in substance (*ousia*). First, things that are posterior in generation are prior in form and substance. For example, an adult is prior to a child and a human being is prior to a seed because the former possess the form already while the latter do not. Furthermore, everything that comes to be proceeds towards a principle and a *telos*. (For the principle is the-for-the-sake-of-which, and generation is for the sake of the *telos*.) And actuality is *telos* and potentiality is grasped for the sake of this. For animals do not see in order to have vision but have vision in order to see. (*Metaphysics* 1050a4–11)

Actuality is prior to potentiality. Because the growth of an animal is a development toward its final form, a mature, fully actualized animal is ontologically superior to a young, potentially mature one.

Objections abound: does this imply that a fetus, which is only potentially an actual child, is worthless compared to an adult, and so can be aborted without a shrug? Are children inferior to adults? More generally: the very notion of value-laden gradations of being or reality is silly. Something is (real) or is not (real). Yet another objection can invoke a distinction famously offered by Hume: there are facts, which can be discerned by reason and tell us about the objective nature of the world. But knowing them, knowing what things are, tells us nothing about their value. For a value and a fact are entirely different. A living being, for example, is an enormously complex, self-replicating organism. It is more complex than a rock. But it is not better than a rock. A human animal thinks hard about the meaning of life, whereas a rabbit does not. But a human being is not ontologically or biologically superior to a rabbit. To think it is, is to project our own sentiments upon the facts.

Aristotle disagrees, and his hierarchical ontology is basic to his view of the world. Stars, composed of an indestructible, weightless element not found on earth, are superior to sub-lunar beings. Inanimate objects like rocks are inferior to living ones like plants. Plants, which have no sense perception at all, are inferior to animals, which in turn also can be hierarchically divided. At the top of the list of animals, of course, comes human beings, the animals that think.

Such a hierarchical view of reality came to be known as "the great chain of being," or the *scala naturae,* and is closely associated with medieval philosophy. It is often visually depicted as a triangular structure that puts God on top, with angels just below, followed by human beings, animals, plants, and rocks. To us, such pictures are laughable because in essence reality is homogenous. Recall, however, Koyré's definition of a cosmos: "a conception of the world as a finite, closed, and hierarchically ordered whole." No hierarchy, no cosmos; no world.[20]

To defend, or at least reconsider, Aristotle's teleologically based ontological hierarchy, consider the opening line of the *Metaphysics:* "All human beings by nature strive to know" (980a21). At first glance, this statement seems easily falsified. What about the slacker who prefers to drink beer when he is not sleeping? Such a man strives to learn nothing. But his existence does not falsify Aristotle's contention. This is because he adds "by nature" as a qualification, and nature is teleological.

An essential feature of the human animal is precisely the urge to know, and when someone actualizes this potential he is completing his nature. Any individual may sleep and drink his life away but in doing so he reveals that he is radically deficient. The teleological conception of nature allows for just such judgments. Just as an eagle born with abnormally small and hence dysfunctional wings is an inferior member of its species, so someone who, for whatever reason, is unable to think clearly or who has a terrible memory falls short of being a complete human being. The very young or very old, or those adults who have suffered some sort of brain damage that has compromised their cognitive abilities, fall on the lower ends of the normal distribution depicted in the "bell curve."[21] They are not "special"; they are inferior.

Or consider this related example of teleological reasoning from the *Politics*: of the animals only human beings have language (*logos*). Other animals have "voice" and with it can indicate pain or pleasure. But language, Aristotle tells us, ". . . is for the purpose of clarifying what is advantageous and what is harmful, and hence what is just or unjust. For this is unique to human beings in comparison with the other animals: they alone have a perception of good and bad and justice and injustice, and so on. When a community shares in these it produces a household and a city" (1253a14–18).

From the above, Aristotle concludes that a human being is "by nature a political animal" (>VI.3). The argument, then, is roughly this: it is observable that human beings have language, with which they articulate and discuss the principles or values guiding their choices. There must be a reason, a purpose or *telos*, for this feature of the human animal. Because it is only in the sharing of values and the pursuit of common goals that a human community is forged, language is for the purpose of entering into such communities. Because the city (*polis*) is the most all-embracing community of which we are members, Aristotle concludes that because we are linguistic beings, we also are political beings whose very nature requires citizenship in order to come to fruition. As a result, a human being without a city is either "a beast or a god" (1253a29; >VI.3). He is out of place (*atopos*, often translated as "absurd"), unable to fulfill the capacities nature has given him and so not recognizable as a human being.

In sum, Aristotle is an ontological and practical elitist. Some species are superior to others, stars are better than dirt and water, and human beings were not all created equal. The slacker described above is inferior to the student hard at work. (Chapters Five and Six explore these issues in some depth.)

Many of us today condemn any form of "elitism" and would attribute Aristotle's to his having lived in a slave-owning, woman-oppressing culture (which he did). His prioritizing of actuality over potentiality, which is the fundamental metaphysical distinction on which his value judgments rest, is, on this account, but a tool to constrain human possibility and freedom. So too is his teleological ranking of individual members within a species and between species and his concept of the *topos*. But if actuality–potentiality, topological physics, and teleology go down the tubes, if the possibility of "natural subordination" is annihilated, then there is no cosmos.[22] An infinite, homogeneous, continually expanding universe, in which there is no up or down, better or worse, and in which nothing has a place, overwhelms an orderly and finite world. And so the notion of ontologically stable standards of measurement becomes entirely bogus. Aristotle's hierarchy may be objectionable, but it is important, at least, to understand what happened to us when it disappeared.

II.7: To Understand Nature, Study Its Best Examples.

Aristotle's teleology has a significant methodological implication for his study of nature: to understand a species, study the best, the most fully actualized, instance of that species. "When it comes to beings that are by nature, one must study to a greater extent those that are according to nature rather than those that are degenerate. So, for example, in the case of human being, one must study those who are in the best condition with regard to both body and *psyche*, and this will be clear. For among those who are bad or are in a bad condition it might seem that the body often rules the *psyche* on account of its debased and unnatural condition" (*Politics* 1254a36–b2).

To find out what human being is, do not go to the psychiatric hospital or the prison. Instead, investigate the best and the brightest. Such an approach is almost exactly the opposite of the one scientists, especially neuroscientists, employ today. Because it is, or at least should be, impossible to perform controlled experiments on the human brain, scientists often take advantage of an accident or damaging illness in order to study its workings. A famous case was one Phineas Gage. In 1848 an explosion propelled an iron rod into his face that entered just beneath his left cheek and exited through the top of his skull. A good portion of his frontal lobe was destroyed. Observers noted with amazement that most of his functioning remained quite normal. This freakish accident, this experiment that nature itself provided, helped scientists begin to understand how different regions of the brain regulate different bodily and psychological functions, and today we now know that the frontal lobe helps us think about the future.

The observation of breakdowns can lead to results that are useful in learning how to fix what is broken or improve what already works well. By sharp contrast, by focusing on what is best, Aristotle only learns what is most "normal" (from the Latin *norma,* a "measure," "standard," or "pattern") or natural. Although his procedure is consistent with his teleology it may nonetheless seem to be inevitably riddled with prejudice. For if a study begins by identifying the best instances of a species it must already know in advance what these are. Presumably, however, it should not be able to do this until the study has been completed. So, for example, Aristotle insists in the passage from the *Politics* cited above that to investigate human beings one must locate people best in body and *psyche*, for these are most "by nature." As a result, he may investigate only those who have well-developed musculature and high scores on their IQ tests. But how does he know that such features actually determine who is the best of the bunch? Why not study those who have thin muscles or a good sense of humor or are exceptionally kind?

Of course, the contemporary approach, which takes its bearings from breakdowns by using them as windows into the ways things work, is equally question begging. For it ignores at the outset the possibility of a best.

II.8: The Finite Is Better than the Infinite.

A basic, perhaps even a foundational, thought has stood behind much of the discussion offered so far: the finite is prior and superior to the infinite. This notion is directly related to teleology for "nature," Aristotle tells us, "avoids what is unlimited. For the unlimited is without-a-*telos* (*ateles*) and nature always seeks the *telos*" (*Generation of Animals* 715b15). A *telos* is an "end" and only something limited has one. To be *teleion*, "complete or "perfect," is to have reached the *telos*, which is a limit. Natural motion is the *entelecheia* of what is potentially insofar as it is potential. It is a coming into the *telos*, an activity that cannot occur in an unlimited fashion.

In *Metaphysics* I.5, Aristotle discusses the Pythagoreans, those early thinkers who believed that the world was intelligibly structured through mathematical principles, especially number. Philolaus, from the fifth century, put it this way: "all the things that are known have number; for it is not possible for anything to be thought or known without this." Clearly, such a statement is a forerunner of the modern conviction, articulated by Galileo and company, that nature is a book whose characters are mathematical. In other words, nature can be "read" or known but only in mathematical terms.[23]

Aristotle addresses the views of the Pythagoreans, as he does all the reputable opinions of his predecessors, in a spirit of both appreciation and critique. He ultimately rejects mathematics as the language of physics. Referring to his contemporaries, the Platonists, whom he takes to be much influenced by the Pythagoreans, he says, "nowadays philosophy has become mathematics" (*Metaphysics* 992b1), and for him this is a criticism. But he retained one of their basic principles: the finite is superior to the infinite. This view was expressed in the Pythagorean table of opposites that Aristotle cites in the *Metaphysics* (986a23–26).

Finite (*to peras*)	Infinite (*to apeiron*)
Odd	Even
One	Many
Right	Left
Male	Female
Resting	Moving
Straight	Curved
Light	Darkness
Good	Bad

The finite is to the infinite as the good is to the bad. Such an evaluation seems preposterous, for the two seem to be no more than quantitative designators and thus to be indifferent to questions of value. Nonetheless, this evaluative hierarchy is a central Pythagorean tenet because, to return to Philolaus, if numbers are what render the world intelligible, and if each number is finite, then the finite itself is somehow responsible for intelligibility. Furthermore, if intelligibility is counted as a good, then so too should the finite. Aristotle accepts reasoning akin to this. He says, for example, that "insofar as something is infinite it is unknowable" (*Physics* 207a26). To think is to think something, in much the same way that to be is to be something (a notion that is discussed shortly).

In *On the Heavens* I.5, Aristotle asks "whether there is an infinite body" and he pleads for the urgency of this question: "for whether there is or isn't does not make a small difference, but all the difference in respect to the study (*theoria*) of truth" (271b5–6). Everything hinges on the answer to this question, which for Aristotle is emphatically negative. What follows is a sampling of his arguments.

Despite the fact that they are divine and eternal, it is impossible for the heavenly bodies to be infinite in magnitude. A body that revolves in a circle cannot be infinite, for if it were, then the straight lines radiating from the center of its circular path also would be infinite. But if they were, so too would be the area encompassed by two of these lines. The body moving in the circular path would then be required to traverse this infinite area. It is, however, impossible to traverse an infinite distance. Therefore, the heavenly bodies that orbit the earth in a circular motion—a fact confirmable, Aristotle thinks, by both observation and argument—are not infinite. As he puts it, "we see that the heaven revolves in a circle, and we have determined by argument that this circular motion belongs to a body" (*On the Heaven* 272a5); a body that must be finite.

To make the same point: we see that the heavenly bodies complete their orbit in a finite time span. Therefore, if the heavens were infinite, an infinite distance would have been traversed in a finite time, which is impossible. (See 272b30.)

That these two arguments rely on what "we see" reveals their limitation. We can only see finite objects, but by itself this fact hardly implies that there is nothing infinite in the universe. It would have this implication only if knowledge were inextricably bound to perception or were required to conform with the sensible phenomena. It is not unreasonable to propose, however, that reality is best accessible and knowable not through perception but through some form of abstract thinking, such as geometry, which can put the infinite to good use. Bruno was an early champion of this line of thought (<I.2). "No corporeal sense can perceive the infinite," he said, "for the infinite cannot be the object of sense-perception." He then generalized: "truth is to but a very small degree derived from the senses as from a frail origin." Real epistemic action resides "in the intellect . . . in the mind, in its proper and vital form."[24] Koyré describes Bruno's position: "for sense perception and imagination infinity is inaccessible and unrepresentable; for the intellect, on the contrary, it is its primary and most certain concept. . . . Accordingly, from Bruno's point of view, the Aristotelian conception of a closed innerworldly space is not only false, it is absurd."[25]

Another argument from the *Physics* relies on a concept broached in Chapter One (<I.4): "place." There can be no infinite body, Aristotle argues, because "every sensible body is somewhere by nature and there is some place for each" (205a10). Recall that Aristotle defines "place" as "the limit of the surrounding body" (211b1). With this definition assumed, however, the argument becomes a tautology: there can be no infinite body because all bodies have a place. This is equivalent to saying that because all bodies are limited there is no infinite body.

Recall that the notions of place and natural direction are tightly intertwined (<I.4). Unless forced to do otherwise, fire naturally moves upward to its place in the heavens. The natural motion of earth is downward. The sun rises in the East, to the right, and sets in the West, to the left. If there were an infinite body these notions would become meaningless. It is best here to let Aristotle speak for himself.

> Every sensible body is in a place, and the forms and differences of place are the up and the down and before and the front and the back and the right and left. And these are not relative to us nor a matter of convention, but have been distinguished in the cosmos itself. And they could not possibly be in the infinite. Simply put, if an infinite place is impossible, and every body is in a place, an infinite body is impossible. Indeed, whatever is somewhere is in a place, and what is in a place is somewhere. (*Physics* 205b31–206a2)

Directionality—up, down, left, right, front, back—is an objective feature of the world and renders it intelligible (<I.2). The moon simply is above the earth; fire goes up, water down. The world makes sense and as a consequence must be finite.

Having eliminated the possibility of an infinite body or entity, Aristotle is not yet done with the infinite. For "if there simply were no infinite at all, many impossibilities would ensue" (*Physics* 206a10). For example, if there were no infinite we would be required to say that time has a beginning and an end, and that continuous magnitudes are not divisible into further magnitudes, two notions that are absurd. We would have to say that numbers are not infinite, which again is obviously false because there is no highest number.

What, then, remains of the infinite? It is, but only in potentiality (206a18). A line segment can be divided into infinitely many smaller segments. Each segment subtracted from the original line is limited, but the procedure of subtraction cannot be completed. The infinite, Aristotle tells us, is "that which is always beyond" (207a1). It is the potential of there always being more.[26] Differently stated, the being of the infinite is "in thinking" (*en noesei*: 203b24). We can always think of a higher number and in our minds subdivide a line segment to infinity. We can always imagine a point beyond. But (against Bruno) Aristotle cautions against "trusting in thinking alone" (208a15). Clever people can cook up puzzles and argue on behalf of paradoxical positions. But the goal of theoretical thinking is not just being clever, or doing elegant mathematics, but remaining faithful to (saving) the phenomena. This requires looking as well as thinking, and listening to what we ourselves say. It requires *theoria* in Aristotle's uniquely phenomenological sense.

That the finite is prior and superior to the infinite also is reflected in one of Aristotle's basic metaphysical principles: "For one man and a man are the same, and being a man and a man are the same" (*Metaphysics* 1003b22). To be is to be this or that; it is to be determinate or singular. To be, in the fullest sense—that is, in actuality—is to be finite. Differently stated, the concept of the finite is intimately connected to that of the "whole." As mentioned above (<I.2), a "whole" is "that from which nothing is absent; for example, a whole man" (*Physics* 207a10). A whole is a complete (*teleion*) unity of parts. This description leads directly to the concept of the finite: "The whole and the complete (*teleion*) are either entirely the same or their natures are akin. For nothing is complete unless it has a *telos*. And a *telos* is a limit" (207a15).

A man is whole because he is a complete (*teleion*) set of parts; the list of his parts comes to an end, and each contributes to the functioning of the man. As mentioned earlier, *teleion* also can be translated as "perfect," which derives from the Latin, *perficere*. Something that has been gone through entirely is complete and thus "perfect." The infinite is that which cannot be gone through. Furthermore the words "perfect" and *teleion* also have evaluative connotations. What is "perfect" is not only complete or "that from which nothing is absent," but it also is maximally good and "cannot be exceeded in its kind. For example, a perfect doctor or a flutist are those who, according to the form of the excellence that belongs to them, lack nothing" (<I.2).

In the infinite universe, nothing is perfect. And so, to paraphrase Bernard, there can be but "progress" and no perfectibility.

A last argument: "the causes of beings are not infinite, either as a linear sequence or a form." Instead, there must be an *archê,* a "beginning," "origin," or "first-cause" (*Metaphysics* 994a1). To borrow a modern example (that parallels Aristotle's own), "water comes from water molecules, a water molecule from hydrogen and oxygen, hydrogen from electrons, protons, etc. Is there an end, or, are there ultimate particles or ultimate matter? For Aristotle, there is an end."[27] One thing cannot come from another and then from another, and so on to infinity. There must instead be a termination point, a first cause, for if there were not and the sequence were infinite, then no real cause would ever emerge. For "if there is no first, in general there is no cause" (994a18–19). If every answer to a "why question" simply generated another question, and did so infinitely, then no proximate answer would ever bring us any closer to the truth and it would be impossible to make sense of the world. After all, compared to or divided by infinity, all finite steps add up to zero.

But we do get closer to the truth. The world does make sense. On this conviction, based in no small measure upon the phenomenon of ordinary life, Aristotle stakes all. Therefore, the causal sequence is not infinite. This line of reasoning will take on great significance in Aristotle's discussion of the first or "motionless" mover, or god, in the *Metaphysics* (>III.5).

This same prohibition against an infinite causal sequence applies to the final cause. If I walk for the sake of health, and seek health for the sake of happiness, and this sequence of means-and-ends proceeds forever, then no individual end I might achieve, and so no action that I might take, can ever bring me closer to my ultimate goal. As Aristotle puts it, "the ones who make the sequence infinite are not aware that they are destroying the nature of the good. And yet no one would undertake to do anything if he were not going to reach some limit" (*Metaphysics* 994b12–14).

This last argument should set off alarms, for in making a claim about the causal structure of the world by invoking an observable fact of our practical lives it seems anthropomorphic. Virtually all of us act in the belief that what we choose to do has an intelligible purpose, or meaning, and thus advances us a bit closer to the actual goal for which we strive. This we could not do were the sequence of goods or means-and-ends believed to be infinite. Why did I put on my shoes? In order to take a walk. Why did I take a walk? In order to improve my health. And why do I aspire to this? In order to be happy. Were the sequence not to end, or not to be thought to end, then human life would be meaningless. But it is not meaningless. For if it were I would stay in bed and never put on my shoes.

To approach to the same point from a different angle: Aristotle insists that possessions like money, power, or fame—all of which are potentially unlimited—cannot be the best of things, nor can their possession constitute genuine human happiness. No amount of money can be highest and so ultimately satisfying because there is always more money to be had. No amount of power or fame can be maximum, for even if one were to rule or be admired by all humanity, there would still be the gods left to conquer. Therefore, these sorts of external, quantifiable, and thus unlimited goods cannot be the cause of the best life.

This privileging of the finite is crucial to understanding Aristotle's practical philosophy as found in the *Nicomachean Ethics* and the *Politics*, which are discussed at length in Chapters Five and Six of this book. For the moment only note this: in seeking knowledge one seeks the causes of things. In order for this search to terminate, the sequence of causes must be finite. Were it infinite, the world would be unintelligible. But in fact just as our daily lives make sense so too does the world.

To reiterate the possible objection: such reasoning is anthropomorphic. Perhaps human beings need to believe that their own sequence of means-and-ends terminates in order to give themselves a reason to get out of bed in the morning. But surely this phenomenon by itself cannot support Aristotle's denial of infinite causal regress as such. Maybe we are just puny creatures terrified by the prospect of our own meaninglessness who project our own wish for meaning, and thus finitude, upon the nonhuman screen of the universe in which it has no place.

The debate between Aristotle and his modern opponents, between the closed world and the infinite universe, hinges on what evidentiary weight is attributed to ordinary human experience. If it is a lot, as it is in Aristotle's phenomenological conception of *theoria*, then the Finite will win. By contrast, if, like Richard Dawkins, we conceive of human experience as being a "prison" that occludes our view of reality, then Aristotle loses. If the scientist must demand of herself to resist the "idol of the tribe"—in other words, to check her humanity at the door of her laboratory—if her singular goal is to figure out how things really work so that knowledge and power can be one, then Aristotle should be junked.

But as Bernard put it, "knowledge that isn't self-knowledge isn't doing much, mate."

II.9: Good Science Appreciates Things as They Are.

A notable feature of Aristotelian science (or theory) emerges from this chapter: it is useless. Even when successful, the Aristotelian scientist cannot do much with her knowledge. Knowing purposes, forms, and seeing a finite world clearly as it shows itself to our naked eyes here on earth does not allow for the sort of intervention into and control of natural forces required for the development of powerful technology. For that only a mathematized conception of mechanical relationships attained from a thoroughly nonhuman perspective is required. Lamentably, at least from the standpoint of most seventeenth-century philosophers, because Aristotelian science subordinates the efficient to the formal cause it squandered its chance to grasp how nature really works.

The goal of Aristotelian theory is to look at, to comprehend and articulate a finite cosmos whose salient features are intelligibility, purposiveness, hierarchy, order, and value. It does not know how to tap the vast reservoir of power contained within the atom or how to manipulate the properties of petroleum in order to fuel the machines. Instead, what it offers is an understanding and appreciation of the world. To borrow a thought from Heidegger, for Aristotle, good "thinking" is like "thanking," two words that seem etymologically related in English and German (*denken* and *danken*), although not in Greek. Good thinking both expresses and results in gratitude, not in the accumulation of power.

Weirdly (to us), Aristotle counts the uselessness of knowledge as a symptom of its value. Recall that in the *Metaphysics* passage discussed above (<II.4), Aristotle recounts the manner in which knowledge comes into being. As it begins with perceptions and then develops through memory into experience, and then finally becomes knowledge, it progresses from awareness of particulars to an understanding of the universal; from simply knowing "that" to knowing the cause or "why?" "Knowledge," Aristotle explains, "comes to be whenever from many thoughts that have emerged from experience one universal conception emerges about these similar things" (981a6). The example suggested above was the person who has experienced the pain of many headaches and then the relief that came from taking aspirin. She may well advise a friend suffering from a headache, and her recommendation may actually work. But she has no explanation for why it worked, and hence no real knowledge. The physician, by contrast, does. She has a *logos* (981a15) . . . a *logos* of the cause.

Still, those with only experience "may have more success than those who have a *logos* without experience. The reason for this is that experience is of particulars, while knowledge is of universals, and action and processes are all particularized" (*Metaphysics* 981a16; >VI.5). A doctor with a firm grasp of the science of anatomy may goof up in treating a particular patient precisely because the patient is particularized and thus only an incidental manifestation of a larger structure. Experience may be more useful than universal knowledge when dealing with real people.

Aristotle concedes this limitation but nonetheless insists that genuine knowledge is superior to even the most efficacious forms of experience. On this point he cites the Egyptian priests who were the first to develop pure or theoretical mathematics. They were able to do so because, to introduce a word that takes on great significance by the end of this book (>VI.6), they were allowed "leisure" (*scholê*). They were "counted as wonderful by others" (981b15) not because they had invented anything useful but simply because they were "wiser." Theoretical knowledge is good not for any consequence or specific application it may generate, but simply in and of itself. "It is clear that we do not seek such science for any other need; but just as we say that someone who is for the sake of himself and not for another is free so is this sort of science alone free among the sciences" (*Metaphysics* 982b25).

A faint echo of this notion that the best forms of knowledge are intrinsically valuable and thus represent true human freedom can still be heard in the phrase "the liberal arts." Unfortunately, as any resident of an American university (where the applied sciences rule supreme) knows, there is little liberty left in the curriculum; there is little *scholê* left in the schools.

Given our own conception of physics, the same laws of motion apply to both the stars and terrestrial objects. Therefore, knowing such laws affords the opportunity to move objects here on earth into space. For Aristotle, the stars are fundamentally different from objects here on earth. Their orbit is invariable, impervious to human intervention, and eternal. All that remains for the human investigator, then, is to look at, think, and learn about them, even if such knowledge is not applicable and generates no technological results. Nonetheless, such study has value, for it transforms the student into a knower. And this is good. First, as we will see below (>V.6–8), it is good for an individual human being to actualize her natural capacity to know and thereby fulfill her *telos*. Such actualizations will be called "virtue" or "excellence." Second, it will turn out that Aristotle's conception of knowledge as intrinsically valuable will play a surprisingly important role in helping to improve the human community (>VI.6–7). For us, what is perhaps most relevant is this: retrieving Aristotle's model of theoretical knowledge, of theory as phenomenological, of thinking as thanking, might somehow be useful in a culture on the verge of being torn apart by the technological conception of science. Our scientists study nature, and then the machines ravish it. Nothing is left untouched. Aristotle's metaphor for knowing remains seeing, and seeing is not touching. This is why such knowledge is useless. But, to state the paradox, a discussion of which concludes this book (>VI.7), precisely in being useless Aristotelian theory may be immensely useful. For it can save the world.[28]

Chapter Three

Being Is Good.

"Being is better than non-being" (*Generation of Animals* 731b30). It's easy for us to agree with this statement, at least when it comes to ourselves. For generally speaking we prefer being ourselves to being nothing; we prefer life to death. But Aristotle's statement is more than a generalization of our own feelings.

III.1: Metaphysics Is Onto-Theology.

Aristotle characterizes the subject of *Metaphysics*: "There is a kind of knowledge that studies being as being and what belongs to it in virtue of itself. This is not the same as those kinds of knowledge that are said to be partial. For none of these investigates being as being as a whole. Instead, they cut off some part of it and study the attributes of it. The mathematical disciplines are an example of this" (1003a21–26).

There is a study—more literally, a "theorizing"—of being as such. Other kinds of knowledge also study being, or reality, in some sense; they all study what is (real). These disciplines, however, cut off and isolate a chunk of being and concentrate on it alone. The expert in arithmetic studies numbers and nothing else; the biologist studies living beings, and so doesn't pay attention to rocks. By contrast, metaphysics studies being uncut; being simply insofar as it is being. A more etymologically precise title for this study is "ontology," the *logos* of *to on*, being.

It is not obvious how ontology could possibly fulfill its task. Normally, when we go about the business of knowing we know this or that. We become biologists who study living organisms or geologists who study rocks. By contrast, because its subject matter is not restricted in this fashion, ontology seems to be about everything. . . . every thing that is. Does ontology, then, study what all beings—animals, plants, rocks, numbers, houses—have in common? After all, each of these things is and is something. Perhaps, then, metaphysics studies the Being that all beings share. This is problematic because Aristotle demands that knowledge, with the notable exceptions of mathematics and logic, must study something real rather than an abstract generality. It is difficult, therefore, to see how ontology could both meet this requirement and yet study everything.[1]

To reformulate this problem: just as "mammal" is the genus under which the various species like "dog" and "cat" are subsumed, and "animal" is an even higher genus than "mammal," so Being might be construed as the highest genus of all. For logical reasons Aristotle thinks that this is impossible.[2] Without going into the details of his technical analysis, the problem with it can be expressed informally: if Being were the highest genus, the most general of all concepts, it would lose its concrete reality and become an abstraction. But, to reiterate, for Aristotle, knowledge is of something real; it is of a being in the world. Again, with the exception of mathematics, an abstract concept cannot function as such an object. Consequently, the subject matter of metaphysics remains obscure.

In Book I.1–2 of the *Metaphysics*, Aristotle tries to elucidate it. In typical fashion, he begins by exploring the "reputable opinions" that have come down to him concerning the question of "wisdom" (*sophia*). Before turning to these, it might be helpful to recall an earlier discussion (<II.4): knowledge, Aristotle says, must be of a universal, rather than a particular. While someone who has "experience" may know her way around the particulars and offer good advice like "When you have a headache take an aspirin," she has no knowledge of human anatomy or physiology. She is not, in other words, a physician who has mastered medical science (*techne*); she has not studied the human body, the human species (*eidos*), as such. As such, she is inferior in "wisdom" to the physician. "We believe that knowing and understanding belong more to *techne* than to experience, and we assume that those with *techne* are wiser than those who have experience. This indicates that wisdom is attributed by all men on the basis of having knowledge. This is because people with such knowledge know the cause, while those with experience do not. For the latter know "that" something is the case, while the former know "why." And to know is to know the cause" (*Metaphysics* 981a24–27).

Aristotle acknowledges that while someone with experience may actually be more effective in dealing with the particulars than one with knowledge, the latter is "more honorable" (981a31), or just plain better, because she is "wiser" and so knows the universal or the cause. Because metaphysics understood as ontology, the study of being as being or the study of every thing, is the most universal of all subjects, it would seem to be the complete and most honorable fulfillment of the human pursuit of wisdom. Still, it is not clear what exactly it studies or how "being as being" avoids becoming an empty abstraction.

Aristotle signals his awareness of such questions when he begins his review of the reputable opinions concerning wisdom, the first of which is "We think that, first of all, the wise man knows everything to the extent that this is possible; he does not, however, have knowledge of every thing taken as an individual" (982a8–10). On this view, the wise man does not know on what day you were born or how many hairs are on your head. Instead, his knowledge of everything seems to be an understanding of just what it is to be; to be a hair or a head or a person who counts hairs on heads. To state the obvious: this description hardly clarifies the subject matter of metaphysics.

The second reputable opinion also sheds little light. "The wise man is able to know the difficult things that are not easy for a human being to know. For perception is common to all human beings; therefore, it is easy and does not indicate wisdom" (982a10–12). These lines suggest that the wise man knows what is furthest from sense perception, and therefore most difficult for human beings to know. Perception, which we all share, is always of particulars: I see this brown dog standing before me right now. Presumably, then, the most universal object would be that which is furthest from sense perception, and as such most difficult to apprehend. But what could this be? Again, Aristotle might here be pointing to Being taken in its most universal or general sense. But he also could refer to a specific being that is furthest from sense perception; perhaps to an object that cannot be perceived at all with the senses. In other words, this reputable belief might suggest not a study of Being in general, but of the highest Being, one unavailable to sense perception.

To clarify, consider a dangerous, because potentially misleading, comparison. Imagine that the God of *Genesis*, the one who created Heaven and Earth and all the beings of the world, exists. Because God is somehow responsible for, or is the cause of, all beings, the study of God would, in a way, be the study of all beings, and metaphysics would become theology, the *logos* of *theos*. If this were the case, the problem concerning the object of metaphysics would have been solved. God is real and anything but an empty concept. Indeed, God can be construed as the Being of beings; the fullest and richest, the most real, of all beings.[3] As such, the study of Him, or theology, would constitute a study of everything.

Aristotle himself endorses the possibility of metaphysics as theology when he lists it, along with mathematics and physics, as one of three "theoretical sciences" (1026a19). Most important and elaborate, however, is his extended discussion of god in Book XII of the *Metaphysics* (>III.5). There we learn why mentioning the biblical God above was dangerous: Aristotle's own version of the divine is fundamentally unlike the God of *Genesis*. It is not personal or moral or loving, nor does it enter into human history. But it is divine (>III.4).

It is conceivable that Aristotle alludes to the divine in his brief mention of the last reputable opinion. On this view wisdom must be "dominant rather than subordinate. For the wise man must not be ordered about, but instead give orders. He must not obey someone else, but he who is less wise must obey him" (982a15–19). A few lines later Aristotle supplies the needed clarification: "the wisdom knowing that for the sake of which each thing is done—this is the good of each thing, and in general what is best in all of nature—is the most dominant kind of knowledge, and it dominates rather than is subordinate" (982b4–8). Metaphysics is not merely the study of what every being has in common; its subject matter is neither the highest genus nor the most universal and abstract of all possible objects. Instead, it studies the ultimate Good. The dangerous comparison with the biblical God remains useful in at least gaining a foothold in this line of thought. Aristotle's god is the ultimate good of the world and so the wise man who has mastered theology and thereby understands the good of every thing should not be ordered around by anyone else.

To sum up: there is a tension in Aristotle's initial examination of the subject matter of metaphysics. It is the study of everything, but not of every thing in its particularity. Instead, as ontology, it studies Being as such. The problem with this description is that the subject matter of metaphysics would then become what all beings have in common, and as a result Being as Being would become the most general, abstract, and possibly empty of all concepts. A countervailing tendency, perhaps even a response to this problem, is to conceive of metaphysics as theology, for "god," whatever that proves to be for Aristotle, is a real being; indeed, it is the most real Being because it is somehow responsible for all other beings. The opening chapters of Aristotle's *Metaphysics* thus allude to the possibility that metaphysics must proceed on the dual tracks of both ontology and theology.

III.2: There Are Substances Out There.

Aristotle's ontological discussion begins thus: "being is said in many ways" (*Metaphysics* 1028a10). Just as he does in arguments about the nature of the heavenly bodies and in defense of his teleology, Aristotle summons ordinary language as evidence about the nature of being itself. He continues:

> Being is said in many ways. . . . For it signifies the "what it is" and the "this something," the "what sort" and "how much" and each of the other predications of this kind. Although being is said in these many ways, it is apparent that of them the primary one is the "what it is," which signifies substance (*ousia*). For whenever we say that this is of a certain sort, we say it is good or bad, not that it is three cubits long or a human being. And whenever we say what something is, we do not say it is white or hot or three cubits long, but a human being or a god. All the other ways of speaking of being are said insofar as they are quantities or qualities or affections or something else of being as it said in this primary way. (1028a10–19)

In this passage, Aristotle returns to a notion developed in his treatise the *Categories.* There are basic or primitive modes of predication. We can say, "The dog is brown" or "The tree is twenty feet high." In the former a quality is attributed to the dog; in the latter, a quantity is attributed to the tree. The verb "is," the third-person singular of "to be," couples or attaches the predicate, expressed by the adjective, to the subject, expressed by the noun. Aristotle's categories are the elemental forms that such predications can take. We can attribute quality, quantity, relation, position, temporality, and so on, to various subjects. To reformulate: we can ask several primitive questions about things. In turn, the answers are the categories. So, for example, we ask, "What is it?," "How big is it?," "Where is it?," "When is it?," and "Of what sort is it?" The answer to the first and most important question will be a "substance"; to the second a "quantity," and so on.

But the *Categories* is not merely a scheme with which to analyze the way human beings talk (or, even more narrowly, the way humans beings speaking Indo-European languages like Greek or English talk). It is a study of the way things are. For, to repeat a familiar point, the way we talk is a map that guides us as we navigate our way through the way things really are. The simple predicative structure of the sentence "S is P" suggests that the S, the subject of the sentence, takes on the lion's share of importance. All predicates must be attributed to a subject. If I say, "The boy is healthy" you know what I mean. But if I just say "healthy" you'll be prompted to ask, "Who's healthy?" "Healthy" floating by itself does no meaningful work until it is anchored in a subject. The ontological correlate to this anchor is a "substance." The Greek word is *ousia*, which is derived from the infinitive "to be" (*einai*). Translated literally, it would become "being-ness" or "entity" (a word derived from the Latin *ens*, a participial form of *esse*, "to be").[4] As with "metaphysics" (a word Aristotle never uses), "substance" is a traditional philosophical term and for this reason will be retained. Aristotle explains why it is the most basic of the categories.

> One could wonder whether walking and being healthy and sitting down signify being, and similarly with others of this kind. For no one of them is with respect to itself by nature nor can they be separated from substance. Rather, that which walks and that which sits and that which is healthy are to be counted as beings. These seem to be to a greater extent because in them there is some determinate substratum and this is the substance and the individual that is made manifest in this sort of predication. For "good" or "sitting" cannot be said without this. Thus it is clear that on account of substance each of the others are, and that being in a primary sense, not with respect to something else but simply, is substance. (1028a20–31)

A substance is a "substratum" (*hupokeimenon*). It is what lies under, and so can receive or absorb predications. As such, only substances exist "separately." The "dog" just is. It has a bunch of properties but unlike them it is characterized by its ontological independence. Even if the dog's properties change—if it loses its hair or some weight—it remains itself; it is what it is and is not another thing. By contrast, a quality like "healthy" cannot stand on its own. Its being is dependent on its belonging to, being attributable to, a substance. For this reason, ontology is actually the study of substance. "And so in ancient times and now and forever the question that has been investigated and puzzled over, what is being?, is really this: what is substance?" (1028b2–4).

A substance is not only a "substratum" lying under predications but is "determinate" (*horismenon*). It is finite, bounded, de-limited, definite. As a result, it is a singular and identifiable "this something" (*tode ti*) and so is receptive to the question "What is it?" It is a tree and neither a rock nor a bird. What tree? That one over there. It is separated from other substances by being what it is and not something else.

To clarify this notion of the "determinate substratum," consider the following: "one man and a man," Aristotle says, "are the same; so too are being a man and a man. In the two phrases, 'one man' and 'being one man' nothing is clarified by appending the extra word" (1003b26–27). To be is to be one, to be a singular "this something," a substance; a cat rather than a dog. Just as the finite is ontologically prior to the infinite (<II.8) so too is determinacy, being this or that, ontologically prior to the indeterminate. If I say "green" you will ask, "green what?" "Green" by itself is indeterminate. But when I say, "The green tree over there," it is clear to what I refer. Substance is the primary sense of "being" for this reason.

Beginning his inquiry into substance, Aristotle says, "It seems that substance belongs most evidently (*phanerotata*) to bodies. Thus we say that animals and plants and their parts are substances. So too do we say this of natural bodies like fire and water and earth and each one of this sort, and the parts of these or what is composed from these (either of parts or of all of them), like the heavens and its parts, namely, the stars and the moon and the sun" (*Metaphysics* 1028b8–13).

In the hunt for substance what appears first on the screen, what is most "evident" or "apparent" (because *phanerotata* derives from *phainesthai,* "to appear"), are bodies, beings standing present before us in their concrete and perceptible reality. The first item on the list tells much. An animal is far and away the most illuminating example of an Aristotelian substance for it exhibits the most natural sort of unity, determinacy, and ontological integrity. It is an organic whole that maintains its unity through time by means of a continuous, mutually enabling interaction between its own parts and its environment. It absorbs materials other than itself from the external world and through its metabolic system transforms it into itself. It changes continually, all the while being itself. Precisely because they maintain their own unity even as their material constituents are constantly changing animals are paradigmatic substances.

Note the first-person plural: "we say that animals and plants and their parts are substances." Of course we do. Of all beings known to us, it is other animals, especially human ones, that stand before us as beings in their own right. To such beings we give proper names. Bob is a friend, Sue is a sister, Mollie a pet dog. We have an urge to name creatures who are most like ourselves. Occasionally we give names to inanimate objects; a favorite car or truck perhaps. But it is animals that compel us with their individual being like nothing else. They are most apparently, and truly, substantial.

Aristotle looks around, using only his naked eye, and sees living beings roughly the size of himself, and he takes them to be quintessentially real. Some coincidence! He declares that what perhaps is no more than a fleeting appearance showing itself during a limited time period to our human and animal-loving eyes is actually a structural feature of the world itself.

As such, he may well be treating his own viewing as an accurate mirror of the world when it is, as Bacon contemptuously puts it, rather "like a false mirror, which, receiving rays irregularly, distorts and discolors the nature of things by mingling its own nature with it." Perhaps there is no more extreme case of such "mingling," such anthropomorphism, than Aristotle's putting animals first on the list of his substances, of beings that are really real.[5]

Matters get worse when Aristotle argues that species are not only real but permanent features of the natural landscape. While an individual animal is born and thereby comes into being, and then perishes or goes out of being—in other words, is resident in the realm of "generation" or "becoming"—"the form or species or whatever we ought to call the shape (*morphê*) in the sensible things is not being generated" (1033b5). The form of the individual animal, its species, is passed from the parent to the offspring, both of which come-to-be and perish. But the form itself does not come into being; it is permanent (<II.4–5).

In the *Categories* Aristotle states that a single sensible body, paradigmatically an animal, is the primary instance of a substance: "Substance, as it is said in its most dominant and primary sense, the one which it is said most of all, is that which is neither said of some subject nor is it something in a subject. For example, the individual human being or the individual horse" (2a11–14).

An individual human being, say Bob, is a primary substance. He stands before us as a determinate unity that can bear attributes. He is tall, bald, and wears glasses. When it appears in a sentence, the noun "Bob" can play the role of the subject. Nor is "Bob" in something else, as for example heat is "in" the water. He just is, all by himself. As such, he is a primary example of a substance.

There is, however, one kind of predication that seems to disrupt this line of thought: "Bob is a human being." By saying this we seem to say that Bob is somehow "in" human being, for he is included in or belongs to the species of human beings. Furthermore, we regularly say things like "a human being has eyes" or "a human being has a brain." But "human being" is not an individual. We don't bump into a species; we bump into guys like Bob. Aristotle comments: "The species in which the primary substances are said to belong are called secondary substances. So are the genera of these species. For example, human being and animal" (2a14–16).

A substance is paradigmatically real, more so than a quality like "green" or "twenty feet tall." But it is not clear what, finally, is more real, the individual or the species, Bob or human being. In the *Categories* the answer is unambiguous: the former, for the individual is the "primary" substance, the species and genus "secondary," and Aristotle says that "if the primary substances were not then it would be impossible for everything else to be" (2b5–6). This hierarchy, however, may not hold in the *Metaphysics.* Whether it does or not is an enduring subject of debate among the scholars and it cannot possibly be solved without a comprehensive interpretation of the entire book. The best that can be done here is to return to *Metaphysics* I.1, Aristotle's account of the development of knowledge.

From various perceptions memory comes to be. From many memories comes "experience" and from experience comes *techne,* the intellectual comprehension of the universal. However complicated the exact process by which this occurs may be, one point is straightforward: somehow, from sensory encounters with individual substances, comes knowledge of the universal form. This process is not one of abstraction, as it would be in a philosopher like Locke.[6] In other words, an abstracting power of the mind does not lift the general out of the particulars. Instead, the universal form is somehow already in the particular and is real in its own right. So, for example, when I look at Bob sitting in a class I not only see an individual but also a human being. As Aristotle explains in the *Posterior Analytics,* "for although the particular is perceived so too is perception of the universal; for example, 'human being,' not 'a human being, namely Callias' " (100b2). If when looking at Bob I am asked, "What do you see?" there are two good answers: "Bob" and "a man." I see the universal as well as the particular and I do so, somehow, at the same time.

To return to the spatial metaphor, the universal is somehow "in" the particular. Or, to use the more technical language of metaphysics, "each thing and its essence are one and the same" (1031b20).

Of all ontological concepts "essence" is the most elusive. It is difficult even to translate the Greek: *to ti ên einai.* The verb *ên* is the third-person singular imperfect of *einai,* "to be," and so the translator's first temptation is "the what it was to be." This is not quite right, however, because the tense of Greek verbs "express two different relations. They may designate the time of an action as *present, past* or *future*; and also its character as *going on, finished,* or simply *taking place.*" Like the present, the imperfect "represents an action as *going on.*" It is thus "a present transferred to the past, retaining all the peculiarities of the present."[7] The English "was" suggests a finished action and thus is misleading. The *to ti ên einai* is closer to "the what it is over a period of time to be." The Latinate "essence" is the traditional term of choice and will be retained.

The "essence" is the "whatness" of a substance; it is what the substance is and so supplies the answer to the question "What is it?" As such, it is intimately related to Form. "Essence will belong to nothing which is not a species (*eidos*) of a genus, but only to a species of a genus" (1030a12). To unravel the intricacies of the relationship between Form and Essence is far beyond the scope of this book. For the moment, it is sufficient to describe the essence as the determinate and primary whatness of a substance.

Aristotle's *Metaphysics* becomes an torturously complex exercise because all these notions—substance, essence, matter, form—require meticulous disentanglement. For example, there are several candidates for substance: "substance is said if not in many ways, in at least four important ways. For the essence and the universal and the genus seem to be the substance of each thing, and the fourth of these is the substratrum" (1028b33–36). In the *Categories* universal and genus were demoted to secondary substances because they do not pack the concrete punch that an individual, or primary substance, does. If I ask you, "What did you just bump into?" you will not answer, "an animal." You'll say, "a dog" or, if you know the dog's name, "Molly." This suggests that the genus is ontologically subordinate to the species and the species to the individual. It is possible, however, that in the *Metaphysics*, where form plays the pivotal role, the hierarchy found in the *Categories* between primary and secondary substances is reversed. Fortunately, this problem cannot be pursued here.[8]

There is another famous problem: if the essence and the individual are somehow the same, and if you and I, as human beings, share the same essence, what differentiates us? Form or essence, after all, "signifies a 'this such' and not just a 'this' or a 'determinate something' " (1033b20). What remains to do the work of differentiating us into individuals, then, is matter. An individual, like Callias or Socrates, is "a this-such form in these flesh and bones" (1034a6). This is curious because, as discussed earlier, matter is indeterminate. It is not actually a this or a that, but potentially this or that. How, then, can it supply the resources to individuate a form? Yet again, this issue must be left behind.

The last sense of "substance" is "substratum" (*hupokeimenon*), and Aristotle only makes matters more difficult by stating that it too is "said in different ways" (1029a2). There is matter, form, and the composite of the two. Your dog Mollie is made of material stuff: calcium, water, and so on. She has a form: she is a dog, the species to which she belongs. And the living, breathing animal you pet is the composite, somehow the combination of form and matter.

To begin to make sense of these concepts, which together have traditionally been called Aristotle's "hylomorphism" (from the Greek *hule*, "matter," and *morphe,* another word for "form"), think again about the nature of living beings, the best example of the form–matter composite. (As Montgomery Furth has put it, "the actual Aristotelian substances are preeminently the biological objects, living things—which means in practice the higher animals, metazoans, the ones he could see.")[9] Better than rocks or plants, animals tell us what it is to be. An animal, developing over time, with all of its mutually enabling parts working together in order continually to maintain the unity of the organism, interacting with the external world but incorporating it into itself through metabolism, reproducing an offspring remarkably like itself, and healing itself, retains its form and is both an individual as well as a member of a clearly delineated species. When Aristotle engages in ontology as the study of substance, he is practicing what Furth calls "bio-metaphysics."

As usual, criticism is required. A famous one came from Locke, for whom the very notion of a substance was deeply suspicious. His account, to explain by means of an example, is roughly this: I look at the apple on my desk. It's been sitting there for an hour and doesn't seem to have changed. It's red, somewhat spherical, and stands about four inches high. These various perceptions "go constantly together." Every time I glance at the apple, it's red, spherical, and four inches high, and no one of these qualities can be detected without the other two. The human mind then, for reasons Locke does not explain, presumes that these simple qualities "belong to one thing, and words being suited to common apprehensions and made use of for quick dispatch, are called, so united in one subject, by one name." In this case, it is "the apple." While Aristotle is confident that behind the name "apple" stands an actual substance that exists out there in the world, Locke is suspicious. "Not imagining how these simple ideas"—red, spherical, four inches high—"can subsist by themselves, we accustom ourselves to suppose some *substratum* in which they do subsist and from which they do result, which therefore we call *substance*." In doing so, however, "we use words without having clear and distinct ideas; we talk like children."

Children do not think carefully or about to what their words refer. But we should. By "substance" we mean some sort of support, something standing under and thereby unifying, the various qualities we have observed constantly going together. What I see on my desk, or so I think, is not merely the three unrelated qualities of being red, spherical, and four inches high, but an apple that has and thereby unifies or holds together these attributes. There is, so I think, a single being on my desk, which corresponds to the singular noun, not a multiplicity of qualities. I call this being a substance and think it most real but, according to Locke, it is but a "supposed but unknown support of these qualities we find existing, which we imagine cannot subsist . . . without something to support them." And in imagining this and calling it substance we do no more than voice our confusion.[10]

For Locke, then, there is a human need to find unity in the multiplicity of perceptions that are constantly conjoined and to call it by a name. Doing this generates a confused concept because a name suggests the presence of something simple and self-standing, whereas in reality our encounter with the apple, which involves seeing its redness and sphericity, is complex. Like Spinoza, who condemns teleology as a "misconception" whose origin is located in "the nature of the human mind," and like Bacon, who believed that human beings have been seduced away from the path of truth by the "idol of the tribe"—in other words, by "human nature itself"—Locke mistrusts the human need to find substantial unity in our experience of the world. Aristotle, by splendid contrast, trusts this human impulse. There really are substances out there, just as we think, and just as the rules governing our language suggest.

III.3: We Know a Substance When We See One.

Locke's critique of Aristotle's substance-ontology can be reformulated. Assume Bob is a substance. To say anything about him that goes beyond merely repeating his name requires a list of predications. He's six feet tall, fifty-four years old, bald, left-handed, and so on. These predicates, however, are all shared by other substances, because Sue also is six feet tall and Jim is bald. As a result, it seems that nothing can be said about Bob just insofar as he is Bob. There seems to be no access, verbal or cognitive, to a substance except through the pathway of predication. This obstruction reinforces Locke's doubt about the clarity of the very concept of a substance. We may think there is a unified substantial being underlying an array of attributes, but this may be no more than mere fancy.

These reflections reiterate the problem of individuation mentioned above (<III.2). Bob may be taken to be an individual substance, but if all that can be said or thought about him is mediated by the many attributes that are predicated of him, and if these are generally applicable to substances other than Bob, then in attempting to articulate it his individuality seems to disappear. The attributes, all of which are universal, impede access to Bob himself. This result seems to clash, however, with the fact that substance is the primary category of Aristotle's metaphysics and as such is required to have the maximum degree of ontological integrity. This it seems to lose if it cannot be articulated except through its non-substantial predicates.

There is a possible solution: intuition, a nondiscursive form of cognitive apprehension analogous to seeing. Perhaps it is possible to know something but be unable to explain it in words. You might say, "I really do see the point but I can't quite explain to you what it is." Typically such a response is counted as either ineffectual or unacceptable. If you really know something then you should be able to explain what you know and maybe even how you came to know it. Invoking intuition seems to be a lazy gesture, a casual waving of the hand toward knowledge.

There is, however, at least one version of intuition that promises to be epistemically respectable. It emerges through Aristotle's discussion of what he calls the "first principles" (*archai*) of "demonstrative knowledge" (*epistêmê*). The best example comes from geometry. All of its propositions or theorems, its epistemic body, are demonstrated or proven. But a proof must begin somewhere. If it didn't the steps would be infinite and the very possibility of a proof would be annihilated. Euclid's *Elements*, to cite the most famous case, begins with a set of definitions, postulates, and "common notions" or axioms. An example of the first is "A point is that which has no part"; of the second, "all right angles are equal to one another"; of the third, "If equals are subtracted from equals, the remainders are equal." From these first principles a series of propositions are proven, each of whose steps is logically justified by reference to an earlier proposition or principle.

Because the steps of a proof procedure are finite, the first principles themselves "cannot be demonstrated" (*Posterior Analytics* 76a31). A first principle is an "axiom," a proposition that by virtue of itself is worthy (*axios*) of being taken as true. It is impossible to prove, but also meaningless to deny, that if equals are subtracted from equals, the remainders are equal. This principle is self-evident; it simply "looks" and so must be counted as true in order for the process of demonstration to proceed.

Because Aristotle firmly believes that a demonstrative science is objectively true about some region of the world, these first principles are more than mere assumptions put into place in order to generate interesting results. Instead, they must be objectively true and knowable, and for this epistemic task a cognitive faculty other than that responsible for demonstrative science is required. This is "mind" or "intuition" (*nous*: *Nicomachean Ethics* 1141a7), which Aristotle says is even "more precise than demonstrative knowledge" (*Posterior Analytics* 100b9). We know, we simply and correctly see, that the remainders of equals subtracted from equals are equal.

Even if first principles cannot themselves be proven, a kind of argument can still be mustered on their behalf. Aristotle offers one in the *Metaphysics* when he defends the "principle of non-contradiction" (PNC), which he takes to be the most basic axiom of all: "it is impossible for the same thing at the same time to belong and not to belong to the same thing and in the same way" (1005b19–20). In minimally formalized language, S cannot be P and not-P at the same time and in the same way. As with his *Categories*, it is not clear whether Aristotle is here speaking about beings—S cannot be P and not-P at the same time, in the same way—or about language: "S is P and S is not-P (at the same time, in the same way)" cannot be true. It does not make sense to say, for example, that "Bob is bald and not-bald at the same time and in the same way." This is a violation of the most basic principle of "logic," which is derived from the Greek *logos*, one of whose meanings is simply "language." But Aristotle's PNC also is an ontological principle: it is impossible for Bob to be bald and non-bald at the same time in the same way. As usual, the conviction that language is a reliable indicator of reality leads to the (altogether fruitful) blurring of the logical and the ontological. In any case, on to the defense of the PNC.

First, the truth of the PNC cannot be proven, for it is the fundamental axiom required by all proof procedures; it is the "ultimate belief" (*eschatên doxa*: 1005b33) to which all who engage in demonstration must eventually be led back. Nonetheless, a case for it can be made by means of what Aristotle calls a "refutative" (*elenchtikôs*: 1006a12) argument. In order for it to get off the ground, there must be an opponent who holds and is willing to defend the view that the PNC is false. Once this happens, however, the opponent has refuted himself, for he maintains that S (the PNC) is false and not true; he asserts an "S is P" statement and, as a defender, is unwilling to contradict himself by also saying "S is not-P." In trying to challenge the basic principle of logical reasoning, he in fact affirms it. Or, as Aristotle puts it, thinking himself to be "destroying *logos* he in fact supports it" (1006a26).

In requiring the opponent to say "it is true that the PNC is false"—in other words, requiring him to make a claim taking the form of "it is true and not false that S is P"—Aristotle may seem to be cheating. It is as if he wants to play a game, the basic rule of which is the PNC, and he says to his opponent, "Sure, you can challenge the rule of my game but only if you first begin by playing according to my rule." In other words, Aristotle might seem to be forcing the opponent to accept the conclusion of the argument (that the PNC is true) before having actually secured its truth by argument; he might seem to beg the question. Aristotle is sensitive to this potential objection, so he moderates the demand placed upon the opponent. He need not say something as elaborate as "It is true and not false that S is P." Instead, he is only required to "say something that is at least meaningful both to himself and to someone else" (1006a21); he must be willing to enter into a conversation in which both partners understand what each other is saying. But in order for this to occur words must have a determinate meaning. A noun must be taken to mean "this" rather than "that," for otherwise communication between the two parties in the dispute would be impossible. So, for example, "human being" must "mean one thing" (*sêmainein hen*: 1006a31); say "two-footed animal." For the moment, it is irrelevant whether the statement "A human being is a two-footed animal" is true or not. What matters is only that for the words to be used meaningfully in a conversation they must be understood by each party. And for this to occur they must be semantically anchored in a determinate manner. If you think that by "human being" I mean a four-footed animal like a squirrel, and I think by it I mean a "two-footed animal," then we will talk at cross-purposes and never get through to each other. If "human being" were allowed to mean both "two-footed animal" and "not-two-footed animal"—in general, if S were allowed to be both P and not-P at the same time and in the same way—then when you used "human being" in a sentence I would not know what you were talking about, and the conversation (*dialegesthai*) would come to a halt.

Aristotle summarizes: "not to mean one thing is to mean nothing" (1006b7). The act of conversation requires the determinacy of meaning and this implies adherence to the PNC. Hence, simply upon entering a debate over the truth of the PNC the opponent is refuted.

Of course, the opponent could refuse to participate in the conversation; he could refuse to speak meaningfully and even celebrate the breakdown of communication. Aristotle contemptuously dismisses this possibility, for were the opponent to act thus he would be "like a plant" (1006a14); a nonrational, uncommunicative, and so nonhuman being.

Aristotle goes further: the opponent who denies the truth of the PNC not only challenges the possibility of meaningful conversation, but he also "destroys substance and essence and will as a result be forced to say that everything is an attribute" (1007a21). So, for example, if the PNC were denied, it would be impossible to determine just what a human being is. Pretend for a moment that the essence of a human being is rationality. If so, then saying "a human being is a rational animal" would count as the definition of a human being, for it articulates the essence—the *to ti ên einai* or "the what it is over a period of time to be" (<III.2)—of a human being. Again, it is unimportant whether this definition is true. What matters is only the demand that the meaning of a noun be defined or limited in order for meaningful conversation to occur. In turn, this requires the

presence of substance and essence, for these are the ontological anchors that render something a determinate "this" rather than a "that." As Aristotle puts it, "to mean a substance is to mean that its essence is not something else" (1007a26–27).

If you and I are going to talk about "human beings"—perhaps in a debate about whether they are all morally equal—we must mean roughly the same thing by the words. We cannot mean that a human being both is and is not a rational animal (at the same time, in the same way). In other words, if we suspended the PNC and allowed contradictions into our midst, then there would be nothing to say about human beings except to list an unlimited number of attributes. This point can be elaborated with a bit of logic.

If the PNC were suspended, then the following compound sentence, which is a contradiction, could be taken as true: "S is P and S is not-P (at the same time and in the same way)." If so, then (by simplification) "S is P" is true. And if this is true, then (by addition) so too is "S is P or Q," at least if "or" means that S must be either P or Q. In other words, once "S is P" is taken as true, then anything—Q, R, T, and so on—can be tacked on by the "or," and the resulting statement is true. If it is true that "the number three is odd," then it is also true that "the number three is odd or green," for the "or" implies that only one of the disjuncts has to be true. Next, return to the first statement: "S is P and S is not-P." It follows (by simplification) that "S is not-P." So now we have "S is P or Q" and "S is not-P." Therefore, "S is Q." This process can be repeated. "S is P or R"; "S is not-P"; therefore "S is R." And this can go on endlessly.

In sum, if the PNC were denied, and the contradiction "S is P and S is not-P" were allowed to stand, it would follow that S is Q, R, T, and so on indefinitely. S would receive an unlimited and unregulated series of attributes.

If the PNC were denied then substance would be destroyed because it would become impossible to say that "S is P" and just leave it at that. If substance were denied then there would be no real S, whose essence can be expressed in a statement like "S is P." S is Q, R, T, and so on forever. Nothing but attributes and it wouldn't matter what they were. No truth, just hot air.

No PNC, no substance. No substance, no meaningful conversation. But there are meaningful conversations. Or, at least, we take ourselves to experience them. We can talk to each other and know what each other, and ourselves, mean. Therefore, substance is real, and the PNC is true.

Back to the original issue: Locke's objections to the concept of substance are powerful. It may be impossible to attain clear linguistic access to substances because we must articulate them in terms of their predicates. Nonetheless, this does not imply that we have no cognitive access to them. The act of conversation itself affords us an intuition of substances. I know they are there because without them we wouldn't be able to make sense of what we were talking about. And this we do. Hence, we do know substances. We somehow see them in our conversational midst.

In a sense, Locke might agree, for he understands that substance has something to do with the human need to think there are unities and to give them names. The difference between him and Aristotle is that the latter trusts these human impulses to be epistemically significant, whereas the former does not.

Aristotle's argument may seem unsatisfying and inconclusive. Perhaps, however, its very weakness reflects his accurate assessment of the phenomena. If substances are given to us in our experience of and reliance upon meaningful conversation, we may well never be able to prove that they are there. The best we can do is refute someone who says they aren't. A world bereft of substances would be one without beings with the ontological integrity to stand behind nouns. It would be a world in which all the many conversations we have with one another would have to be dismissed as epistemically worthless. As a result, we need substance to make sense of ourselves.

Aristotle offers another way of thinking about intuition in his discussion of truth in the *Metaphysics.* In general, "someone who believes that what is separate is separated and what is combined is combined attains the truth (*alêtheuei*), and he who thinks in opposition to the way things really are thinks falsely" (1051b3–5). So, for example, if you think that Bob is a man, you think truly because "Bob" and "man" are in fact combined; in other words, Bob really is a man. If you think that Bob is a woman, you think falsely because in fact "Bob" and "woman" are separate from each other. Such a conception of truth only applies, however, to composites (such as predications and states of affairs). When it comes to incomposites or simples, there is no separating or combining to be done. You cannot be right or wrong, you cannot "truth" (which in Greek is a verb) or "falsify" in the same way that you can about Bob's being a man or a woman. Instead, you either see it or you don't. To shift the sensual metaphor, when it comes to a simple substance like Bob, there is only "touching" (*thigein:* 1051b24). "It is not possible," Aristotle says, "to be wrong about the 'what-is-it' " (1051b25–26). When Bob is standing before you, you simply see it is he. In other words, in the apprehension of a substance, independent of its predicates, there is only intuition; a nondiscursive seeing of it.[11] (The subject of truth is discussed further below: >IV.7.)

III.4: God Is Alive and Good.

Next: the theological side of metaphysics.

There are three kinds of substance. The first is "natural" (1071b4) and includes ordinary beings—dogs, trees, and the like—that move, come into being and perish, and have both form and matter. The second kind also is natural and is found among the heavenly bodies, those eternal entities made from the fifth element, whose only motion or change comes in their circular orbit around the earth. The third is the subject of metaphysics, at least in its theological dimension.

> [The third substance] must be discussed because there must be some everlasting substance that is motionless. For substances are the first of beings, and if all were destructible, then everything would be destructible. But it is impossible that motion either came into being or perished, for it always was and will be. Nor can time come into being or perish. For if there were no time, then there would be no before or after. Like time, and for similar reasons, motion is therefore continuous. For time is either the same as motion or an attribute of it. (*Metaphysics* 1071b4–10)

Because substances are the most ontologically primary of beings—more basic than, say, qualities or quantities—if they were to perish, everything would perish. But everything will not perish, and that is because motion and time are eternal. Therefore, in some as yet unspecified sense, substances too are imperishable.

This argument depends on Aristotle's conceptions of motion and time and the fact that they are either the same or somehow interconnected. In Book IV of the *Physics*, he musters two arguments in order to eliminate the first option. First, when something changes, the motion is in the thing changing. When a tree loses its leaves in the autumn, the change has taken place in the tree. It has not taken place in the house next to the tree. Time, by contrast, does not occur in a thing but instead is present and the same everywhere; it applies to the tree and the house alike. So, while the tree was losing some leaves between 3:00 and 4:00 P.M. on Tuesday, the house was simply standing there during the same hour. This consideration suggests that time and movement or change are not the same. Second, changes can be faster or slower. If there is a frost on Tuesday night, a large quantity of leaves may have dropped before noon Wednesday and the tree may therefore have changed much more quickly on Wednesday than it did on Sunday. Time, by contrast, cannot be faster or slower. In fact, the very notions of faster and slower are determined by the constancy of time. A thousand leaves dropped in one hour on Wednesday. This is a faster rate of change than what occurred on Sunday, when only ten leaves fell during an equivalent hour. This comparison is made possible by the constancy of the temporal unit used to measure the different rates of change. Time, therefore, is not identical to motion (*Physics* 218b13–15).

And yet if we were utterly unaware of any change or motion, we would be similarly unaware of the passage of any time. Thus "it appears (*phaneron*) that time is neither motion nor separated from motion" (219a1). The challenge, then, is to articulate the inextricable bond between the two. To do this, Aristotle deploys the notion of the "before and after." When there is motion, for example a change of place (locomotion), there is a "here" and a "there." Before I threw it, the ball was here in my hand. After I threw it and it completed its journey, it ended up over there in your hand. I was able to determine the beginning of the ball's flight, its end, and an in-between during which it made its trip. Analogously, there is a "before" and "after" in time that measures the duration of the ball's journey from here to there, and so is dependent upon but conceptually distinguishable from it. So, "whenever there is a before and after, we say there is time. For time is this: the number of motion according to the before and after" (219b1–2). Time is not motion, but the counting, the measuring, the dividing up into before and after, and the measuring of the in-between of motion.

Recall that time is triadically structured (<I.2). The present moment or "now" divides the "before" (the past) from the "after" (the future). Building on this, Aristotle syllogizes: "If it is impossible for time to be, and to be intelligible, without the now, and the now is a mid-point between beginning and end—the beginning of the future time, and the end of past time—it is necessary that there always be time. For the final moment of time that has passed will itself be a now, since it is impossible to grasp time without the now, so that since the now is both beginning and end, it is necessary time always comes from it in both directions. And if this is true of time, then apparently it also must be true of motion, since time is an affection of motion" (251b19–28).

The concept of a beginning or end of time is incoherent. A first moment of time would have no "before" and a last moment of time would have no "after," and so, because time is necessarily triadic, neither is conceptually possible. Time, therefore, is everlasting. Because of the bond that necessarily cements the two, so also is motion.

This conclusion has significant implications because "there is no motion apart from beings (*ta pragmata*: *Physics* 200b33). If there is a change, then something is changing. It is either moving from place to place or its qualities are changing or it is getting bigger or smaller. Motion and time cannot be found, except in abstract argument, apart from moving and thus temporal beings. Therefore, if motion is eternal, there must be an eternally moving substance.

Of course, we already knew that, for the heavenly bodies have already been shown to be eternal (<I.6). But these are moving and have matter. Because a basic Aristotelian principle is that "everything that is moved must be moved by something" (*Physics* 241b34), something must cause the stars to orbit the earth eternally. Furthermore, because the causal sequence cannot be infinite (<II.8), what moves the stars cannot itself be moved by something that is itself moved by something else, and so on without end. "If there is no first, in general there is no cause" (*Metaphysics* 994a18–19). There must thus be a being that causes the motion of other beings while itself not moving. This is Aristotle's infamous "first" or "unmoved" or "motionless" mover. The next passage is meant to shed some light on what it is.

> If there is an object that can move other things or can act upon them, but it is not actually doing so, there will be no motion. For it is possible that what has a potentiality will not actualize it. So there will be no gain if we postulate an eternal substance unless a principle is present which is able to cause change. Even this is not enough, for if it is not actualizing there will be no motion. Furthermore, if the substance of this principle has potentiality, even if it is actualizing, this will still not be enough. Motion will still not be eternal since it is possible that what is potentially will not come into being. Therefore, there must be a principle whose substance is actuality. (*Metaphysics* 1071b12–20)

We observe—in fact, it is undeniable (except by someone playing a debater's game)—that natural phenomena, beings in the world, move. It has been proven (syllogistically) that motion is eternal and that consequently there are eternally moving substances. Therefore, what is required next is an answer to the question, what is the cause of the eternal motion of the heavenly bodies? Such a "mover," something that causes motion, must itself be eternal. But, more important, it must be eternally and continuously actual.

Motion is the actualization (*entelecheia*) of the potential insofar as it is potential. A basin of cool water is potentially hot, but it doesn't change until fire, which is actually hot, is brought near it and then heats it. When this demand for actuality is applied to the search for the cause of the continual and eternal motion of the stars, the result is a being in unadulterated actuality. For if this being had even the slightest dab of potentiality then it might not become actual. For this is, after all, what being "potential" means: it might not be. Hence, the cause of the eternal motion of the heavens must be permanently and continuously actual.

If this being is purely actual, then because motion is the actualization of the potential as potential it must be motionless. Therefore, something with no trace of potentiality cannot move or change.

There is more: a substance whose very being is actuality has no matter. An everyday natural substance, the dog or the tree, has form, analogically pegged to actuality, and matter, analogous to potentiality. Such a being necessarily goes through changes and eventually will perish. Even the imperishable stars have matter, albeit of an eternal and weightless kind, which is why they circle the earth forever and don't fall down. But their cause, and the cause of everything else, must be permanently, ceaselessly, continuously actual.

The conception of a motionless mover that Aristotle develops is literally extraordinary. Ordinary things are moved by movers that are themselves moving. The downward thrust of my fingers pushes the keys on my keyboard downward. A moving mover moves something else. How, then, can there be a motionless mover? "The object of desire and the intelligible object move things in this way; namely, without themselves moving. Of these the first things are the same. For what shows itself to be beautiful (*to phainomenon kalon*) is desirable, and what is first of all beautiful shows itself to be something to wish for" (*Metaphysics* 1072a24–29).

I'm hungry and want to eat. The food on my plate looks fine (*kalon*) to me, and so I am moved by it. My hand grasps the fork and I push it downward until it engages with the food, which I then carry upward toward my mouth. The food has caused me to move while itself being motionless (at least in relationship to my hand). Thus works an object of desire.

So too with an object of thought. I see this written on the board: $X^2 - 20X - 300 = 0$. It beckons me, for I want to solve the equation. The scribbles on the board have moved me to think about them without themselves moving. Such is the power of the intelligible object.

Applying this line of reasoning to the heavens results in the conclusion that the first mover is motionless and functions like an object of desire.

It is thus like a final cause or *telos*. It "moves other things as an object of love, and the other things that are moved then cause motion" (1072b4).

This sounds loony: stars love the motionless mover and as a result orbit the earth in perfect circles. And here you thought that stars were nothing but exploding gases that obey the laws of physics and don't feel a thing. It only gets worse. The motionless mover seems to experience pleasure: "its actualization," Aristotle says, "is pleasure" (1072b16). (Note that Aristotle does not say that it feels pleasure.) This statement, which sounds as preposterous as stars that love, can only be understood by examining the link Aristotle forges between pleasure and the most fundamental of all metaphysical principles, actuality.

In the *Nicomachean Ethics*, Aristotle begins a discussion of pleasure by comparing it with vision.[12] "Seeing seems to be complete at every moment and it lacks nothing that, coming to be later, will complete its form. Pleasure seems to be like this" (1174b13–17). When I turn my head and see the orange basketball on the floor, the experience of seeing is complete and whole, rather than being sequential or broken up into parts. To clarify by means of a contrast, consider the building of a house. It is complete only when the house is finished at the end of the process. Each task beforehand—laying the foundation, constructing the walls, and so on—is both incomplete and different from the other tasks required for building the house. A house with only a foundation is not really a house, just a part of one. Only when the house has all its parts is it complete. By contrast, seeing is complete at every moment that the visual apparatus is activated.

This notion can be explicated grammatically by reflecting on the relationship between the present and perfect tenses of verbs. Both are primary tenses, which means that "they denote present or future time." They differ in that the present "represents an action as going on at the time of speaking or writing; as *grapho*, *I write* or *I am writing*." The perfect, by contrast, "represents an action as already finished at the present time; as *gegrapha*, *I have written;* that is, *my writing is now finished* . . . it implies the performance of the action in past time, yet states that it *stands completed* at the *present* time." In the case of an action like writing, the two tenses express something different. While "I am writing," the page is incomplete and I cannot yet read it. After "I have written" the page, which took me ten minutes, the writing is done and I can read it. The perfect tense differs from the aorist, which "expresses the simple occurrence of an action in past time." So, to continue the example, "I wrote" the page can refer to something I did yesterday or a year ago, and the page may not be before me now.[13]

The key point here can be made with Aristotle's own example: when it comes to perception, "one sees" and "one has seen" (*Metaphysics* 1048b23) at the same time. So too does "one think" and "has one thought" at the same time. At each and every moment the activities of seeing and thinking are "complete" or "perfect," both of which translate the Greek *teleion*. Such actions are neither developmental nor processes whose end point is distinct from the activity leading to it. Therefore, when formulated linguistically the perfect and present tenses have the same semantic content. The case is different in Aristotle's own example of learning. "I learn or am learning": this means that I am now busy at work in the classroom studying, say, arithmetic, which I do not yet know. "I have learned": I now know arithmetic; I am a knower rather than a student and so no longer need to study or acquire knowledge. Instead, I can use the knowledge I have to solve a problem. The phrase "I have learned" signals the termination of a process or what Aristotle here calls a "motion" (*kinesis: Metaphysics* 1048b27). It is "incomplete" or "imperfect" (*ateles*) and requires time to attain its goal. By contrast, seeing suffers no such distinction between process and end result. "She sees," "she is seeing," and "she has seen" describe one and the same *energeia*, "actuality" or more literally "being-in-a-state-of-work."

Like seeing, feeling pleasure is complete at every moment rather than being a process whose end result is distinct from it and which, once attained, signals its termination. If writing a page or building a house is a "motion" that takes place "in time," pleasure, like seeing, is an undivided experience; "it is something whole and is in the moment" (*Nicomachean Ethics* 1174b9). Delightfully all absorbing, the experience of pleasure takes us out of the flow of time. Of course, this does not mean that the temporal duration of a pleasurable experience cannot be measured. You were, for example, enjoyably absorbed in your massage from 8:20 to 9:00 P.M. But, as usual, Aristotle is keenly fixed on what takes place inside the experience. If you were really feeling pleasure, you didn't look at the clock at all.

A conceptual pair has been forged: actuality and pleasure go hand in glove.

Aristotle continues his discussion of pleasure in the *Nicomachean Ethics* by elaborating its relationship to sense perception. "All sense perception is actualized in relation to a perceptible object and it is completely actualized when it is in good condition and is in relation to the finest of the perceptible objects. . . . With regard to each sense the best actualization is of that which is in the best condition with respect to the best of the objects that fall within its purview. And this is the most complete and the most pleasant" (1174b14–20).

You have twenty-twenty vision and are looking at the orange basketball on the floor, which in a well-lighted room has been placed at a good viewing distance away from you. The conditions for seeing it, your well-functioning eyes and the object itself, cumulatively optimize the activity of seeing. You see the ball as well as anyone could. By contrast, someone near-sighted or who is struggling to see in a poorly lighted room sees the ball in a manner inferior to yours. In the first case the capacity to see is fully and best actualized, and so will be most pleasurable. Of course, most of the time when we are engaged in the everyday business of seeing, smelling, tasting, touching, and hearing we are not explicitly aware of feeling pleasure. Nonetheless, at the very beginning of the *Metaphysics* Aristotle rightly says that we enjoy or take pleasure in, we feel "affection" (*agapêsis*: 980a22) for, the exercise of our senses. This is palpably true on special occasions, when we listen to good music or eat delicious food or have a massage. It also is obvious when the use of our senses is obviously beneficial. When, for example, you were about to cross the street but saw a car coming and so returned to the sidewalk, you felt grateful for your ability to see. But independent of such occasions and simply "on account of themselves" (*di' hautas*) the senses are enjoyable when they are at work. This is because their work is an actualization, an *energeia*.

The *telos*, the purpose, of the eyes is to see. Therefore, a person with excellent vision who sees a maximally visible object in a well-lighted room maximally actualizes a natural capacity. And this feels good. Furthermore, the better our vision is—or more generally, the healthier we are—the better it feels. If you are sick, a food that normally is experienced as delicious will taste lousy.

By explicating pleasure through the comparison with seeing, and by linking it to actuality, Aristotle treats it (almost) as a physiologic phenomenon. "There is a pleasure for every form of sense perception, as there is also for every thought and theorizing. And the most pleasant is the most complete. And the most complete is that which is in the sense that is in the best condition and is taking up the best of objects. . . . Pleasure thus completes the actualization. . . . It is a *telos* that comes to be upon the actualization, like the bloom of youth comes upon those who are in their youthful primes" (1174b20–33).

Pleasure is like the bloom of a plant at the peak of its flowering. It is found in an organism fully "at work" (*energeia*) at the peak of its power. It is the youngish dog, unleashed, running joyfully through the park, taking pure pleasure in the exercise of its legs. It is the young girl who skips rather than walks and the middle-aged adult who fulfills his *telos* by thinking, which is the work (*ergon*) most characteristic of his specific animality (>V.1–2). Pleasure completes the activity but not by being a distinct goal apart from it, as the house is distinct from the process of building. As long as the eyes are healthy and the object is fully visible, there will be pleasure in seeing. In contemporary lingo, there is a feedback loop that is generated by and informs the activities of living beings. Even if it does not consciously experience pleasure, a healthy snail is reinforced in the performance of its snail activities, particularly nutrition, and thus continues to perform them. Only thus does it move forward to stay alive.

Aristotle's conception of pleasure is inseparable from his teleology. The eyes are for the purpose of seeing. If your vision is excellent and all the other conditions for good seeing are met, if you are a healthy animal, you'll feel good.

This train of thought can be extended. As Aristotle explains at length in his treatise *On the Psyche,* which is discussed in Chapter Four below, "life itself is an actualization" (1175a12). As such, it is inherently pleasurable and thus "desirable" (1175a16). Life is "sweet" (*Politics* 1258b30), and "to be alive is better than not to be alive" (*Generation of Animals* 731b30). A healthy penguin pursues life and so seeks to avoid being eaten by a seal. Neither animal has formulated a doctrine of the goodness of life, and some animals may even lack a nervous system capable of receiving much by way of pleasure. Nonetheless, they are alive. This means that they actualize their capacities; minimally, their metabolic systems are at work. And if there is actualization there is positive reinforcement; there is pleasure.

As pure actuality and thus as pleasure, Aristotle's motionless mover is both alive and divine (*Metaphysics* 1072b25–26). It is good and so is the object of desire. Aristotle makes it clear, however, that it is not morally or personally good. "For what sort of actions could we assign to [god]?" (*Nicomachean Ethics* 1178b10). To be courageous, for example, requires that the agent endure fear. But the divine surely fears nothing. To be temperate requires controlling one's bad desires, of which the divine has none. Because all moral actions require a deficiency or need of some sort, "it appears that everything to do with such actions are trivial and unworthy of the divine" (1178b17–18). The goodness of Aristotle's motionless mover, then, is the ontological complement of its actuality. To be is to be actual, determinate, intelligible; to be form. God is alive and good in the same sense that the cosmos as a whole, which is a hierarchical order of different beings each of which has its own place, is good.

Because "everyone believes that the gods are alive and in a state of actuality (*energein*: 1178b19), Aristotle's god must be "doing" something. The following passage takes the first step toward characterizing what this might be. "Since its actualization is pleasure, its mode of being, which it engages in forever (which for us would be impossible), is like that which is best for us during a short time. And on account of this wakefulness, perception, thinking are most pleasurable, and hopes and memories are as well" (*Metaphysics* 1072b14–16).

To identify what pleasure might characterize the motionless mover, Aristotle points to "us" (*hêmin*). What it "experiences" is like what we experience if only incompletely and for a short time. For us, being awake, perception, and thought are the most pleasurable actualizations. Perception requires a body, which the motionless mover does not have (because it has no matter and does not participate in potentiality). What remains is thinking. The motionless mover is not only alive and "divine" (1072b24); it is "mind" or "intellect" (*nous*). To reiterate, the divine can neither do nor think about a practical action like being generous. Instead, the only activity that belongs to it is "theoretical" (*theorêtikê*: 1179b22) (>V.7, VI.7).

The divine thinks and so must think about something, for if it thought nothing surely it wouldn't be worth fussing about. Because it thinks something it must think of either something other than itself or itself. Next, recall the argument made about perception: seeing is most fully actualized when the object is optimally visible and the eyes are in the best condition. Analogously, if thinking is to be maximally actualized, as it must be in the case of the divine, the mind must be in the optimal condition and its object must be the best and most fully intelligible object. But only one object meets this requirement: the divine itself. Therefore, divine "thinking (*noêsis*) is a thinking of thinking (*noêseôs noêsis*: 1074b34)." With no trace of potentiality to it, the divine mind thinks itself permanently, continually, ceaselessly.

The cosmos is finally caused by a motionless mover, the ultimate object of desire, which is pure mind thinking itself. Perhaps this sounds a bit similar to the God we read about in the Bible. But Aristotle's divine being is not an Intelligent Designer of an orderly world (<II.2). It does not think about or ingeniously craft animals and plants, and so surely does not make the animal kingdom for the benefit of humankind. Nor does it enter into history, create the world (which as eternal is not subject to creation), or love us. To reiterate, it has no moral or personal qualities at all and it partakes of no actions of the sort with which we are accustomed. It is full actuality and all it does is think . . . itself.

Still, as distant as this theological conception may be from the book of *Genesis*, all those medieval philosophers who found in Aristotle's treatises a philosophical buttress to their religious convictions weren't just making it all up. Consider the following.

The motionless, first mover, Aristotle's god, is the ultimate object of love and is Good. But there are, he says, three ways in which the Good can be conceived as being present in the cosmos. The first, which comes closest to our conception of the biblical God, is as "something separate and itself with respect to itself"; in other words, as an "absolute" Being. (The word derives from *absolvere,* "to set free, release, complete, finish, bring to an end.") The second is in the very "order" (*taxis*) of the parts that make up the whole. The third is a combination of both. Aristotle explains through a comparison. An army finds its goodness in both its order and in the general who commands it.

> Everything is ordered in some way; water-animals and birds and plants. But these do not lack a relationship of one to the other. Instead, there is a relationship. For everything is related towards one (*pros hen*).[14] It is like a household (*oikia*) in which the freemen are least able to act in a random fashion, because all or most things are ordered, while the slaves and wild animals have little share in the common life and so do act in a random fashion. For such is the principle of each of these, which is their nature. I mean, for example, that it is necessary for everything to come together in order to be distinguished. Thus it happens in other cases in which everything has a share in the whole. (*Metaphysics* 1075a16–25)

Aristotle is a metaphysical "ecologist" (which derives from *oikos,* "household"). The world is a cosmos, an ordered whole in which all beings have their place. In a Greek household, the "freemen," male citizens, had significant responsibilities to the community that their social status required them to execute. Hence, despite being "free" they were not permitted simply to do what they wanted. (How this sense of "freedom" differs from our own is discussed in Chapter V.4 below.) Only by performing the various tasks uniquely appropriate to them were freemen "distinguished" from other elements in the city, such as slaves or women (>VI.3). But only by being part of a community composed of diverse elements could such tasks be identified as unique. In other words, to determine that X is different from Y, both X and Y must together belong to some set of objects that can be compared with one another. If they were absolutely separated, there would be no way of comparing them. To be distinct, therefore, requires participation in a common and ordered whole in which distinctions can be made between the various parts. This is an "ecological" notion: each individual is part of and thereby contributes to the whole. Each can be distinguished only by having "come together."

Back to the comparison with the army: just as an army becomes good because of both its order and the general who commands it, so too is "the

Good" of the whole found both in the order of the parts and in the cause of the order of the whole, the motionless mover or god.

The world makes sense and it does so in two basic ways, which correspond to the ontological and the theological sides of metaphysics. First, beings or substances have a form, an *eidos*: things "look" like what they are. A dog looks like and is a dog rather than a mouse or a tree. A human being is not an ant. Because of the primacy of form, itself inextricably bound to actuality, beings are intelligible and thus can be studied for what they are. Just as the goodness of an army is manifested in the order of its well-disciplined troops, so is the world composed of intelligible beings. But just as the army has a commanding general, the order of the world and its beings is ultimately caused by a "one": the motionless mover, god, fully actualized mind thinking itself. All beings in the world are ultimately related to it. There is a first cause, an ultimate source of intelligibility.

For centuries the scholars have debated just what this ultimate mind is and whether it could be assimilated to the God of the Bible. The proposal here is modest: in addition to being the cause of the circular orbit of the stars, the first mover is the cause of order and intelligibility of the world. This does not address how exactly "mind" thinks itself, moves the heavenly bodies as an object of love and thereby causes the world. Instead, it only treats god as the cause of a world that makes sense . . . to us.

Aristotle thinks from the ground up. Our daily lives are informed by our encounters with intelligible objects. We bump into dogs and cats, and when it rains we cover our heads because we know that water comes down from the sky. Ants are below us on the ontological ladder and so we don't feel guilty when we inadvertently stomp on them or, when they are doing some damage, deliberately poison them. The stars are above. The world is an *oikos.* Things fit. Because Aristotle demands that the sequence of causes be finite (<II.8), there must be a first, completely actualized and so motionless mover. Somehow it "thinks." And when it does it thinks itself as cause of the world. It explains why the whole world makes sense.

For a philosopher like Hume, all of this is nothing but pathetic anthropomorphizing, and he offers this bit of deflationary analysis to calm it down. "The idea of God, as meaning an infinitely intelligent, wise, and good being, arises from reflecting on the operations of our own mind and augmenting, without limit, those qualities of goodness and wisdom."[15] Aristotle thinks quite differently. "We desire (*oregometha*) because something seems beautiful rather than it seeming beautiful because we desire it" (*Metaphysics* 1072a29–30).

We do not project our own conception of beauty and order upon the world and only then find it to be good. In loving the world we do not narcissistically love ourselves. Instead, the beings of the world, especially living ones, actually are beautiful and this is why they engage us. Most of all we want to understand them and so it is that "all human beings by nature strive to know" (*Metaphysics* 980a20). Correspondingly, we do not project an amplified version of our own best attributes onto a blank screen and call it "god." Instead, we reason carefully about the world, which at its fundament is intelligible, and realize that there must be a first cause with the various attributes that have been discussed in this chapter. There must be a reason why the world is intelligible. And it is god.

III.5: To Stand Firmly on the Side of Life.

Addressing an audience of American bishops in 1998, Pope John Paul II said, "Above all, society must learn to embrace once more the great gift of life, to cherish it, to protect it, and to defend it against the culture of death, itself an expression of the great fear that stalks our times. One of your most noble tasks as Bishops is to stand firmly on the side of life, encouraging those who defend it and building with them a genuine culture of life."[16]

The pope was right. We live in a culture of death, and there is no more urgent task than the struggle against it. In the infinite universe of modern science the distinction between the living and the inanimate either cannot be drawn or is metaphysically trivial. Bereft of *telos*, with nothing but the blind forces of physics and duplicator machines roaming the earth, being is not paradigmatically expressed in substance and animals are given no privileged place in the cosmos. "Soul" is but a name given to the consciousness produced by a material clump, also known as "the brain." There is nothing special about being alive and no one belongs anywhere in particular. Such is the culture of death. And it must be opposed (before it's too late).

Aristotle joins the pope in standing "firmly on the side of life." As he puts it, "*psyche* is better than body, the animate [that which has *psyche,* is *empsuchon*] is better than the inanimate; being is better than non-being, and living is better than not being alive" (*Generation of Animals* 731b29–30). His is a bio-metaphysics in which animals are paradigmatic substances. He thinks that life is good and a "gift," at least in the biological sense of it having been given to us without our having asked for it. He is, in short, "pro-life." But his position is quite different from that held by those who typically march under this banner. For them the slogan mainly refers to their opposition to abortion, euthanasia, stem cell research, and human cloning. (The more thoughtful of such marchers realize that in order to be consistent their commitments should lead them also to oppose capital punishment, debilitating poverty, environmental degradation, and most if not all forms of war.) By contrast, Aristotle endorses the limited use of abortion and infanticide. He recommends, for example, that there be a law prohibiting the rearing of a "deformed child" and says that in a well-governed city "the number of children born must be limited and if in violation of this stricture there are offspring due to copulation, abortion must be performed before there is sensation and life" (*Politics* 1335b20–25).

Aristotle's view on infanticide, anathema to us, emerges from his teleological conception of nature. A species is defined by a form, which gives every individual within it a *telos*. If a child is brain damaged and will never be able to perform a normal range of rational activities, then it does not have the potential to reach its *telos* and become a well-functioning adult. As a consequence, it does not have the same value as that belonging to a fully actualized or well-formed individual and euthanasia becomes a legitimate option. When it comes to abortion Aristotle draws a firm line: only those that occur before the fetus possesses "sensation and life" are "holy" (1335b25). This constraint tracks the traditional notion of "quickening," the time at which (typically around twenty weeks) the mother can feel movement and which was long considered to be the moment when the fetus attained an individual life. Of course, advances in embryology and genetics have rendered this notion obsolete. The scientific details are not relevant here, for the significant point is only that Aristotle draws a line somewhere in order to permit some abortions. He does so because while a fetus clearly has great value—it is a potential human being—it is not on a par with actual human beings. So, for example, a city is well advised to maintain some form of population control. Not to do so is irresponsible and will "necessarily cause citizens to live in poverty, which in turn creates political conflict and malfeasance" (*Politics* 1265b10–12). The well-being of an actual city takes precedence over the value of a potential human being, and thus abortions performed early in the pregnancy are permissible.

Life is good and naturally pleasurable, for it is *energeia*. But all instances of life are not equally good. There is, in other words, a difference between life and a good life, between one fully actualized and one less so. And this distinction is grounded upon a teleological conception of nature.

"Life is good" may sound pathetically cheerful. But listen to what Aristotle actually says:

"Perhaps there is present in living itself, just by itself, some portion of beauty (*to kalon*),[17] at least if a life is not overwhelmed by an excess of hardship. It is clear, at any rate, that most human beings will endure much bad suffering in order to cling to life because there is a kind of joy and natural sweetness to it" (*Politics* 1278b25–30).

Life (as actualization of natural capacities) is sweet, but it can go bad awfully fast if overwhelmed by misfortune and suffering. Even more pressing, this teleological thought has a dark side built into it. A living being is born and then develops toward its mature state, its *telos,* where it operates at the peak of its powers and experiences maximum pleasure. But then it goes downhill and eventually dies. As human beings get very old they decline and life becomes worse. In the *Rhetoric,* for example, Aristotle paints a bleak picture of the character of the really old. Generally speaking, they are bad tempered, mistrustful, small-minded, cowardly, miserly, and bereft of strong desire and hope. They incessantly talk about the past, have no sense of humor, and are unpleasant. Aristotle may generalize far too quickly, but his remarks testify to an indisputable point: when we get old our powers diminish and we begin the process of decay. Most important, after the age of forty-nine, which Aristotle takes to be the peak of rational ability (1390b14), our most significant capacity begins to slide. Eventually, for someone suffering from advanced Alzheimer's, for example, euthanasia might be both a reasonable and justifiable option. Aristotle's teleologically based commitment to the value of life implies that death and therefore the approximation of death in advanced age, however natural, is bad.[18]

To elaborate Aristotle's view on death by means of a contrast, consider briefly the thought of the ancient Greek thinker Epicurus (who was born some twenty years before Aristotle died). He was an "atomist" who maintained that there was nothing in the world but indivisible simple bodies ("monads") and the void through which they moved. Upon this theoretical foundation he constructed an ethical doctrine in which happiness is the ultimate good of life and is finally equivalent to pleasure. In turn, the key to pleasure is the elimination of stress or anxiety and the consequent attainment of tranquility. Above all else, tranquility requires the elimination of the fear of death, which is at the root of human anxiety. "Get used to believing that death is nothing to us. For all good and bad consists in sense-experience and death is the privation of sense-experience. Hence, a correct knowledge of the fact that death is nothing to us makes the mortality of life a matter of contentment, not by adding a limitless time [to life] but by removing the longing for immortality. For there is nothing fearful in life for one who has grasped that there is nothing fearful in the absence of life."[19]

For Epicurus, there is no good reason to fear the dreamless sleep of death because it brings nothing but the cessation of sense-experience, which is required for the awareness of pain. To make the same point on ontological grounds, death is simply the rearrangement of the atoms that comprise us. The soul does not survive the destruction of the body and so there is no afterlife or eternal damnation to fear. Because we are material beings whose atoms will be recycled, death is no big deal. Understanding this simple truth brings about the pleasurable state of tranquility the Epicureans prized so highly.

Aristotle would disagree: death *is* something to us; the termination of our good lives. Death, more particularly an early death, is thus to be feared. Indeed, enduring rather than eliminating the fear of death is courage, which is a virtue. (See *Nicomachean Ethics* 1155a10–30). Furthermore, on this account a "longing for immortality," which Epicurus dismisses as irrational and stress inducing, is rational. For life seeks to perpetuate and to generate beyond itself, a fact conspicuously in view in sexual reproduction. "For this is the most natural function of living beings, to the extent that they are complete and neither maimed nor the product of spontaneous generation: producing another like itself. An animal produces an animal and a plant a plant in order that they might have a share in the eternal and divine as far as possible. For every living being strives for this" (*On the Psyche* 415a26–415b1).

No individual animal can actually become immortal or divine, and so it seeks to overcome this lack, to respond to the inevitability of death, by reproducing itself. It does so in order to participate in the divine in the only manner available to it: through the perpetuation of its species. Recall that the species are a permanent feature of the natural world (<II.5). All beings, even snails, are thus able to participate in the eternal in this limited fashion. When it comes to human beings, as we shall see in the second half of this book, the story gets complex. For in addition to being able to copulate we can aspire to the divine through our thinking.

Life is a gift. No one asks to be born. As such and although it is good, it never fully belongs to us. Instead, it is vulnerable and forever subject to the awful intrusions of bad luck.[20] Aristotle explains when, in the *Nicomachean Ethics,* he addresses the traditional saying (attributed to Solon) that no man is happy until he is dead. On the one hand, this is absurd; happiness is a form of activity (>V.1–2), while death terminates all activity. On the other, the saying brings into clear focus the contingencies that necessarily infect all human lives. A man may have had a long and good life, but at the very end catastrophe may break loose and ruin everything. Chance intrudes and so no life as it is being lived is entirely safe from disruption. While it is true that the best and most virtuous of human beings will endure misfortune as well as anyone can, the fact remains that "supreme happiness" (being *makarios* or "blessed": 1101a7) is out of reach while a person is alive. Only after death can the value of a life be fully and safely evaluated (by someone who is alive). A good death, then, is required for a life to be counted as completely good. And yet "to be alive is better than not to be alive."

To sum up: Aristotle would join forces with Pope John Paul II in urging us to oppose "the culture of death, itself an expression of the great fear that stalks our times." This commitment requires more than opposition to abortion and euthanasia. Instead, it requires a wholesale reconceiving of the world; a world where first being, but then life, can be conceived as good. And this requires the metaphysical doctrines of substance, form, *telos*, and *energeia,* all of which emerge from reflection upon the lives we live down here on earth.

Chapter Four

Truth Is Easy.

"Truth is like the proverbial door that no one can miss"

—*Metaphysics* 993b5

"Human beings hit upon the truth more often than not"

—*Rhetoric* 1355a7–10

IV.1: If the Eye Were an Animal, Vision Would Be Its Soul.

"Soul" is a word that embarrasses scientists and most contemporary philosophers. Perhaps it conjures up an image from Dante's *Inferno*, where disembodied beings with fully intact characters and the capacity to feel pain remain for eternity to receive the endless punishments they deserve. Or it may suggest a mysterious notion of a nonmaterial substance that somehow acts within or upon the body. In the hands of a lazy thinker, "soul" can function as a deus ex machina in order to explain human consciousness or personal identity and so hard-nosed thinkers have long sought to replace it with a proper understanding of the brain.

This is a catastrophe. Soul is real. But it is not what Dante thought it was. It is what Aristotle calls (in Greek) *psuchê*, the origin of our words "psyche" and "psychology."

Psuchê is derived from *psuchein*, "to breathe." In its earliest appearance in Greek literature it means "life-breath" or "animating force" and it is often prominent in descriptions of someone's death. When Homer depicts Pandaros being killed by Diomedes, for example, he says "his life (*psuchê*) and strength were scattered" (*Iliad*, V.296). At the end of his life a man breathes his last. The difference between a corpse, which is a quickly decomposing heap of organic elements, and a living man who remains intact is the presence of *psuchê*. Aristotle's "psychology," his *logos* of the *psyche* (the term used in this book), remains faithful to this primordial sense of the word, which itself is faithful to the phenomenon of, the witnessing of, someone's dying.

Consider *On the Psyche* II.1, in which Aristotle gradually works his way toward a definition of the *psyche*. He begins by arguing that it must be a "substance" (*ousia:* 412a19). This, however, is not sufficiently specific because there are three subdivisions of substance: "matter, or that which in itself is not a 'this something'; shape or form, according to which something is said to be a 'this something'; and third, that which comes from both of these" (412a7–10).

> Bodies seem most of all to be substances, and especially natural ones, for these are the origins of other bodies. And of natural bodies, some have life while others do not. And we say that life is self-nourishment, growth and decay. Consequently every natural body having life is a substance and substance understood as a compound. Since it is this sort of body, which has life, the body is not the *psyche*. For the body is not something that belongs to an underlying subject; rather it functions as an underlying subject and as matter. Therefore, the *psyche* must be a substance in the sense of the form of a natural body potentially having life. And the substance is actuality (*entelecheia*). (412a11–22)

Unlike other passages, where animals are first on the list of substances, here it is natural bodies in general, which in turn are divided into the animate and inanimate. Because bodies occupy the level of matter and because some bodies are alive while others are not, the *psyche*, that which is responsible for being alive, must be other than the body-as-matter. Hence, the *psyche* is defined as a substance in the sense of form of a natural body potentially having life. ("Organic" is added to the definition at 412b5.) What differentiates a living from a dead or inanimate object is the presence of *psyche,* a life-force that acts and actualizes the potentialities of the body; that keeps it intact and whole through the passage of time.

Even this definition is not sufficiently specific, for there are two senses of "actuality." To explain, Aristotle deploys the example of knowing "arithmetic" (417a32), which was discussed briefly in the Introduction. I may have learned arithmetic as a child can thus perform operations like addition and subtraction. In this sense, I am an actual knower of arithmetic. But even if I have this knowledge I am not using it right now. However, when presented with a problem—say, 3945 + 592—the knowledge I possess will kick into gear and I will solve it. Having arithmetic in my epistemic repertoire counts as a first level of actuality but only in the midst of actually working through a problem do I rise to a second level of actuality; namely the full-blown exercise of the knowledge I possess. Clearly, then, first actuality also can be construed as a high degree of potentiality. Even if not actually doing so, I am capable of computing sums.

The word Aristotle uses to express the exercise of knowledge already possessed is *theôrein*, literally "theorize" but usually, although inadequately, translated as "contemplation" (>V.8).

To generalize this point, Aristotle deploys an analogy: while asleep, I am alive and so my *psyche* is present as the actuality of my living body, but I am not engaged in, for example, seeing. While awake and with open eyes actively seeing things, I am working at a higher level of actuality. Sleeping is to waking as having knowledge is to *theôrein*.

Aristotle uses *theôrein* to illustrate the salient and most philosophically attractive feature of his conception of the *psyche*. Rather than being a static thing it is the *energeia*, activity, the being-at-work of the living body. It is the *entelecheia*, the state of having-of-a-*telos* and being actively directed toward its attainment. Two additional analogies illustrate further what this means: (1) If an axe were a natural body, being able actually to chop wood would be its *psyche*. When an axe becomes so severely rusted that it can no longer chop, it is an "axe" only in name (412b11–15). (2) "If the eye were an animal, vision would be its *psyche*" (412b18–19). An eye that cannot see—say one in a painting or carved in stone—is an "eye" only in name. To sum up: the seeing eye, the chopping axe, and the person actually having knowledge of arithmetic are three illustrations of Aristotle's conception of *psyche* as the actuality of a body.

These remarks show that Aristotle's *psyche* is utterly unlike the disembodied beings inhabiting Dante's *Inferno*. In fact, Aristotle explicitly distances himself from such a conception when he says, "thus it is clear that neither the *psyche* nor its parts, if its nature allows for parts, are separate from the body" (413a5). However, in a statement that has sparked a vast debate, he also says this: "concerning the mind (*nous*) and the theoretical capacity nothing is yet apparent, but it seems that this is a distinct kind of *psyche* and this alone can be separated just as the eternal is separated from the perishable" (413b24–27). With this notorious mention of a separable "mind" Aristotle may well seem, and for centuries was seen, to veer closer to Dante than might be comfortable for those who would want him to remain a thinker who thoroughly "naturalizes" the world (<II.2). Explaining

how the two sides of his psychology—his insistence that *psyche* and body are not separate and his statement that mind is separate—cohere (if they do) will require significant work (>IV.5, VI.7).

IV.2: The World Is Nourishing.

Aristotle lists the ability to nourish itself as the first and most essential attribute of a living being. It is the basic life-function, the most primitive form of *psyche* shared by animals and plants alike. But the "nutritive *psyche*" (*threptikê psuchê*: 415a23) plays a role in his "psychology" that goes far beyond merely being placed first on the list. As Aristotle outlines its structure, which turns out to be tripartite (<I.2), he provides a template by means of which other psychic activities can be articulated. Notably, and of paramount importance in understanding a human being's relationship to the world, both perceiving and thinking turn out to be analogous to eating.

The "nutritive *psyche*" can be broken down into three elements: (A) that which nourishes a body, namely food; (B) the living body that is nourished by the food; (C) that which actually does the nourishing, namely the nutritive *psyche*.[1]

When I look at a cookie (A) sitting on the table it is something unlike me. By contrast, after I have eaten the cookie, after it has become digested, it has become part of and thus identical to my body (B). The becoming actually alike of what is potentially like, the process or activity of digestion, is the work of the "nutritive *psyche*" (C). This triadic scheme (presented at 416b20–21) can be represented thus:

A — B

That by which the body is nourished → The body which is nourished
(the food)

↓

C

That which does the nourishing
(the nutritive *psyche*)

This diagram helps to reiterate the key point made above: the *psyche*, at least in its work as nutrition, is the activity of the body as it is being nourished. It is the actualization of a living body's metabolic capacities through which external objects become integrated into the organism. It is the primal expression of life, namely the ability of an organism to maintain itself over time by interacting with and incorporating those elements in the external world that are capable of nourishing it and keeping it alive and whole.[2]

At its most basic level, being-alive requires the organism to make some small portion of the world identical to itself; it must eat. For it to survive and reproduce itself its immediate environment must thus be hospitable; it must supply nourishment. A living being, then, has a home or place in the world; it has a "niche" (from the Latin *nidus*, "nest").

To jump two steps ahead: if thinking is like eating, it too will reflect our being-at-home in the world.

IV.3: Perceiving Is Like Eating.

The triadic structure of the nutritive *psyche* establishes a template by means of which perception, the capacity to register awareness of the external world through the sense organs (which distinguishes animals from plants), can be articulated. Because it is analogous to eating it can be diagrammed thus:

A^P B^P

The perceptible object → The organ of perception

↓

C^P

That which does the perceiving
(the perceptive *psyche*)

Like food, the perceptible object, say the red scarf hanging in my closet, is potentially identical to the sense organ, my eyes. As the work of digestion entails the potentially identical nourishment becoming actually identical so the work of perception, the *aisthêtikê psyche,* involves the potentially identical object becoming actually identical. When I open the closet and see the scarf in some sense it becomes identical. This does not mean that my eyes literally become the scarf or that they become red; instead the sense organ becomes identical to the perceptible object in form.[3] Perception "is the reception of perceptible forms without the matter, like the wax receives the impression of the ring without the iron or the gold" (424a20).

The interaction between the elements—or worse, the mechanisms—comprising this process is difficult to explain. Before even attempting to do so, consider instead the fundamental consequence of Aristotle's account. If the object and the sense organ do somehow become identical, if perception is the reception of sensible forms without the matter, then by and large we apprehend external objects as they really are. I see the red scarf. Somehow the redness of the scarf causes my eyes to become identical to the sensible form "redness." I thereby see the scarf for what it really is: red. In short, human beings more or less perceive things accurately. This is the basis of Aristotle's "extraordinary confidence in the . . . adequacy of the senses to tell us, fairly directly, about the most important causes in the world."[4]

To appreciate the significance of this theory of perception, consider a view radically at odds with it. Consider what Galileo had to say about heat. First, "motion is the cause of heat." What we call "hot" and "cold," two words that seem to name different qualities, actually refer only to differences in the velocity of particles. Hence, Galileo says that the "commonly held conception" of heat is far from the truth. For example, you might say, "The fire is hot." The grammatical structure of this sentence, even the way it sounds, might suggest to you that heat belongs to or is "in" the fire as a quality or attribute. By means of a simple thought experiment Galileo urges you to ignore this suggestion. If you put your hand into the fire it will feel terribly hot and painful. If you remove your hand to a safe distance it will feel pleasantly warm. Your perceptions have changed but the fire has remained constant. Therefore, the qualities hot and warm cannot belong to the fire itself. Instead, "heat is altogether subjective." It is something that results from the interaction of the fire with your perceptual and nervous systems.

These kinds of "relativizing" arguments can be reproduced for all perceptions. The scarf looks bright red when the light is strong but dull red when the light pales. The water at room temperature feels warm to the cold hand and cool to the hot hand. The apple tastes sweet now but bitter after having eaten some ice cream. In each case, the conditions of the perceiver change, whereas the object does not, and so Galileo generalizes: "I think therefore that these tastes, odors, colors, etc., so far as their objective existence is concerned, are nothing but mere names for something which resides exclusively in our sensitive body, so that if the perceiving creatures were removed, all of these qualities would be annihilated. . . . But just because we have given special names to these qualities . . . we are tempted into believing that [they] really and truly exist."

When uttered as predicates in ordinary sentences using the verb "is," adjectives like "hot," "red," and "sweet" tempt us to think that behind them stand objective qualities that belong to beings in the world. But this is false. To use what has become standard terminology, these are "secondary qualities." They do not inhere in the object itself, but instead are the result of the object's interaction with our sensory apparatus. By contrast, even if there were no perceiver, "primary qualities" would still be there. And these are entirely different from hot, red, and sweet. As Galileo puts it, "I cannot believe that there exists in external bodies anything other than their size, shape or motion (slow or rapid)."[5] Only these sorts of quantitative determinations belong to objects in themselves. The world is essentially composed of material bodies in motion. Therefore, in order to grasp the nature of reality the natural sciences must ruthlessly employ a mathematized, a depersonalized language purged of adjectives like "sweet" and "red." What we take to be red must be reconceived not as a color we see but as the reflection of light at a certain measurable wavelength.

Locke articulated the distinction between primary and secondary qualities in the following terms. A quality, he said, is "the power to produce any idea in our mind." Primary qualities are those that "are utterly inseparable from the body in whatever state it is." To illustrate he offered an example of a grain of wheat. Grind it up and its color and smell will change. Nonetheless, every part of the grain retains the same qualities of "solidity, extension, figure and mobility." Such qualities thus belong to the object, and therefore "the ideas of primary qualities of bodies are resemblances of them." By contrast, secondary qualities "are nothing in the objects themselves but the power to produce various sensations in us by their primary qualities." So, to return to Galileo's example, a fire at a safe distance produces a feeling of pleasant warmth on the skin. If the hand actually touches the fire it will register extreme heat and pain. The fire has remained constant. Therefore, fire itself, which is no more than particles in motion, is neither warm nor hot. The feeling of warmth is in us and is the result of the interaction of these particles with our nervous system and brain. The ideas we have of secondary qualities "have no resemblance" to the objects that caused them.[6]

Locke's quintessentially modern conviction is that human beings who operate solely from within their ordinary (linguistically saturated) experience of secondary qualities are cut off from reality.[7] They live inside a bubble that separates them from the very objects that cause their perceptions. They mistakenly think that the scarf is red and that honey is sweet. To liberate them from what Dawkins, who echoes this line of thought, calls their "prison," to open up the pathway to genuine knowledge of reality itself, this bubble must be shattered. Only through a science cleansed by its devotion to mathematics can the truth about primary qualities, about the universe, be grasped. Differently stated, ordinary, nonscientific human beings live in the midst of "systematic error."

This notion of "systematic error" is dear to the heart of contemporary psychologists and neuroscientists. Daniel Gilbert, for example, makes it the cornerstone of his recent book *Stumbling Towards Happiness.* To summarize his argument briefly: human beings do a terrible job of accurately predicting what will make them happy in the future and so end up quite miserable most of the time. This is because they so regularly are wrong about themselves.

Gilbert begins his dissection of systematic error with an account of perception. Most of the time, he says, we act with "the belief that things are in reality as they appear to be in the mind . . . we feel as though we are sitting comfortably inside our heads, looking out through the clear glass window of our eyes, watching the world as it truly is (73, 88)."[8] This feeling, however, is delusive. To take a simple example, the human eye has a blind spot in its field of vision (which occurs at that point of the retina where there are no light-sensitive rods or cones). But the brain does compensatory work and is able to "fill in the scene." When we look at the world, an entire visual field opens up (<I.2). But the whole that our brain registers does not necessarily correspond to what is outside of it, for a great deal of work has been going on to produce the image. In general, perception does not register the world as it is. Instead, to an important degree the brain interprets or even creates its own perceptions.

Gilbert reiterates the primary–secondary quality distinction: "objective stimuli in the world create subjective stimuli in the mind, and it is these subjective stimuli to which people react" (155). This is why they get things wrong. Furthermore, "to ensure that our views are credible, our brain accepts what our eyes see. To ensure that our views are positive, our eye looks for what our brain wants. . . . We may live at the fulcrum of reality and illusion" (171).

Memory studies are particularly useful in documenting systematic error. Another simple example: Gilbert claims that the human brain creates illusions by compressing a vast amount of memories into "a few critical threads." As a result, memory is more of a "reweaving" than a "retrieving." So, in one experiment subjects were asked to remember a list of words related to sleep: "nap," "dream," and so on. The word "sleep," however, was not on the list. Nonetheless, when asked to reproduce the list by memory, subjects typically added "sleep." They were refashioning the list they had actually read into what they thought it should be. After all, it is reasonable to expect that "sleep" would be included on a list of words that have to do with sleeping. But it wasn't.

Because anticipation of the future is regularly shaped by memories of the recent past, "most of us have a rough time imagining a tomorrow that is terribly different from today" (114). This is particularly true with imagining future emotional states. To cite a familiar experience, if you and your partner are presently enjoying a gratifying sexual relationship, you may decide to get married. You imagine your long-term happiness as a continuation of the pleasures you are now experiencing, but in doing this you probably ignore other considerations that are in fact more relevant in determining whether such a marriage will be viable for the duration. No wonder, then, that the misery of divorce is so common.

Gilbert (2006) cites a number of studies to show the many ways ordinary human beings delude themselves. For example, "96 percent of the cancer patients in one study claimed to be in better health than the average cancer patient" (167). We "mispredict the circumstances under which we will blame others" and those "under which we will blame ourselves" (178). "Our most consequential choices . . . are often shaped by how we imagine regret" (178), but we frequently are wrong in predicting what we will regret and how bad it will feel. We often become frightened of events whose probability of happening is actually quite small, for "we mistakenly conclude that they are more common than they actually are" (200). In general, Gilbert concludes that "people are typically unaware of the reasons why they are doing what they are doing" (173). And thus human beings live within the prison of systematic error. We are, he says, "strangers to ourselves" (174) and so it is no wonder that most people are unhappy.

Of course, Gilbert the scientist who cheerfully purports to know the truth about these matters hardly takes himself to be a stranger to himself. Instead, he's confident that he knows a lot about what makes us tick. Therefore, he must either count his own assertions to be false or claim himself to be something other than the human beings he studies.

Aristotle sees the world differently. We live in "systematic truth," not error. When we look out through the clear window of our eyes, we see what's actually out there. The scarf really is red, for "this is a world in which colours, sounds, and smells are as real as the primary qualities, and they are the chief factors in the causal explanation of perception."[9] As a result, those of us who use our capacity to see, remember, think and talk carefully have a real shot at happiness (>V.1–2).

An entire book would be required to do justice to Aristotle's theory of perception.[10] What follows, then, is no more than a brief sketch.

First, the ability to perceive objects in the external world through sense organs differentiates animals from plants. Not surprisingly, Aristotle offers a teleological explanation of why. A plant is stationary, at least in

Aristotle's sense: it occupies a single place and engages in no locomotion. Of course, it grows and moves toward the sun, but it does not move itself away from or out of its own place. As such, it receives nourishment from the very place in which it originated: the soil in which it grows. Plants "draw up nourishment from the soil continuously" and so there is no need, no teleologically sound reason, for them to have perception.[11] Most animals, by contrast, can move from place to place and thus must have perception in order to identify what counts as food for them so that they can then move toward it. "Nature does nothing in vain. . . . Thus, if any body were capable of locomotion but did not have perception, it would perish and not be able to reach its *telos*, which is the work of nature. For how would it be nourished? Those animate bodies that are stationary [like plants] have as their nutriment that from which they have arisen but it is not possible for a body that has *psyche* and a discerning mind not to have perception" (*On the Psyche* 434a32–b4).

At its most primitive level, the *telos* of perception is the survival, through nutrition, of the animal. Of course, perception can offer more than that, especially to us. "But in animals that have understanding (*phronêsis*) these senses are present for the sake of living well. For they report many differences from which comes understanding of both intelligible objects and of practical matters" (*On Sense and Sensible Objects* 437a1–5).

In *On the Psyche* Aristotle begins his analysis by discussing the "special" objects of each form of perception. "I call a special (*idion*) object of perception that which cannot be perceived by any other sense and in respect to which it is impossible to be wrong. Color is the special object of sight, sound of hearing, flavor of taste" (418a11–13).

Two points, the first of which reformulates the statement above: "perception of the special objects of perception is always true" (427b12). (As such it is similar to the intuition of substances: <III.3.) Second, a special object of perception is not a "mental item";[12] not what Locke called an "idea." Instead, it is a real being in the world outside of the human mind. Or, as Aristotle puts it, "perception is certainly not of itself but of something other than perception, which is necessarily prior to perception" (*Metaphysics* 1010b35–11a2). The "special objects" cause animals like us to have the corresponding perceptions.

Each of the five sense organs (the B^P in the diagram above) is a material thing capable of being affected by only a small portion of external reality. The human ear, for example, can be properly affected—that is, affected in such a way as to cause hearing—by only a limited range of sounds, those that are produced by a "blow" (419b11) to a particular sort of object, say a stick hitting a piece of bronze.[13] The sound travels through and moves the air until it reaches the ear. Air that is "lodged deeply" (420a11) inside the ear is then affected by the moving air, and sound is registered. Without having received the actual bronze or the stick, without having become literally identical to either, the ears have been affected by the form of the sound, and the animal hears.

The monumental question facing Aristotle's theory of perception (and the contemporary one) is how a body in motion—in the case of hearing, moving air—causes a perception, an awareness, which itself is not simply another motion. Or, to return to the diagram above, hearing is found in C^P not in B^P; the ear, the organ of hearing, does not by itself do the hearing; it is the living animal that hears. How this works is, to put it mildly, hard to explain. Consider what Myles Burnyeat has to say: "We are forced to conclude that the organ's becoming like the object is not its literally and physiologically becoming hard or warm but a noticing or becoming aware of hardness or warmth. All these physical seeming descriptions—the organ's becoming like the object, its being affected, acted on, or altered, its taking on sensible form without the matter—all these are referring to what Aquinas calls a 'spiritual' change, a becoming aware of some sensible quality in the environment."[14]

This comment can be translated into a complaint: at the last stage of his analysis of perception Aristotle abandons his best, his most naturalistic and scientific commitments. As a good anatomist (as the author of the *Parts of Animals*) he studied the structure of the ear. He understood that perception required causal interactions between material things in the world. The stick striking the bronze moves air toward the air lodged deeply within the ear. But he did not, perhaps because he could not, explain what it means to receive form without matter, and to have this register as a perception. In other words, he did not explain why some causal relations between material objects—the moving air hitting the air within the ear—generate awareness, while others, such as moving air hitting a wall, do not. Awareness, which itself is not material, somehow arises from the interaction between material objects. And Aristotle's only explanation for this occurrence is that the perceptive *psyche* hears the sound. He thus seems to let the phenomenon of awareness stand as its own explanation rather than searching for a finer-grained materialistic explanation (on the level of efficient causality).

In similar fashion, by claiming that secondary qualities are really out there in the world, and, as Burnyeat puts it, "all that is needed for perception to take place is for these qualities or forms to act on the corresponding faculties in us to bring about an awareness of themselves," Aristotle quit too early. "One might say that the physical material of animal bodies in Aristotle's world is already pregnant with consciousness, needing only to be awakened to red or warmth. . . . In a certain sense an animal's perceptual capacities do not require explanation. For Aristotle such capacities are part of animal life and in Aristotle's world the emergence of life does not require explanation. For Aristotle it is the existence of life which explains why animals have the physical constitution they do, not the other way round."[15]

Burnyeat's statement that for Aristotle "an animal's perceptual capacities do not require explanation" raises a question: what level of explanation does perception require? The neurological mechanisms at work in hearing are far better understood today than they were two thousand years ago. Nonetheless, it is not yet obvious how much progress there has been in explaining how a chunk of matter, namely the brain, gives rise to conscious awareness. To make a sharper point: in the age of neuroscience we have become infatuated by, perhaps addicted to, mechanical explanations, for these give rise to powerful technologies. Today a good deal is known about which regions of the brain are responsible for what psychological functions. As always, this knowledge comes to the forefront whenever there is a breakdown. For instance, "the hypothesis that the brain contained localized sites for specific abilities and functions . . . was not fully confirmed until the early 1860s, when Paul Broca demonstrated that an injury to an area of the frontal lobe in the brain's left hemisphere caused a loss of speech."[16] Such knowledge opens up the possibility of repair. Today the mechanisms of memory are gradually becoming better understood and so there is hope that a pharmacologic treatment may be available in the not too distant future to prevent or repair the damage done by Alzheimer's. As our neurologic tools become more powerful we have come to expect that the medical industry will continually expand, its tools and drugs will become more and more effective, and eventually pain and perhaps even death will become obsolete.

But recall what Tom Stoppard's Bernard had to say: "Don't confuse progress with perfectibility." The former can proceed infinitely, while the latter requires a *telos.*

Back to Aristotle: "Perception occurs in being changed and acted upon, as has been said, for it seems to be a kind of 'alteration' (*alloiosis*: 416b33)"; "it is a form of being acted upon (*paschein*: 424a1)." Beings in the world—the red scarf, the hot fire, the sweet honey—affect our sense organs.

In the act of perception, a sense organ changes from a state of potentiality (my eye can see a red object but is not seeing it now) to actuality (when the red object is placed in my field of vision, I see it). That "actuality" has two senses has already been mentioned. If motion or change is the actualization of the potential insofar as it is potential, then it also must have two senses.

Think of it this way: A child (C) does not yet know arithmetic. After he has studied it in school he has become a "knower" (K), one who knows arithmetic. At the moment K is not trying to solve a problem, nor is he thinking about numbers at all. As such, he is at the first level of actuality (or the second level of potentiality). By contrast, when presented with and then engaged in the solving of problems, he is actually using his knowledge; he "theorizes" (T).

This sequence contains two different kinds of change. After C, the potential knower of arithmetic, has gone to school and become K, a knower, an "alteration" has taken place. C has moved from one contrary to another: from being a not-knower of arithmetic to being a knower. This is a "change" in the truest sense of the word. (See *Metaphysics* 1048b27.) By contrast, when the knower moves from merely having the knowledge of arithmetic to actually using it, when K becomes T, something other than a true alteration goes on. It is, says Aristotle, a "progress into itself and into actuality" (*entelecheia:* 417b7). Only when using his knowledge is K fully becoming what he really is, namely one who knows arithmetic.

Applying this scheme to perception, Aristotle arrives at this: the three elements comprising the perceptual scheme are "the male seed" (M), the human being able to perceive from the moment of birth (B), and the human being actually perceving (A). A real alteration, like the one between C and K, takes place only in the transition from M to B. When a child is born, it, like all living animals, can perceive. Before being born, however, it could not perceive. (All questions concerning embryology must be deferred.) Therefore, a change from one contrary to another, a real alteration, has taken place. But when a living being changes from being able to perceive, which itself is a first degree of actuality, to actually perceiving, when it moves from B to A, something else has occurred: like the transition between K and T, there is a "progress into itself." In other words, a real alteration has not occurred. In seeing the scarf, in B becoming A, B becomes itself. (See *On the Psyche* 417a21–b5.)

This is important: in perceiving beings other than ourselves, we become ourselves.

When we accurately hear, feel, touch, taste, and see things in the world like the red scarf, we "progress into ourselves and into *entelecheia*." In other words, our living bodies are teleologically directed toward a truthful apprehension of perceptible objects. And so we are at home in the world, which is our "niche" (<IV.2).

To return to the analogy with the nutritive *psyche*: the cookie on the table is actually unlike but potentially like my body. By means of digestion it is incorporated into my body. Both its form and its matter become me. Perception is more complex, for in seeing the red scarf I do not actually incorporate the woolen thing into my body, just its sensible form. Nonetheless, perception is structurally similar to nutrition. "Just as has been said, the perceiver is potentially such as what the perceptible object actually is. So, when it is being affected it is not like [the perceptible object], but having been affected it has become like it" (418a3–6). Both nutrition and perception, then, are workings (*energeiai*) of the *psyche*, ways of being-alive in a world in which we fit well.[17]

There is more to our sensory lives than just the hearing of sounds and the tasting of flavors and so a theory of perception must do more than explain how individual senses perceive their "special" objects. Most important, perhaps, is the fact that when we see an object, we are aware *that* we see it. This awareness is made vivid by its absence in sleep. When you are sleeping, your sense of touch is still alive and so when I lightly move a feather across your ear it is likely that you will move in response. By contrast, if you are awake your sense of touch not only registers the sensation, but you also become aware that you feel the feather on your ear. (See *On Sleep* 455a17). Even the simplest of perceptions—feeling the feather or hearing the sound—is never actually an isolated event for it is always integrated into a more comprehensive experience of "awareness that." This, however, cannot originate in any of the five special senses. After all, each is paired with a "special" or uniquely perceptible object that is materially constituted so as to be able to affect only the corresponding organ. Thus, the awareness "that" one hears cannot be explained by hearing alone.

The story gets more complicated. In addition to the apprehension of the "special" perceptibles and the awareness *that* they are being perceived there are the "common-sensibles" (some of which correspond to what Galileo and Locke called "primary qualities"). "The common-sensibles are motion, rest, number, figure, magnitude. For these sorts of objects are special to no single sense, but are common to all. For motion is perceivable by both touch and sight" (418a17–20).

I see the train approaching me from the west. I see it as both green and moving. If it were to graze my arm when I wasn't looking, my sense of touch also would register motion. If my power of smell were as great as a dog's I might even be able to smell its approach. To reiterate, individual senses only perceive special objects that are materially constituted in such a way as to affect specific sense organs. The common-sensibles like motion, however, are accessible through a variety of senses. Although they are somehow perceived by individual senses they are not "special" and hence cannot simply be perceived by hearing, vision, and so on. Consequently, there must be some sort of "common-sense" by which they are apprehended.

It is tempting to posit a special organ in the body responsible for the apprehension of common-sensibles, and Aristotle does conceive of "the place around the heart as the origin (*archê*) of the senses" (*Parts of Animals* 656a23). He also says that "the passages of all the sense organs stretch towards the heart" (*Generation of Animals* 781a21).[18] Furthermore, about memory he says that "the 'image' or *phantasma* is a result of the common-sense being affected. And so it is apparent that recognition of such *phantasmata* resides in the primary perceptive part" (*On Memory* 450a11–14).[19]

Apparently, then, this primary or common-sense has a variety of responsibilities. It apprehends the common-sensibles, those that can be perceived by more than one sense, as well as "images" in the ordinary meaning of the term (>IV.4). It perceives and thus discriminates between different sense objects simultaneously. It perceives that we perceive. Perhaps, then, the heart is a centralizing perceptual organ that does work going beyond the special senses. For example, to quote Everson, Aristotle's explanation of how I perceive that I see is as follows: "For this to occur, not only must the primary sense organs undergo some change, but that change must be communicated to the controlling organ." Everson then quotes *On Dreams* 461a30: "For one judges that one is seeing and hearing and perceiving even when one is awake because the change [from the sense organ] arrives at the source [of the perception]." Continuing, he says, "in ordinary perception, then, there is thus a change which runs from the affected primary organ to the controlling organ and this physiological process is necessary for the subject's awareness of the perception."[20]

Of course, Aristotle was unable to explain the mechanisms by which such "awareness" occurred, because even if they do exist, they surely aren't located in the heart. Nonetheless, he did at least gesture toward some sort of physiologic correlate of the "common-sense." Finally, however, he explicitly rejects the possibility of a central organ: "it is impossible for there to be a special sense organ that perceives the common sensibles" (425a14). If there were such an organ then the perception of the common-sensibles would be like that of the specials. This it is not, however, because a quality like motion is apprehensible by both sight and touch. Everson explains how it might occur: "the change brought about in the organ by the [special] sensibles will have accidental features which are determined by the common sensibles with which it forms an accidental unity."[21] So, for example, I see the red scarf moving as it blows in the wind. It could well stop moving and yet would remain as a red scarf; its moving is an accidental feature. Even so, my perception of it as red and moving is a unified whole. I do not see a red object, see it is a scarf, see it moving, and then add the three elements together. Instead, the experience is unified. I simply see the red scarf moving.

Aristotle makes a similar point when he discusses how it is that we perceive differences, another function of a unified "common-sense":

> Each sense, which resides in the sense-organ insofar as it is a sense-organ, is of an underlying sense-object and it discerns differences between its various objects. So, for example, vision apprehends the white and the black while taste apprehends the sweet and the bitter. And the other senses function similarly. Now, since we discern white and sweet and discriminate between each of the other sense-objects in relation to each other, we must perceive by something that they differ. We must perceive this by some sense since they are sense-objects. . . . Furthermore, it is impossible to discern that sweet is different from white by means of separate senses. Instead, both must be clearly perceived by some one sense. For even if I perceived something and you perceived something else it would be clear that they differ from each other and there must be some one thing that says they are different. For sweet is different from white and the same one thing says they are different. Consequently, as it says so it thinks and perceives. (426b8–22)

In tasting the sugar I sense that it is white and sweet and thus am aware that white is not sweet. For me to do this requires some sort of common-sense able somehow to apprehend this difference. Aristotle explains by means of an analogy. If you perceive a red scarf and I perceive a blue one neither of us would know that our individual perceptions were different from the other's unless we communicated. Correspondingly, to detect that white is not sweet there must be some "voice" that "says they are different." The ability to differentiate white and sweet is like "saying" insofar as it is a unifying "voice." To apprehend difference there must be some sort of basis for comparison or vantage point from which the comparison is registered; some sort of common ground or means of unification (<I.2).

In sum, perception is a unified experience and so constitutes what Everson calls the "perceptual system." I see the red object, and am aware that I see it; I see that it's moving; I notice its shape; I am aware that it is not blue: all in one. Aristotle lacks what to us would count as a satisfying physiologic (neurologic) explanation of how this all happens. What he does have is a theory of perception that saves the phenomena. I see the red scarf blowing in the wind and it's really red, moving, and out there. The upshot of this section, then, is that Aristotle's theory of perception saves us from becoming, to use Daniel Gilbert's phrase, "strangers to ourselves." The honey tastes sweet and so we say that it is. And if our bodies are healthy and our senses functioning normally then most of the time we'll get it right.

IV.4: We Are Wrong More Often than Not.

So far this chapter may seem to have painted an exceptionally rosy picture. Aristotle is confident that the senses apprehend objects accurately. Because the process of attaining knowledge begins with and remains rooted in the apprehension of the "special" perceptibles and about these we do not err, we are able to know the world for what it is. In fact, Aristotle goes so far as to say, "the theorizing of truth is easy." Even though no single person can obtain an adequate grasp of all of it, none of us entirely fails, for "truth is like a proverbial door which no one can miss" (*Metaphysics* 993a20–b10).

But Aristotle also says this: "being mistaken is more familiar to animals and the *psyche* spends more time in being mistaken [than it does in perceiving objects accurately]" (*On the Psyche* 427b1–2). Such a statement may seem to clash with the notion of "systematic truth" developed in this chapter. It doesn't. But it does serve to render Aristotle's picture less naïve than it may initially appear, for with it he acknowledges that the human encounter with the external world is fraught with error. The faculty largely responsible for the unsettled or misguided side of life is called *phantasia,* which the following example will begin to elucidate.

"It appears (*phainetai*) that the sun is a foot long." This "appearance," however, is mistaken, for anyone who has given the matter some thought "is convinced that the sun is greater than the inhabited world" (428b3–4). Simple perceptions of special sensibles are always true but not so with "appearances," with what Aristotle calls, using a word impossible to convey in a single English translation, *phantasia.* "Imagination" often comes close, and in the following passage it does seem like the right choice.

> For *phantasia* is different from perception and thought although it does not come to be without perception, and without it there is no "supposing" (*hupolêpsis*). That it is not the same kind of

> thinking as "supposing" is apparent. For as an experience *phantasia* is up to us and we can have it whenever we wish, since it is possible to make something appear before our eyes. . . . By contrast, whether we hold an opinion is not up to us for it is necessary that it be true or false. Furthermore, whenever we hold an opinion that something is terrifying or frightening or encouraging we straightaway experience the corresponding feeling. But in the case of *phantasia* we react similarly to how we react when someone includes in a picture something terrible or encouraging. (427b14–24)

To identify what *phantasia* is Aristotle first tells us what it is not: perception. The latter is always true (at least when it comes to the "specials"), while the former, even though it depends on and is derived from perception, is not. He later adds another distinction: perception is continual and present in all animals while *phantasia* is sporadic and absent from creatures like ants and bees (428a10).

Next, *phantasia* is distinguished from the ability to "suppose" or form a judgment (or opinion, or belief). The latter is not entirely "up to us." I am right in believing that 2 + 2 = 4, but the truth of this belief is not up to me. Consequently, while I can say the words "two plus two equals five," I can't really mean or believe them because I know they are false. Truth places a constraint on my capacity to hold sincere beliefs. By contrast, as long as my faculties are reasonably intact it's up to me whether to summon up an image of my wife or Bob or anyone else. Hence, Aristotle concludes that *phantasia* is not the same as judging or forming beliefs, and here the word does seem translatable as "imagination."

Another argument: If I really believed that the terrorists had landed, then I'd be scared. By contrast, if I imagine terrorists landing—if, say, I am writing a story about terrorists—I may not feel any fear at all and instead only apathetically observe the image of them in my mind. The conclusion is the same: *phantasia* is different from forming beliefs and once again seems to mean "imagination."

But other contexts make it clear that *phantasia* isn't always "imagination" in the visualizing sense we take to be typical of the word. One has been noted already: that the sun "appears" (*phainetai*) to be one foot long is a product of *phantasia*: it is a *phantasma*. Here "appearance" rather than "image" would seem more appropriate, because what it names occurs simultaneously with the perception itself. One scholar thinks that *phantasia* as "appearance" is so broad as to be "the faculty in virtue of which any *phainomenon* is experienced."[22]

Furthermore, the story is complicated considerably by the fact that memories are treated as *phantasmata* (*On Memory* 450b24), as are dreams (458b16). The latter in particular do not conform to the description offered in the passage cited above, because the "appearance" of a dream is not up to us and it does generate feelings attached to its "images." If I "see" a small and aggressive animal in my dream, I become frightened.

Alfredo Ferrarin, in his masterful essay, says this about *phantasia*: its "definition is general enough to accommodate visualization, memory, dreams, teleologically directed activity. *Phantasia*'s main but not exclusive effect is that of enabling us to visualize and make present to ourselves absent things." Whether the "image" is a visual one I present to myself of a friend, or a memory in which the past is made present "*qua absence*"; whether I feel fear because of an "image" I have of "forthcoming evil" or hope as "the image of an imminent good," *phantasia* "represents, in the broad sense stands for, the thing that generated the *phantasma*. . . . The image is the thing in its absence, the thing as a representation."[23]

Amplified by this understanding of the many tasks to which *phantasia* can be put, the statement that "the *psyche* spends more time in being mistaken [than it does in perceiving objects accurately]" begins to make more sense. For in making the absent present *phantasia* opens up the possibility, even the likelihood, of a gap between them. I conjure up, I make present, a visual image of an old friend I haven't seen in years. Likely it is imperfect.

In this context, a useful take on *phantasia* is offered by Malcolm Schofield, who suggests that various senses of this term can be collected and classified as "non-paradigmatic sensory experiences." What Schofield intends to convey by this cumbersome phrase is that the verb *phainesthai*, from which *phantasia* derives, "expresses scepticism, caution or is noncommittal about the veridical character of sensory or quasi-sensory experiences."[24] In other words, the verb is used in order to say, "It looks thus and so—but is it really?" Schofield cites the following passage to support his claim: "Furthermore, whenever we actualize [our senses] accurately on the sensible object, we do not say that 'this appears to us to be a man.' Instead we say this whenever we do not perceive clearly whether it is true or false" (428a12–15). When I see a man approaching and say, "It looks like, appears to be, Bob," it means that I'm not sure who it is.

Our perceptual and cognitive lives are dense. Apprehension of special perceptibles, for example, is never actually separated from our perception of common-sensibles: I do not see only bright orange, but instead a bright orange circle. In a similar fashion perception is inseparable from the *phantasia* always at work. The top of the bottle seen from my present location looks like an ellipse, when it is actually circular, a fact I discover when I look straight down upon it. The object approaching looks like a dog, but in fact I see it as a fox. I have a dream about Bob but in it he has the hair he lost twenty years ago. I generate a visual image of my wife but don't get her eyebrows quite right. I see a tall man walking toward me, but from a distance he looks short. The parallel lines of the train track seem to converge far down the road. When I peer into the water the stick looks bent. An array of processes is at work even in the apparently simple glance at the sun. Nonetheless, they somehow constitute a unity and are experienced as a single cognitive act, even though upon analysis their elements—the apprehension of the special perceptibles, the discrimination between them (the white is not sweet), the perception of the common-sensibles, the "appearances," and so on—can be abstractly isolated from one another.

Through the work of *phantasia,* by which we represent what is absent, the door is opened wide for error to enter our lives. Still, "truth is easy," for it remains the case that we regularly and reliably make contact with reality through perception. As Ferrarin puts it, "the greater the contact (howsoever understood) with presence, with the thing, the greater the truth." Because we are perceiving animals who live in the world, we live in truth (>IV.7). But we also live in time, which "is the cause of destruction" (*Physics* 221b1), and so what is present becomes absent. "If contact is the guarantee of faithfulness, removal and distance are the main causes of falsehood and *phantasia* is all the more likely to err the more it is removed from the thing and connected with absence."[25] The distant future, which we can only imagine, flows through the present into the past, which we can only remember. And so if I bring to mind a visual image of a friend I haven't seen in years it surely will be imperfect. This does not mean, however, that its defects cannot be corrected, or that years ago I did not see him for who he was. Even if time "wastes things away," including my memories, this does not mean that I cannot "hunt" them down, "recollect" them, get them right (*On Memory* 451b18). Even if "things get old by time, and forgetfulness rather than learning occurs because of time" (*Physics* 221a31), it is nonetheless possible for me to concentrate hard and determine what it is I know.

Truth is "easy," for making contact with reality is the groundwork of our lives. But maintaining and extending our access to the truth requires continual work.

This discussion has implications for the central thesis of this book, that Aristotle is a "phenomenologist." He treats the phenomena as evidence and takes his bearings from the way beings in the world show themselves to us in ordinary human experience. But we have just learned that being mistaken is a structural feature of that experience. After all, the stick looks bent in the water and the tall man approaching looks small. Fraught with error, the phenomena may not deserve the epistemic credit Aristotle gives to them.

But Aristotle's theoretical procedure is never heavy-handed. He does not simply count every phenomenon that comes his way as being truthful. He knows that the sun is not a foot long. In a similar vein, even though he invests heavily in the epistemic value of the *endoxa*, the reputable beliefs (<I.1), which are themselves phenomena, he doesn't think that every opinion or traditional view is equally truthful, and he is aware that they sometimes conflict with one another. The Pythagoreans, for example, were right in believing that the finite is prior to and better than the infinite, but wrong in conceiving of the structure of reality as numerical (<II.8). And, to return to an example from early in this book (< Introduction), Socrates himself was not entirely correct in denying that, in general, Aristotle's theoretical work is discriminating, cautious, and meticulous. He explains his approach in the following passage, which also was cited in the Introduction. "It is necessary, just as in the other studies, to set down the phenomena (*tithentas ta phainomena*) and first of all to review the puzzles. In this way, the reputable beliefs (*ta endoxa*) about these affections will be shown; if not all the reputable beliefs then most and the most authoritative of them. For if the difficulties are dissolved and the reputable beliefs are left intact, then the showing will have been adequate" (*Nicomachean Ethics* 1145b2–7).

Aristotle begins with the phenomena and the reputable beliefs or opinions; he "sets them down." And in so doing he often discovers "puzzles" (*aporiai*). These he works through, measuring them against each other, his own observations, and *logoi*. At the end, what is best among the "reputable beliefs" will be left intact. To elaborate, recall the following sentence (<I.8): in concluding that the heavenly bodies are eternal, he says, "it seems that the *logos* bears witness (*marturein*) to the phenomena and the phenomena to the *logos*" (*On the Heavens* 270b5–6). Here "the phenomena" refers to the (putative) fact that "all human beings have a conception of god," which they locate in the highest region of the cosmos. Of course, most people have an anthropomorphic image of a Zeus who lives high in the sky and carries a thunderbolt, and in thinking thus they are quite foolish. But they are not all wrong, for the heavenly bodies are in fact eternal and divine. In general, even if they don't get things all right people don't get them all wrong.

A few lines later Aristotle says that his assertion that the heavenly bodies are eternal is "sufficiently" confirmed "through perception." To the naked eye it certainly looks like the orbits of the heavenly bodies have never changed a bit. This is an "appearance," reinforced by memory, that can be trusted, at least with respect to securing "human conviction" (270b13).

Furthermore, in all of recorded history, no one has observed or reported any changes up there. Naked-eye perception, religious tradition, memory, scientific observations, appearances—all of which can be construed as "phenomena"—work together to provide "witness" for or to confirm the *logos,* the theory.

Finally, the overall picture is roughly this: perceptions of special sensibles are always true. But *phantasia* is ever at work—in imagination, memory, and "appearances"—and so error is a structural possibility of ordinary experience. Even if it cannot be eliminated entirely it can be held at bay by means of repeated observations, sustained and systematic recollection, rigorous analysis, a careful consideration of prior theories, dialogue with others, and the observation of ordinary human practices and language.

IV.5: Thinking Is Like Perceiving (Which Is Like Eating).

Phantasia is (conceptually) located somewhere in between perception and thought. It originates in and requires the former: "*phantasia* seems to be a motion and not to come to be without perception . . . it comes to be by the actualization of a sense and it is thus necessary that it be similar to the sense" (*On the Psyche* 428b11–14). Memories are characterized similarly: they require images, and as such memory "belongs to the primary perceptive capacity" (*On Memory* 450a12). So too with dreams: "The capacity of *phantasia* is the same as that of perception . . . and since *phantasia* is the movement produced by a sense in the course of its being actualized, and the dream appears to be some sort of *phantasma*—for a *phantasma* in sleep is what we call a dream—it is apparent that dreaming is the work of the perceptual part but belongs to this part in its relationship to *phantasia*" (459a17–21).

And yet *phantasia* is not the same as perception. Nor is it the same as thought. Recall that Aristotle has argued that *phantasia* cannot be "supposing" (*hupolêpsis*). Alternatively, "there is no 'supposing' without *phantasia*" (*On the Psyche* 427b16). More forcefully, he says this: "the *psyche* never thinks without a *phantasm*" (431a17), and when it "theorizes it must at the same time theorize some *phantasm*" (432a9). The following passage from *On Memory* attempts to explain: "It is not possible to think without a *phantasm.* For what occurs in thinking is the same as what occurs in drawing. For in this case, though we do not make any use of the fact that the size of the triangle is determinate, we nonetheless draw it with a determinate size. Thinking is similar. Even if one is not thinking of something with a size he puts before his eyes something with a size, even if he doesn't think of it as having a size" (450a5–10).

A geometer trying to prove a theorem about the equilateral triangle draws a diagram. It necessarily will have specific dimensions, but in these the geometer is not interested. Instead, the diagram is used only to represent equilateral triangularity as such. Nonetheless, to think the triangle, the geometer must do so through the "image." "Thinking," as Ferrarin puts it, "uses images as particular examples and illustrations of intelligible forms. Which is to say it sees the universal in the image, but disregards precisely what makes the image an image, its particularity. Thinking ignores whatever is subjective and particular about the image and uses it as a representation of the form we think it in."[26]

Trouble looms: if the *psyche* never thinks without images or *phantasmata,* and these derive from perception, then thinking should be inseparably connected to the body. And yet in *On the Psyche* III.4–5 and in his description of the motionless mover as "thought thinking itself" (<III.4) thinking certainly seems separable. To make any headway on this notorious dilemma we must ourselves think about thinking.

In *On the Psyche* Aristotle begins his account of "that part of the *psyche* by which the *psyche* knows and thinks (*phronei*)" by offering a comparison with perceiving. "If thinking (*noein*) is like perceiving, then it must be a being affected (*paschein*) by an intelligible object (*noeton*) . . . for just as what is perceptive is to the perceptible object, so too does the mind (*nous*) stand in relationship to intelligible objects (*noêta*)" (429a10–18).

Like perceiving, thinking is some sort of reception of forms that are other than the mind itself. In this case, however, it is intelligible rather than sensible forms. Another point of comparison is that thinking too has a tripartite structure. Recall that the template for all psychic functions was provided by the nutritive psyche:

A B
That by which the body is nourished → The body that is nourished
(the food)

↓

C
That which does the nourishing
(the nutritive *psyche*)

Analogously, perceiving looks like this:

A^P B^P
The perceptible object → The organ of perception

↓

C^P
That which does the perceving
(the perceptive *psyche*)

Because thinking is like perceiving, its structure too should be diagrammed similarly. There are, however, going to be some wrinkles.

A sense organ, say the human ear, is capable of being affected by only a small bit of the material world. In contemporary lingo, it can detect sound waves ranging approximately between 20 and 20,000 hertz. It cannot process sights or smells, and hears only a fraction of the sounds that a dog or cat can hear. These constraints on human hearing derive from its dependence on the physical limitations of the bodily organ. The decisive difference between thinking and perceiving is that the mind "thinks everything" (429a18). It can think about sounds, shapes, colors, images, numbers, people far and wide, forms, and on and on. Therefore, Aristotle reasons, the "mind must be unmixed." If it had a specific material constitution of its own, if it were "mixed" with some earth or water, as is the ear, the range of intelligible objects would be as limited as is the range of detectable sounds. But it is limited not at all. Hence, it is in no way "mixed" with the body.

Aristotle makes the same point by saying "of it there is no nature but this: that it is potentiality. . . . That part of the *psyche* called the mind—and by 'mind' I mean that by which the *psyche* thinks and supposes—is nothing in actuality before it thinks" (429a21–24). Because it can think everything, the mind is potentially everything; it is the "place of forms," at least as they are in potentiality. Later Aristotle coins the phrase "passive (*pathêtikos*: 430a24) mind" as a label, and with it we now have two of the three elements of the anticipated triadic structure:

A^T → B^T
Intelligible Object Passive Mind

Aristotle indicates what the "intelligible objects" of mind might include: "magnitude and the being of magnitude are different . . . water and the being of water" (429b10–11). We can see the water and touch it with our hands, and this we must do in order to begin the process of knowing. But to determine what water itself is, to somehow grasp its "essence," thought is required. Aristotle does not elaborate, nor is he particularly helpful here. Only this: thought takes up intelligible objects, intelligible forms.

A third element in the diagram is required. Just as the nutritive and the perceptive *psyche* are the actual, living work of nutrition and perception, so too, if the analogy holds when it comes to thinking, must there a "C^T," an "active mind." Aristotle never uses this phrase, but certainly has something like this in view in the following passage.

> Since in all of nature there is both matter in each kind of being, and this is what all of them are potentially, as well as another cause and an active (*poiêtikon*) element that makes them all—just as a productive art acts upon its material—these different elements must obtain in the *psyche.* Thus, there is the sort of mind that becomes all things as well as the sort of mind that makes all things, as a kind of disposition. And this is like light. For in a certain way like makes what is potentially visible actually visible. (430a10–17)

The diagram, and thus the analogical sequence of the three types, activities or functions of *psyche,* is now complete:

A^T B^T
Intelligible Object → Passive Mind
↓
C^T
Active Mind

Nutrition is the most blunt and basic activity of living organisms, for the external object literally is absorbed into the body and made identical to it. Perception, found only in animals, is a more internalized process, for it receives only the sensible form and not the matter. Nonetheless, perception is not "up to us," for it requires that a perceptible object (A^P) affect a sense organ (B^P). If a glowing hot coal is placed on my hand, I have no choice but to feel the heat. If my ears are severely damaged, then I'll hear nothing. By contrast, thinking takes place within the mind itself. Both B^T and C^T are "in" the mind and so, not being reliant on external objects or material organs, I can think of the square root of sixteen any time I wish.[27] The "passive mind," the analogue to the sense organ, is "unmixed" with the body. The active element of this process also is mind, "active mind," and it too is "separate" from the body, perhaps even more so than is passive mind. "And this mind is separate and unaffected and unmixed, being actuality (*energeia*) in its substance. For the active pole and the first principle (*archê*) are always more honorable than what is affected and matter. . . . And only in being separated is this just what it is. And this alone is immortal and eternal and without it there is no thinking. . . . By contrast, the passive mind is mortal" (430a17–22).

From the moment *On the Psyche* was "published" there was disagreement about what these lines meant. First, exactly what work the passive and active minds are each required to do is not clear, nor is the relationship in which they stand to each other. The latter is compared to light, which supplies the necessary condition for what is potentially visible becoming actually visible. Thus it seems that the active intellect somehow makes thinking possible. Even more obscure is the description of it as separated, immortal, and eternal. Franz Brentano reports that Theophrastus, who was both a student of and the successor to Aristotle as head of his school, took the active intellect "to be something belonging to the human nature." By contrast, Eudemus, a "philosopher who is said to have followed his teacher's path most faithfully, seems to identify the active intellect with God."[28] Such an identification is hardly implausible considering the description in the *Metaphysics* of the motionless mover as "thought thinking itself" (<III.4).

This debate has raged for millennia. No wonder: the description of the active mind as separated and eternal is terribly sparse and seemingly at odds with the naturalized picture of the *psyche* (as the form of an organic body potentially having life) that prevails throughout most of *On the Psyche*. In fact, this passage even embarrasses some scholars and so one writes, "I cannot understand this chapter, and none of the secondary literature has so far helped me to do. . . . I wish [Aristotle] had never written it."[29]

No serious attempt is made here to crack the code. Only a few comments: Aristotle is a "syllogistic" thinker (<I.2, <I.6) who believes that from top to bottom the world is an orderly whole, a cosmos. His reliance on the tripartite and analogical structure of the *psyche* reflects this conviction and perhaps is what drives him toward his description of active mind. For if thinking is like perceiving, which is like eating, then each slot in the diagram must be filled. (Just as in *On the Heavens* Aristotle insists that some body not found on earth must fill the empty slot of circular motion: <I.4.) Or perhaps "active mind" is postulated by the need to account for the phenomenon of a mind that can think everything. If this is what it can do it must be unlike the ear; it must be "separate."

Recall, however, that Aristotle says that "the *psyche* never thinks without an image or *phantasm*" (431a17) and that *phantasia* is dependent upon perception, which is dependent upon the body. This would seem to imply that thinking requires and hence is inseparable from the body, an implication at odds with active mind's being "separate." Ferrarin proposes a solution. While human beings do depend upon images in order to think, while "an image is both inevitable and prior for us, for our apprehension and our memory . . . it is not prior by nature. . . . Images are inevitable because of the finitude of our thinking, which first must learn, and then knows. But thinking in itself is actual and free and does not need images, as we see in the case of the prime mover, thinking itself without the aid of images."[30]

We have and depend on our bodies; we live in the world. But even if our thinking begins in perception and is imagistic we think through images to essences. The geometer studies the diagram but in thinking about the equilateral triangle as such the particularity of the diagram fades away. Thus, even in our finite state we actualize a thinking that goes beyond images. Projecting (syllogizing) what occurs in our experience to its extreme, we arrive at the notion of "thinking in itself" as pure actuality. As such, the active mind must be both separate and eternal.

One last stab: thinking just is separating. What, for example, occurs in thinking about the question "Was the war in Iraq a good one?" To begin doing so images from the media will float by, past events will be brought to mind, hopes and fears will be felt. But at some point we face a simple question: what makes a war good anyway? And in concentrating on that alone the mind turns away and departs from the particulars, the images, the memories and simply thinks about what the good is. Of course, moments of intense concentration are brief for all but the most powerful of thinkers. But when they occur, when we are lost in a thought, we are out of this world. There is separation.

Charles Kahn expresses this point helpfully. Aristotle, he says, attempts "to do justice to our split nature as human beings. On the one hand we are part of nature, a functioning organism like any animal, and that is what is covered by the hylomorphic definition [of the *psyche*]. On the other hand we somehow transcend the animal's position within nature by our access to the noetic domain . . . the realm of science and ethics, art and technology. . . . So the lack of unity in Aristotle's account of the soul can be seen as an accurate reflection of the complex, paradoxical structure of the human condition."[31] Fully extended or projected, this feature of our experience becomes an "active mind" separate and eternal.

Does this mean that after our bodies perish some little "part" of ourselves will live on? Probably not. Instead, thinking is of a piece with the urge to sexually reproduce, pleasure, and our experience of the "free-time" of leisure (<II.5; >VI.7). We are occasionally able to move beyond the temporal flow of past-present-future that constitutes our daily lives. Pleasure, for example, "is something whole and is in the moment" (*Nicomachean Ethics* 1174b9). All absorbing, the experience of pleasure, like that of intense concentration, takes us out of the flow of time (<III.4). Of course, the temporal duration of a massage or a study session spent trying to prove a mathematical theorem can both be measured. But Aristotle, perhaps more so than any other philosopher, is keenly attuned to what takes place within the experience. If you were really thinking hard, you didn't look at the clock at all. You were gone.

A reminder: there is perhaps no concept or word in Aristotle's vocabulary more significant than *energeia*, "being-at-work," "actualization," "actuality." (It is often conjoined with *entelecheia.*) It goes hand in glove with Aristotle's teaching on pleasure. It is essential to a theory of the *psyche* because organic life is the being-at-work of the body and is latent in the definition of change or motion as "the *entelecheia* of what is potential insofar as it is potential" (*Physics* 201a11). Material objects, including all animals and ourselves, are ever changing and so regularly commute between the actual and the potential. As such, they are in time. When we're maximally engaged in our activities, however, and as fully actualized as we can possibly become—during tremendous physical exertion in athletic competition, or in moments of extreme pleasure, or in the act of concentrated thought—we lose track, we jump out of time and forget that our lives are flowing away before our eyes. Such jumping is an intrinsic feature of human experience, and active mind, separate and eternal, tells us what it is and thereby saves it.

Not nearly enough has been said about this issue, so discussion of the "divine" life of the mind is continued in Chapter V.3 below. There too the salient point is that Aristotle's account of thinking does not require anything supernatural. Instead, it will be part and parcel of his "phenomenology." His account will be firmly rooted to the ground, even as it appears to head off into outer space.

IV.6: We Can Say What We Think.

A working conception of systematic truth has been developed in this chapter. The senses make contact with beings in the world; *phantasmata* are often erroneous but they can be corrected; like perceiving, thinking thinks forms and, like nutrition, becomes identical to them. But one ingredient must be added before the story ends: language (*logos*). We are able to say what we think, and in doing so speak truthfully.

> "Spoken words[#3] are symbols (*sumbola*) of affections (*pathêmata*) in the *psyche*,[#2] and written words are symbols of spoken ones. And just as written words[#4] are not the same for everyone, neither are spoken ones the same. However, what these are primarily signs of (*sêmaia*), namely the affections of the *psyche,* are the same for everyone. And what these affections are likenesses of (*homiômata*), namely real beings,[#1] are also the same" (*On Interpretation* 16a4–8).

This dense paragraph (to which superscript numbers have been added for the purpose of clarification) succinctly conveys Aristotle's conception of what language both is and can accomplish. First and most important, there are "real beings"[#1] (*pragmata*) out there in the world. These "affect" the *psyche*.[#2] A basic way in which they do so is through perceptions. The red scarf is a real being and it affects my perceptual system when I see it.

Both "real beings" and "affections" are "the same for everyone." In other words, there is only one world out there and all human beings experience it, are affected by it, in roughly the same way. Because we are all members of the same species, we possess the same sort of perceptual and cognitive faculties. By and large the way we see, hear, taste, touch, smell, and ultimately think about the "real beings" of the world is largely the same.

Most important in this account is that the affections of the *psyche* are "likenesses" of "real beings." This formulation reiterates the central point of this chapter: our perceptions, as the reception of sensible forms without the matter, are "like" the objects that caused them. As a result, they can be trusted, at least usually, to give us reliable information.

When it comes to language, the story becomes more complicated. "Spoken words"[#3] are not the same for everyone. The Italian "*cane*" is different from the English "dog," even if what is signified by both is the same object. Spoken language is a conventional operation, and the meaning of "spoken words" is largely arbitrary. If everyone agreed, "cat" could just as easily signify what is now meant by "dog."

As various and conventional as "spoken words" are, and "written words[#4] are even more so, they share one feature: they are "symbols of affections in the *psyche*." "Symbol" derives from the Greek *sumbolon*, which means "a sign or token by which one knows or infers a thing." In making a contract, for example, the two parties would break a bone or a coin in half, and each would keep one as a sign of their agreement. Language "symbolizes" mental affections. The word "red" stands for the color seen in the scarf; that is, for the "affection of the *psyche*" caused by the red scarf. In turn, because such affections (which may be *phantasmata*) are "likenesses of real beings"—in the case of perception, because the sense of vision apprehends the visible form without the matter—language is one step removed from actual things in the world. To reiterate, because this one step is the "affection of the *psyche*," and because at least when it comes to sense perception such affections are usually accurate apprehensions, there is an indirect but reliable connection between what we say about the world, and the actual things in the world that affect us. This connection makes it possible for language to articulate the truth about those actual things.[32]

Questions abound. How exactly is my perception of red "like" the red scarf that caused it? The former takes place in me, the latter is out there in the world. In what sense does language, say the word "red," symbolize what took place when I saw the red scarf? Deborah Modrak thinks that Aristotle can answer questions like these, and she may be right.[33] For the moment, however, only recall a statement made by Daniel Gilbert: "we feel as though we are sitting comfortably inside our heads, looking out through the clear glass window of our eyes, watching the world as it truly is." For Gilbert, this feeling is quite wrong and in fact is the source of much human misery. Aristotle, by contrast, comes close to believing it. Furthermore, he has a great faith in human language to be able to say what we see; to say the world "as it truly is."

IV.7: We "Truth" the World.

A language like Greek or English uses nouns, verbs, adjectives, and other parts of speech. They can be combined to form a meaningful sentence, which Aristotle calls a *logos*. "*Logos* is significant (*sêmantikê*) speech"—speech that signifies or means something (<III.3)—"of whose parts some, upon being separated from the *logos*, are also significant" (*On Interpretation* 16b26–27).

When I utter the sentence "The dog is brown," you understand what I mean for it "signifies" something. So too does "dog" by itself mean something. There is, however, a difference. "Dog" by itself is neither true nor false. It's just an "utterance," a *phasis* (which comes from the Greek *phêmi*, "to say"). But it is neither an "affirmation"—a *kataphasis*, a saying that this belongs to that, as "brown" is said or affirmed about (*kata*) the dog—nor is it an *apophasis*, saying that this does not belong to or is "away from" (*apo*) that.[34] For a *logos* to be true or false there must be either "a combining or a dividing" (16a12). The affirmation "The dog is brown," can be true or false because "brown" is combined with "dog." So too can the denial, "the dog is not brown," in which "brown" is separated from "dog," be true or false. In the *Metaphysics,* Aristotle puts the point this way: a true affirmation is "of what is combined"; a true denial is of "what is separated" (1027b20). "The dog is brown" is true if "dog" and "brown" really do belong together; in other words, if the dog really is brown.[35]

True and false beliefs are characterized similarly: "the person who believes that what is divided is divided, and that what is combined is combined, 'truths.' " Furthermore, "it is not because we believe truly that you are white that you are white. Instead, because you are white we who say this 'truth' (*alêtheuomen*: *Metaphysics* 1051b7–9)." This use of "truth" as a verb in the previous two sentences sounds weird in English, but corresponds well to the Greek *alêtheuomen.* It is discussed shortly.

Every affirmation or denial is a sentence or *logos*, but not every sentence is true or false. A prayer, for example, is neither (*On Interpretation* 17a4). To cite the crucial word, which must be kept in the Greek for a while, not every sentence is *apophantikos* (17a2). Only the affirmation and denial, the *logos apophantikos,* the "statement-making sentence," can be true or false.[36] And so only it can "truth."

Apophantikos may seem to be related to *apophasis*, "denial," but it is not. The *phan* bit does not come from the same word as does *phasis* (which is from *phêmi*, "to say"). Instead, it derives from an old friend: *phainesthai,* "to come to light, come to sight, be seen, appear." Heidegger's comments about the *logos apophantikos* are helpful because they are so well attuned to the root word *phainesthai.* "[The *logos apophantikos*] lets something be seen (*phainesthai*), namely, what the discourse is about. In discourse *apophansis* so far as it is genuine, what is said is drawn from what the talk is about, so that discursive communication, in what it says, makes manifest what it is talking about, and thus makes this accessible to the other party. This is the structure of logos as *apophansis.* . . . Because the *logos* is a letting-something-be-seen, it can therefore be true or false."

As suggested above, "truth" can be a property of certain kinds of sentences, like "The dog is brown," which is true if "dog" and "brown" are in reality "combined." But Heidegger insists that the meaning of truth goes beyond this. As he puts it, because the *apophantikos logos* "is a definite mode of letting something be seen, the *logos* is just not the kind of thing that can be considered as the primary locus of truth."[37]

Not only sentences (or beliefs) are true or false. Nor is truth simply the "agreement" or "correspondence" between a statement and some reality or fact that the statement addresses. For there also is a sense in which being itself can be true. Indeed, at one point in the *Metaphysics* Aristotle says, "being in the most dominant sense is truth and falsity" (1051b3).[38] And remember a point that was so important earlier: perception of special sensibles is "true." Perception is not linguistic. Hence, truth is not exclusively linguistic nor found only in the correspondence between statements and reality. For consider this: in Greek "truth" can become a verb. In the *Nicomachean Ethics,* Aristotle says, "those faculties by which the *psyche* truths (*alêtheuei*) by means of affirmation and denial are five in number" (1139b15). These five can be divided into two broad categories: "practical" and "theoretical" truthing (1139a27).[39]

You might be an astronomer who studies the stars. They are eternal and their orbits are immutable. Because the stars are "necessary"—in other words, they do not change and so there is no chance of them being other than they are—studying them does not empower you to alter or affect them in any way. In peering at the night sky you see, and eventually you might come to understand, what is there. This is a form of theoretical truthing. You might then write a book titled *On the Heavens*, and if you did good work your theory or *logos* might be true . . . about the heavenly bodies. Whether it is or not can only be determined by argument, observation, and investigation of those bodies.

But there's more to truth than that. For example, in wondering how much money you should give a friend who has recently lost all of his own, you try to discern the truth of the matter. Perhaps your friend squandered away his money at a casino and simply resupplying him will only reinforce his already bad habit of gambling. Or perhaps he was the innocent victim of a robbery, and without an infusion of cash his family will suffer. You must think through the particulars here, which are contingent matters upon which you can actually exert some influence, and come up with the right answer. If you get it right, then you've "truthed" the situation. This is a practical mode of truthing, an apprehension of what is particular and contingent. If you can do this consistently well, then you have the "virtue" called "practical wisdom" (*phronêsis*). And if you have this, then you must do more than simply know what you should do or utter the true sentence, "I should give my friend 100 dollars." You must act. Your truthing isn't complete without action (>V.6).

A similar situation obtains when it comes to "art" (*technê*), which Aristotle here defines as a form of truthing that leads to production. A builder knows how to build houses. As in "practical wisdom," whose area is the particular, human, and contingent, there is nothing necessary about any given house being brought into being. A builder sees what is required to bring his task to completion, and when he does this well, when he has gotten it right and the house is standing there stable and true, he has "truthed" the situation.

Practical wisdom and "art" suggest that truth is not only a property of statements or beliefs. Because "truth" also can be a verb, it expresses an action, a mode of human comportment toward some chunk of the world. In (diluted) Heideggerian terms, truth is a mode of being, a mode of "uncovering." Heidegger arrives at this formulation by taking his bearings from the Greek word *alêtheia*, which he reads, rightly or wrongly, as etymologically derived from an "alpha privative," the negativizing prefix "a," which is equivalent to the English "non-" or "un," and the verb *lanthanein*, "to escape notice, to be unseen." Truth is "un-coveredness." It is a mode of interaction with the world in which what was concealed becomes unconcealed. "Being true, disclosure, is a mode of Being of human life and refers first of all to the world."

To elaborate, consider a view against which Heidegger, who here follows Aristotle closely, is arguing. For thinkers like Descartes and Locke, the most pressing question is how the mind and what goes on "in" it, its ideas or representations, can possibly make contact with, how it can "truth," the external world. For both, the urgency of this question is reinforced by the primary–secondary quality distinction. Ordinary experience and language suggest that the fire is hot and the scarf is red. For both modern thinkers, however, these are but secondary qualities that do not inhere in the objects themselves independently of the perceiving agent who records them. Our "ideas" of them do not resemble actual objects in the world. Instead, we live in a bubble, separated from the world, and so the question of how the human mind makes veridical contact with or "truths" the world becomes the fundamental philosophical problem.

Not so for Aristotle. For him we are animals at home in the world. The fire really is hot and we can feel it as such. Recall his statement that "it would be ridiculous" to try to prove that nature exists outside of ourselves (*Physics* 193a5), for it is amply "apparent" (*phaneron*) that it does. Nature shows itself to us in our everyday encounters with the external world. We observe the sun as it orbits the earth. Aristotle begins his theorizing with the fact that we live in the world. Our encounter with external objects is through the analogously ordered activities of nutrition, perception, and thinking. In a sense, all three are forms of "truthing." Even the squirrel scratching for food in the dirt can get it right. He finds his food, eats it, and thus continues to live. To survive, an animal must have a niche in which the world makes itself hospitable and truth is possible.

For all these reasons, then, "theorizing the truth is easy" and "no one can miss a door." The door is standing there fully in view, and as a result we walk through it rather than the wall. It stares us in the face and invites us to open it.[40]

To close this chapter on a conciliatory note: Aristotle's disregard for the mind–body problem and all the epistemological grief it has caused for the past four hundred years can easily be dismissed as terribly naïve and poorly supported by the facts. Perhaps, then, as suggested in the *Preface,* the critic should conceive his work as a massive thought experiment. Instead of Descartes's "evil genius," who devotes all his energy to deceiving us—in other words, instead of assuming that our ordinary perceptions, beliefs, and traditions are false—imagine there were a benevolent and thoroughly humane genius, one who guaranteed that the "reputable opinions," the *endoxa,* the phenomena that guide our lives were epistemically reliable. If so, then the world, from top to bottom, would look just as Aristotle says that it does. And, as ours is increasingly not, it would be one fit for human habitation.

Chapter Five

The Theoretical Life Is Divine.

In *On the Psyche*, "active mind" is described in what seem like otherworldly terms. It is "separate," "immortal," and "eternal" (430a22–23). Because the account of the divine as "thought thinking itself" in the *Metaphysics* uses similar language, it might seem that God somehow enters into the thinking lives of human beings. Such, at least, was Eudemus's interpretation (<IV.5) and it is one that has resurfaced throughout the centuries.

The purpose of this chapter is to fulfill a promise made a while back (<IV.5): namely, to show that Aristotle's conception of active mind as "divine" is neither a wild flight of a religious imagination nor a betrayal of his naturalism, but instead is steadfastly worldly. As unlikely as it may initially appear, his account of thinking is faithful to the contours of ordinary experience. Being "divine" or "eternal" isn't all it's cracked up to be. In fact, divinity and eternity are available to us, although only sporadically, throughout and within our lives.

This proposal is developed by discussing the *Nicomachean Ethics*, Aristotle's account of an excellent (or "virtuous") human life.[1] More specifically, this chapter takes its bearings from a notorious question that has long stumped the scholars: do the concluding chapters of this treatise (Book X.7–8) coherently fit together with the rest of the work?[2] Here Aristotle says that "complete happiness" is the actualization of the "supreme" virtue, which in turn is the work of what is best in us, namely "mind" (1177a17–20). He describes such work as "theoretical" (*theôretikê*), and argues that it is the most continuous, pleasant, self-sufficient, and leisurely activity available to human beings. Furthermore, it "alone seems to be liked because of itself" (1177b1), for it supplies no benefit other than itself.[3] Finally, theoretical activity actualizes what is most divine in us and allows us best to approximate the gods, whose "activity is superior in blessedness" and is itself "theoretical."

These lines cause headaches for readers because they seem to conflict not only with Aristotle's generally naturalistic stance but also with much of what has preceded them in the *Nicomachean Ethics* itself. For in earlier sections of the book Aristotle treats "practical" or "moral" activity as a form of genuine excellence. (These terms are discussed shortly.) He seems to grant that a just, courageous, or generous human being, someone "moral" who spends his time interacting well with fellow human beings, can live a fine life without having to be particularly theoretical. In fact, in earlier chapters Aristotle suggests that such activity can be an end in itself. But when he reaches the conclusion of the *Ethics* he seems to shift course drastically, for his extraordinary praise of the "divine" life of the mind unexpectedly demotes practical, "moral," or simply "human" excellence to a secondary status.

Whether the *Nicomachean Ethics* is coherent is not merely a scholarly question, for in addressing it an urgent personal question is raised as well. What is the relationship between a practical or moral life, one spent being decent to fellow citizens, neighbors, friends, and relatives, and a theoretical life, one devoted to thought? For example, is it possible for a selfish, cruel, or unjust person to be an excellent thinker? Conversely, must a generous and morally serious man also be an intellectual? Must a philosopher cease thinking, sacrifice his intellectual work, in order to assume his fair share of responsibilities to his friends, family, and fellow citizens? In short, to use the terms now inscribed in the tradition, what is the relationship between "theory" and "practice?" By examining the *Nicomachean Ethics,* by explaining how its ending coheres with its beginning and middle, this chapter tackles these questions, as well as ones sparked by the "active mind" passage in *On the Psyche.* It explains how a theoretical life, even if it is, as Aristotle says, "divine" and "separate," is nonetheless distinctly human and an essential dimension of our being-in-the-world. Finally, when this book concludes in Chapter Six, it explains how in its own way the theoretical life also is significantly practical.

To begin, then, at the beginning:

V.1: Life Is Meaningful.

Aristotle's *Nicomachean Ethics* is different from what today typically fits under the heading of "ethics" or "moral philosophy." It is not a study of right or wrong action, of what one ought to do, nor does it aim to solve a series of moral problems, puzzles, or dilemmas.[4] Instead, its topic is human "excellence," which in Greek is *aretê* and which also can be translated as "virtue." Aristotle's question is not simply which actions are morally permissible, but what sort of human being we should aspire to become. To answer it a comprehensive account of being human is required. As a result, the *Ethics* is closer to an "anthropology"—a rational account, a *logos*, of *anthrôpos*—than it is to the "moral philosophy" that is taught in contemporary universities and whose subject matter tends to be organized around issues like abortion, euthanasia, human rights, the environment, and so on.

As an "anthropology," the *Nicomachean Ethics* does not treat human being simply as one animal among many. *On the Psyche* and other biological works perform that task. Instead, it offers an account of *anthrôpos* in just one of its distinct modes of being. Unlike other animals we live and interact with each other within political communities, which are themselves guided by a set of articulable civic values. As Aristotle puts it in the *Politics*, we are the "political animal" (1253a7). ("Political" is derived from the Greek *polis*, "city" or "city-state.") This is the ethical or moral or practical, the value-guided and communal, dimension of our lives that biology cannot address.

The *Ethics* begins thus:[5] "Every art (*technê*) and every investigation, and similarly every action (*praxis*) and choice, seem (*dokei*) to aim at some good; hence the statement that the good is that at which everything aims is well said" (1094a1–3).

These remarks are expressed on the level of appearance: "seem" translates the verb *dokei*, which is the root of *doxa* ("opinion" or "belief") and *ta endoxa* ("the reputable opinions"). A quick, introspective glance reveals that our own lives appear to be purposive. We take ourselves to act for reasons and to make choices in order to achieve goals that seem good to us.

You are reading this book. Perhaps it has been assigned by a professor or you only picked it up in order to distract yourself from the computer screen. It doesn't matter what reason or goal you actually had in mind, only that in choosing to open this book you had one. Thus, when Aristotle says, "the good is that at which everything aims" he means that human life is thoroughly purposive or teleological.

The second point is equally commonsensical: purposes, goods, or goals are ordered in a means–end sequence. Assume that you are reading this book in order to get a passing grade on an examination. If so, then your reading is a means toward the achievement of a "higher" good: the attainment of the grade. In turn, the grade is itself a means to an even higher good: graduating from college, a goal you aspire to in order to gain entrance into graduate school. And this you aspire to in order to secure a professorship. And so on.

The question Aristotle next poses is, does this sequence of means and ends terminate or does it go on forever? If it does terminate, it would do so with an end that is not a means to anything higher but instead is simply good in itself. Unlike reading a book in order to pass a course, or taking medicine in order to become healthy, the "highest good" would be one chosen for itself.

But does such a "highest good" exist? Aristotle thinks so: "If then among our actions there is some end which we wish for because of itself, and because of which we wish for everything else, and if we do not choose everything because of something else—since if we did it would go on indefinitely and as a result desire would be empty and vain—clearly this would be the highest good" (1094a18–22).

This passage can be construed as an indirect argument. Assume the opposite of what Aristotle actually believes; namely, that there is no highest good and that the means–end sequence thus proceeds indefinitely or infinitely. You read the book in order to get the grade, to get into graduate school, to become a professor, and so on and on forever. If this were the case, then "desire" or "striving" (*orexis*), indeed life itself (which is animated by *orexis*), would be "empty and vain." No good or purpose or goal would have any substantial value because it would be but a means to something else, which in turn would be but a means to something else again. If the sequence of means and ends were infinite, then the achievement of any single item would advance the agent no closer to the end. After all, compared to (divided by) infinity all finite achievements shrink to nothing. If the sequence of means–ends were infinite, then desire and life itself would be "empty and vain." They would be meaningless.

Life, however, is not "empty and vain." It is meaningful. Therefore, so the indirect argument runs, there must be a highest good to terminate the sequence of means–ends.

Aristotle neither spells out this argument nor explicitly states that life is not empty and vain. Perhaps it is because he takes this notion to be altogether apparent (*phaneron*). Chapter Two of this book suggests the broadest reason why: "Nature is purpose." Aristotle's teleology implies that life, whether of a human being or a plant, has "meaning." As mentioned earlier (< Introduction), this word, so famously associated with philosophy, has at least two senses. The first is the semantic, as in " 'Table' means a piece of furniture with a flat top placed horizontally on legs." There is also the purposive sense: "I meant to turn the lights off." Both are operative in the phrase "Life has meaning," for it is both purposive and its purposive structure can be explained or articulated.

Consider the following scenario: When Bob gets up in the morning, he dutifully trudges off to work. He does so because he cares about making some money, for his goal of buying a car matters to, is meaningful to, him. If he didn't believe this, and feel it in his bones, he would stay in bed. But he doesn't. If life were meaningless, if no single achievement could actually advance us any closer to our goal, then the vast majority of human beings would be living in utter self-deception. Aristotle rejects this possibility. Recall the definition of the *endoxa*: they are beliefs "that seem right to either all or the majority or to the wise; either to all of the wise or to most or to the most well known and generally accepted to be wise." Even if it is not explicitly articulated or philosophically defended, that life has a purpose is a belief held by normal human beings and revealed in their daily actions. Because normal human beings tend to get things right, this *doxa* has significant epistemic value.

Recall an earlier section of this book (<II.8): "The finite is better than the infinite" because it is intelligible and allows for the possibility of being *teleion*, "complete" or "perfect." This conviction, which figures so prominently in Aristotle's cosmology and physics, is directly expressed here in the argument that the sequence of means and ends must be finite. If it weren't, life as we know it would be annihilated.

Aristotle's physics was attacked (beginning around 1600) on the grounds that his cozy little cosmos was really no more than a projection of his own entirely human predilection for what is familiar and like himself; namely, what is finite. No doubt some would hurl the same accusation at his argument that life is meaningful as well.

V.2: Happiness Is Objective.

Believing he has demonstrated the existence of a highest good, an end choice worthy in itself, Aristotle goes forward to explain what it is. Such an explanation, he thinks, will be useful. Just as an archer must see the target well in order to hit it, so must a human being, who is ultimately aiming for the highest good (whether she quite realizes it or not), understand what it is. It is surprisingly easy to give it a name: "both the majority of people and those who are refined call [the highest good] happiness (*eudaimonia*: 1095a19).

If I ask Bob, "Why are you flipping burgers?" the content of his answer ("to make money") is different from the content of the question ("burgers"). This pattern recurs with all goods or ends, except the final one. Bob wants money in order to buy a car, and a car in order to get to the beach quickly. But when this sequence comes to a halt, the content of question and answer merge. So, if I push Bob hard enough, asking him, "Why do you want to get to the beach?" and so on, eventually he will answer, "Because I want to be happy." If I then ask him, "But why do you want to be happy?" he can only repeat himself: "Because I want to be happy." Happiness is the final and highest good, that for the sake of which we do all else. It is what makes human life meaningful.

Unfortunately, identifying happiness as the highest good does little to advance our understanding. Most people already know this (1097b23) and so it is little more than a platitude. So, Aristotle proposes a strategy with which to push the inquiry forward. "Perhaps [happiness] will become more clear if the function (*ergon*) of human being could be grasped" (1097b24–25).

It is not obvious why, in order to discover what happiness is, we must inquire into the human "function," nor is it even clear what this word means. Naturally a clue comes from the Greek. *Ergon* is at the root of *energeia*, translated above as "actuality," but literally coming closer to "being-at-work." An *ergon*, then, is a "work, a deed, an action." The reason translators use the English "function" is found in the following passage: "Is it possible that a builder and a shoemaker have their functions and activities (*praxeis*), but of a human being there is none? Is a human being by nature a 'do-nothing' (*agron*)?[6] Just as there appears (*phainetai*) to be a function of the eye, the hand, the foot, and in general of each of the bodily parts, should one also attribute to a human being some function besides all of these?" (1097b28–34).

This passage suggests two analogies. First, just as a carpenter has a function, namely to build houses, so too must a human being have a function. This assertion may be hard to swallow. Specialized professions require a specific set of skills that are directed toward accomplishing a single end. A builder knows how to work with his tools in order to build a house. Such is his function. But attributing a function to the entire species may be another matter altogether. Differently stated, a builder's function can be construed as an artificial limitation imposed by a socially useful division of labor. A builder builds houses well but would make lousy shoes and so is well advised to stick to his trade. Attributing a function to the human species, however, might seem to illicitly transfer what is artificial to what is natural. The needs of a society shape the builder's function. But nature might not do the same to the species.

The second analogy invokes the parts of the body. Just as the eye and the hand have a function to perform in the self-maintenance of the entire organism, so too, Aristotle suggests, might human being as a whole have a function. This argument smacks of teleology. The special work, the *telos*, of the eye is to see; the function of the hand is to grasp. Similarly, Aristotle suggests, the human being as a whole must have a work proper to it.

Here Aristotle may have made the logical mistake of arguing from the parts of a thing to the whole. For example, if all the components of a machine are tiny it does not follow that the entire machine is tiny. Similarly, even if all the parts of the body have a function this need not imply that the being as a whole must have a function.

Before this objection is addressed, allow Aristotle to continue: "What then would this [function] be? For living is apparently shared with plants, and something special (*idion*) is being sought. For this reason both nutrition and growth should be eliminated. Next would come some sort of life of sense perception, but this appears to be common to the horse, the ox, and every animal. What remains is some sort of life of action (*praktikê*) belonging to that which has reason (*logos*)" (1097b30–98a4).

The work that differentiates humans from other animals is being rational. (*Logos* can mean "reason," "ratio," as well as "speech" or "language.") This assertion sparks more controversy. First, why must a function be "special" rather than being shared by other animals? Second, even if it must be special, why is rational activity selected for humanity? Why not being humorous or caring or anxious or creative or capable of violence on a massive scale?

This passage has generated a huge literature among the scholars. Michael Pakaluk helpfully suggests that it be read in an "intuitive way." He explains by asking the following questions: "What special talents set us apart from other animals? Would we not be 'wasting those gifts' if we lived no differently from animals that lack the ability to think and to direct their behavior through thinking?"[7]

You may love your cat dearly and admire his abilities, both physical and cognitive. Unless you are delusional, however, you will not attempt to reason with him. If, for example, you are a vegetarian who thinks there are good reasons not to eat meat, you will not try to persuade your cat to stop killing mice. By contrast, should your carnivorous human friend refuse to argue or even discuss with you the merits of eating meat, you would find her response lacking. Similarly, if another friend of yours spends eighteen hours a day sleeping, and the remaining six eating and drinking and fornicating, you will be repelled by his behavior.

On this "intuitive" level—which is meant to parallel the tentativeness of Aristotle's own argument—there is a palpable difference between a cat and human being and between those human beings whose behavior is consistently subpar and those we respect. To be human is to do more than eat, drink, grow, reproduce, and die. It is to participate in the practical life of reason. Even if not buttressed with elaborate argumentation such, at least, is Aristotle's entirely reasonable intuition.

Aristotle reiterates this point in another passage tinged with biological-teleology.

> As we say, nature does nothing in vain. And human beings alone of the animals have *logos.* Now a voice is a signifier of what is pleasant or painful and so it belongs to other animals. For their nature has reached this point; namely, to have perception of pleasure and pain and to be able to signify this to each other. But *logos* is for the purpose of clarifying what is beneficial and what is harmful, and thus even what is just and unjust. For this is special (*idion*) to human beings in comparison with the other animals. Only human beings have a perception of what is good and bad and just and unjust and related matters. (*Politics* 1253a9–18)

We share the capacity to nourish and reproduce ourselves and to perceive the external world with other animals, but having *logos* is the distinctive feature of being human.[8] Because this passage appears in the *Politics* (>VI.3) Aristotle slants the meaning of *logos* here in a practical or political direction. It is, he says, for the purpose of articulating what is beneficial and harmful, and eventually what is just and unjust. This is a truncated sense of *logos* for we know it can do more than discuss values. The *logos apophantikos* (<IV.7), for example, is capable of asserting the truth. Still, the main point of the passage holds: what makes us into who we are, our "special" work, is our capacity to enter into some sort of rational discussion. That discussion may be internal, and so would be called "thinking," or can be held with other human beings. It may be about what is good or bad, and so would be "practical," or about what is simply true or false, and so would be "theoretical." But it is all *logos* and it is who we are.

Even if Aristotle's convictions and reasoning about the human function are correct, its relationship to happiness remains obscure. Some light can be shed by the following passage: "For just as the good and the 'well' of the flutist and the statue-maker and every other artist, and anyone else for whom there is a function and an activity, seem to be in the function, so too does it seem to be the case for human being, if it has some function" (*Nicomachean Ethics* 1087b25–28).

A flutist has a function: to play the flute. To be a good flutist is to exercise this function well. The good of the flutist, then, resides in her functioning or working well. The problem here is that "good," as it pertains to the flutist, may differ from the "highest good" (happiness) that orients all of human life. The former is a technical skill and so may have little or no connection to happiness as we ordinarily understand it. After all, even an excellent flutist may be a miserable creep.

To clarify, consider the Greek word *eudaimonia*. "Happiness," the standard translation, is potentially misleading. The Greek begins with *eu*, a prefix meaning "good" or "well," which is still found in English words like "euphemism" and "euthanasia." A *daimon* is some sort of "spirit." *Eudaimonia*, then, means "a spirit in good shape" and also can be translated as "prosperity," "well-being" or "flourishing," the last of which, like several of the arguments above, smacks of teleology. A healthy child running joyfully through the park or a plant in maximum bloom is "flourishing." "Happiness" is ill suited to capture this sense of *eudaimonia* for it is derived from the same Middle English word as is "happen": *"hap, happe*; good luck or chance." When I say, "I happened to see Bob yesterday," or "I happened upon Bob yesterday," I mean that there was some measure of "happenstance," chance occurrence or accident, involved. "Happiness" thus suggests a condition or state that "happens" to us. By contrast, *eudaimonia* as "flourishing" is a condition the agent generates from within and is achieved through actualization (*energeia*). The flutist flourishes if she has practiced long and hard and then performs her piece well. So too does the tree that has grown in good soil and has received lots of water and sun. In short, *eudaimonia* refers to an objective condition. Whether the flutist flourishes or not, executes her function well or not, can be objectively ascertained by expert judges in a musical competition. Whether a tree is in good shape can be judged by an arborist. By contrast, "happiness," as typically heard by an English speaker, just happens. It smacks of the subjective, of an emotion or *pathos* that one just feels, and so does not capture the full semantic value of *eudaimonia*.[9]

Imagine that your friend sleeps eighteen hours a day and spends the remaining six eating and drinking. His family is wealthy enough for him not to take a job, he is of cheerful temperament and always seems, when awake, to be smiling. You are quite puzzled by his demeanor and so you ask, "Are you happy?" He says, "Yes." You, a hard-working person who sleeps only six hours a day, are skeptical and so ask again, "Are you *really* happy?" Again he answers, "Yes," and he does so with a sincerity you take to be genuine. The question is, can he be wrong about his experience and understanding of his own happiness? Differently stated, is a claim to happiness "incorrigible," incapable of being corrected? Some claims are clearly of this sort. If I ask you, "Does your head hurt?" and you answer me as honestly as you can, "Yes, it does," you cannot be wrong. If you feel yourself to be in pain, then you really are in pain. By contrast, if I ask you, "What's the matter?" and you answer, "I have a brain tumor," then you might well be wrong. If you go to the hospital and have the proper tests, the existence of a brain tumor can be ruled out. Your belief in a brain tumor is corrigible, but your honest report of your own pain is not.

To us "happiness" generally suggests something incorrigible. By contrast, Aristotle's *eudaimonia*, understood as "well-being" or "flourishing," is distinctly corrigible. Your friend is simply wrong in reporting about and evaluating his own condition. He thinks he is happy, and he feels a certain contentment or pleasure, but in fact, because he is not hard at work doing what human beings are uniquely and naturally suited to do, he is far from genuinely flourishing. As a result, you should seriously reconsider having him as your friend.[10] In sum, only to the extent that *eudaimonia* is kept in mind should "happiness" be used as a translation and in discussion of the *Nicomachean Ethics*.

The concept of an *ergon* is paired with that of *aretê* or "excellence" (or "virtue"). If I know the *ergon* of an object I can determine its *aretê*. So, for example, I know the function of my glasses is to improve my vision. Because I know this, I can evaluate my glasses. If I can see distant objects clearly when I am wearing them, then I have a good pair.

An objection: surely I could conceive of the function of my glasses to be the enhancement of my appearance, and not just the improvement of my vision. In other words, Aristotle may be overconfident in his ability to ascribe functions even to simple artifacts like my glasses. If so, then he could be really wrong about the function of the human species.

In any case, with the terms discussed above now in place, Aristotle's definition of happiness should at least make sense: "it is a certain kind of activity (*energeia*) of the *psyche* according to excellence" (1099b26). It is excellent rational work.

V.3: Good Life Comes from Good Habits.

The next task is obvious: Aristotle must tell us what rational activity is. He begins by dividing it into two kinds: "one as obeying reason (*logos*), the other as conceiving and having reason" (1098a4–5). To explicate, consider the relationship between a parent and a child, or a teacher and a student. The former gives commands to the latter, who, if all goes according to plan, will obey. That Aristotle attributes rational activity to both parties may seem odd. After all, obeying seems to be passive rather than active. But this is not so. It is reasonable, for example, for a university student to follow the "commands" of the professor written on the course syllabus. Presumably, the professor knows her subject, as well as how to teach it. A good student realizes this and understands that he will benefit by following the path outlined on the syllabus. Furthermore, the student can understand those commands well enough to follow them. As a result, even if operating at a lower level than the professor, the student nonetheless is doing some rational work in obeying her.

The above suggests a ranking: the professor is "higher," more advanced and rationally active, and better, than the student. Only as such is it rational for the student to obey. Aristotle reinforces this hierarchical notion by quoting the poet Hesiod:

> The man is all-best who himself works out every problem . . .
> That man too is admirable who follows one who speaks well.
> He who cannot see the truth for himself, nor, hearing it from others,
> store it away in his mind, that man is utterly useless. (1095b10–13)[11]

Of the three lives here proposed, best is the fully rational man who can think through every problem himself. Second is a good man who, even if he cannot comprehend everything on his own, can both understand what the rational man tells him and realize that he should obey. Finally, there is the worthless man who neither thinks for himself nor is willing or able to listen to his superiors.

This ranking can be articulated in terms of the human function. It is rational activity but of this there are two inflections: the obedient and that which actually conceives. Each can be done well and so to each belongs a specific excellence or virtue. This distinction will emerge shortly as that between excellence "of character" and "of thought" (1103a15), and at least two questions are sparked by it. Is one superior to the other, and what is the relationship between the two?

To sum up so far (by paraphrasing 1197a25–b6): we act for reasons and toward ends. Of these there are many. Some we choose as means toward the achievement of something else. Money is the best example, for unless we are pathological we seek it only in order to buy stuff we want. It is obvious, then, that not all ends are "final" (*teleia*: 1197a27) or "complete" or "perfect." But the highest good, what is most excellent, does show itself (*phainetai*) as "final" for it is pursued only for the sake of itself. Here, though, Aristotle adds a wrinkle: "So if the highest good is one it alone will be final and this will be what is sought, but if it is more than one, that which is most final of these [will be what is sought]" (1097a28–30).

There is one highest good and it is happiness, which is "activity of the *psyche* according to excellence." Specifically, it is rational activity. And of this there are two forms, obeying and conceiving, with their two corresponding excellences: the virtues of character and thought. Perhaps, then, there are two forms of happiness, with one being higher and "more final" than the other.

These comments spark the notorious question. At the end of the *Nicomachean Ethics*, Aristotle states that "complete or final happiness" (*teleia eudaimonia*: 1177a17) is found in theoretical activity and demotes practical activity to secondary status. The distinction made here in Book I between the "conceiving" and "obeying" inflections of rationality provides the background for this subsequent move. Excellence of the former is theoretical work; of the latter, practical.[12] The question, however, still remains: what is the relationship between the two? The example of the student–teacher relationship is the key. Before becoming a teacher who "conceives" one must first be a student who "obeys." In turn, this suggests that the relationship between obeying and conceiving is developmental. This should hardly be surprising. After all, organic development, the directed growth toward a *telos*, is basic to Aristotle's understanding of all natural beings.

As mentioned, by means of the distinction between conceiving and obeying Aristotle arrives at two distinct forms of excellence. "For we say that there is excellence of thinking (*dianoêtikê*) and excellence of character" (*êthikê*: 1103a5). An example of the former is "wisdom" (*sophia*) (<III.1); of the latter, generosity. To excellence of character Aristotle devotes most of Books II–V and to it we therefore turn first.

Excellence of character emerges from habit. In fact, in Greek the two words are closely related. *Ethos* means "custom" or "habit," while *êthos* is "a lengthened form of *ethos*, and means "an accustomed seat," "haunt," "manners and habits," and "character." Translated into Latin, both words became *mos* (plural, *mores*), the root of our word "moral." For this reason, many translators use the phrase "moral virtue" to refer to this dimension of human excellence, and it is used here. The key to understanding it, however, is not to lose sight of the original meaning of *ethos*. Begin, then, by reflecting upon the nature of habits.

Every night before going to bed you put tomorrow's clothes in the same place. Despite the availability of several routes, your walk to work always takes you on the same path. Your routine upon entering the office is unfailing: turn the computer on, put your coat away, make the coffee. So many of our daily activities are performed with little or no thought or deliberation, and thus often transpire almost without being noticed. But they are not automatic as, say, the mechanism of an alarm clock is. The machine is set to ring at 7:00 A.M. and unless there is a mechanical or electrical breakdown it will do so. However automatic it feels the habitual pattern of arranging your clothes is different from the workings of the clock. You can put your clothes on the floor instead of the chair if you should so choose. Similarly, a habitual action is not involuntary, as is breathing. For even if it is difficult it is not impossible to break one's habits.

Habit is thus located in a gray zone, somewhere in between a fully self-conscious and deliberate action and an automatic, mechanical, or involuntary form of behavior. To clarify the two extremes, please do this: raise your right arm above your head. Now think carefully about whether you wish to smack your cheek. You can do it if you want, but you don't have to. There may be good reasons to do it: to bring color to your face, to wake yourself up, to enjoy the sensation of pain. But you may decide that these reasons aren't good enough to compel you to act. You have to figure it out, and when you finish, you'll act accordingly. And when you do, you will act in the bright light of full self-consciousness. An example of the other extreme, namely an involuntary behavior, has already been mentioned: breathing. The organic workings of your respiratory system are largely beyond your control. Draping your clothes over your chair before you go to bed lies somewhere in between. It is neither illuminated by the light of deliberation nor involuntary or mechanical for you can, if you choose, put your clothes on the floor.

Many habits are developed through the imposition of external command or even force. In fact, the development of habit is the actualization of the "obeying" component of our rational capacities. Acting habitually is thus a low-level manifestation of rational activity. Perhaps your mother insisted that you lay your clothes upon your chair every night, and to this day you repeat that procedure. After so many years doing so has become "second nature" and as a result failing to do so can even spark a bit of pain.[13]

Aristotle applies this line of thought to moral action: "by doing just things we become just; by doing moderate things we become moderate" (1103b1). As he realizes, this statement might provoke an objection: in order to do just things must not someone already be just? How, then, can someone become just by doing just things? (See 1105a17–20.) The answer is supplied by the following analogy. A child may write a word properly by luck or at the prompting of someone else (1105a23). He does not really know how to write but only by such exercises will he learn. The model implied by this example is developmental. The child learns how to write by writing. Similarly, a parent may force a child to wash the dishes in order to ensure that the labor of running a home is equitably distributed. The child has no desire to do the work, nor a real understanding of why the parent's demand is just. With age, however, the parent's admonitions will become internalized and if the child eventually does his job willingly or even cheerfully he will be counted as good.

If habits coalesce into a cluster they become a second nature. They become part of our "character." Our *ethê*, the plural of *ethos*, become our *êthos.* Just as *ethos* is the etymological root of "ethics" so too is habit the origin of an excellent character. It is not, however, the pinnacle of "ethical" success. For that requires thinking and acting knowledgeably.

You may have put your clothes on the same chair night after night for decades and now you do so thoughtlessly. At some point, however, you may wish to bring this habit into the light of day for examination and decide whether it is worth keeping. Through reflection you may determine that it is. Having your clothes nicely ready to go allows you to start your day more efficiently. Habitual action is thus like the soil from which can grow a thoughtful conviction. In other words, full-blown rational activity emerges from its lower-level predecessor. Recall the example of the student who "obeys" the professor's syllabus. Someday that student may himself become a professor who knows what he is doing when he writes his own syllabus, but first he had to follow his teacher's instructions.

The *Nicomachean Ethics* ascends gradually from habit-driven moral virtues like courage and generosity, which are actualizations of the rational capacity to obey, to intellectual virtues that fully actualize the capacity to conceive. It concludes with the highest virtue of all, namely the divine activity of theoretical thought. Unfortunately, how these two modalities of excellence cohere is far from obvious.

V.4: Freedom Isn't All It's Cracked Up To Be.

Aristotle's identification of habit as the origin of morally excellent activity needs to be challenged. First, by locating the cause of being moral outside of the agent—in, for example, the parents who raised a good child—he seems to devalue the moral worth of the agent himself. Even if I still do my fair share of work around the house I am not fully responsible for such good behavior. Perhaps my parents, who made me do this for years, deserve the lion's share of credit. If my actions emerge from the gray zone of habit rather than from a fully illuminated act of the will then what I do can't be terribly admirable.

For a philosopher like Kant, Aristotle's conception of moral virtue is unacceptable for just this reason. Genuinely moral action for Kant requires the free will taking full responsibility for itself, a condition that he calls "autonomy."[14] The habitual dishwasher who in working the sponge still hears his mother's voice hardly seems to embody that. Differently stated, for Kant the *Nicomachean Ethics* insufficiently esteems human freedom. A strong bit of evidence for this is the following. Aristotle argues that his conception of moral virtue as the acquisition of good habits is confirmed by what goes on in actual cities: "by inculcating [good] habits in the citizens lawmakers make them good" (1103b3). Indeed, he goes even further when he says, "what the law does not order it forbids" (1138a7).

These statements express a view antithetical to ones we typically hold dear. First, the notion of "making" someone good is anathema to our modern "liberal" (derived from "liberty") sensibilities. Imagine a law that required all citizens to awaken at 6:00 A.M. and have a good breakfast. Imagine further that this law had some teeth; in other words, punishment would be meted out to violators. Even if we were to agree that it is good to awaken early and eat well we would nonetheless condemn such a law as paternalistic, authoritarian, and disrespectful of our autonomy.[15]

Another objection: Aristotle's conception of ethical development, and so of moral behavior, seems to grant undue significance to chance. I chose neither my parents nor my neighbors but they may have exerted great influence upon me. If I had happened to grow up in a section of the city infested with crime I likely would have turned out worse. It is arguable that chance should not be philosophically permitted to play such a prominent role in the moral life.[16]

Aristotle himself raises this very issue when he wonders "whether any human being can be happy as long as he is alive" (1100a10). This strange question (first reported by Herodotus) was posed by Solon, the Athenian statesman of the sixth century. To grasp its import, consider a life like that of Priam, the legendary king of the Trojans. He was a good man possessing great wealth, family, and political power but he suffered catastrophic losses at the end of his life when the Greeks destroyed the city of Troy, killed his sons, and enslaved his wife and daughters. He had lived in the excellent actualization of his capacities until he was old and then his world was shattered through no fault of his own. He was, in short, a victim of terribly bad luck.

On the one hand, even a happy life is susceptible to disastrous interruption. On the other, Aristotle insists that a truly "happy man will never become wretched" (1101a6–7) for he can withstand misfortune better than anyone else. Because happiness is actualization of the *psyche*, it is to a substantial even if not total degree within our own control. But no man can entirely withstand disaster on the order that Priam experienced it. Therefore, Aristotle draws a distinction: being "blessed" (*makarios*: 1101a7) is a condition even superior to being happy for it combines happiness with great good fortune.

If a young man were killed in an accident or by a virus, he could not be counted as entirely happy. This is why Aristotle adds a qualification to his definition of happiness. While it is the actualization of the *psyche* according to excellence it requires in addition "a complete (*teleion*) life" (1098a18). No man is happy until he is dead: even if this is not quite true, Solon's adage is a reminder that human life is precarious and attainment of the highest good, happiness, is not entirely up to us.

Finally, one might accuse Aristotle's position of being internally inconsistent. It begins with the notion that the highest good is *eudaimonia*, which is the actualization of our best potentiality and thus is an achievement that belongs to us rather than a condition that simply "happens" to us (<V.2). This is why, for example, honor cannot qualify as the highest good: "for honor seems to reside more in those who do the honoring than in the one honored, and we suspect that the good is something that belongs to us and is difficult to take away" (1095b24–26). As the example of Priam shows, however, it is not impossible for *eudaimonia* to be taken away even from the truly excellent man.

Aristotle does not contradict himself. Instead he gives voice to the precarious balance that is human life. We work hard to make our lives as good as we can and if we succeed, which is a possibility, we achieve happiness. Because happiness is a result of our own activity it belongs to us and emerges from our characters. Still, its possession is far from ironclad. The moral life is not a crystal-clear equation in which moral worth equals a good will or the performance of a set of requisite actions. It is the murkier affair of living in the world, actualizing human possibilities and suffering defeats beyond our control.[17]

V.5: Moral Evaluation Requires Stories.

Even though it does identify adultery, theft, and murder as unequivocally wrong (1107a11), the *Nicomachean Ethics* generally does not provide guidelines for the moral evaluation of actions or intentions. It is instead, to use contemporary lingo, a "virtue ethics." It takes its bearings from the question "What is human excellence?" or "What sort of person should I aspire to be?" rather than "What should I do?" Furthermore, "moral virtue" as excellence of character is not equivalent to or determinable from the performance of any single action. As Aristotle puts it, "What issues from the virtues is done justly or moderately not only if the act itself has been done justly or moderately. Instead, it requires that the one acting be in a certain condition when he acts. First, he must act knowingly; second, he must choose to act and make the choice for its own sake; third, he must act while being in a stable and unchangeable condition" (1105a28–32).

A group of us are walking on a city street when a beggar approaches asking for money. You pull out your wallet and give him twenty dollars. This looks like an act of generosity. But from this single episode I cannot determine whether you are truly a generous person. Perhaps you just inherited a million dollars and are feeling ridiculously flush. Or perhaps you're trying to make an impression on the rest of us. Are you a generous man? From this one act I cannot not say.

Character abides. It is who we are. To be counted as generous one must act generously through good times and bad. As Aristotle puts it, a virtuous man "must act while being in a stable condition." But there's a problem: how is it possible to identify and know this stable condition in someone else, or even in oneself? Can a person's character ever be accurately grasped?

If I believe that you are generous then I must have witnessed or even benefited from your generosity over a long period of time. I must have many memories of you that I encapsulate under the heading "generous" and be convinced that in the future, even if you have a headache or are broke, you will nonetheless do your best to be generous. Equipped with such a conviction and believing that I know who you are, I can then count on you.

Differently stated, calling you "generous" or "virtuous" requires me somehow to size you up as a whole. This is, however, a precarious venture. I may have long believed that I know you well but then on Thursday you unexpectedly let me down. Your betrayal shook my confidence in my ability not only to know you but other people in general. And then there is the distressing fact that character can change. Recall, for example, that Aristotle paints a bleak picture of those who are very old (<III.6). Generally speaking, he thinks, they are bad tempered, mistrustful, small-minded, cowardly, miserly, bereft of strong desire and hope. They talk repetitively about the past and have no sense of humor. By contrast, young people tend to be impetuous, passionate, trusting, hopeful, and eager for companions. (See *Rhetoric* II.12–13.) Whether these stereotypes are accurate or not, the upshot of this analysis is clear: even if character remains reasonably stable for a long stretch, it is nonetheless subject to serious change.

Recall that a whole is triadically determined because it has a beginning, middle, and end (*telos*). In discussing this earlier (<I.2) several examples were invoked, one of which is particularly apt here: the "narrative whole." Aristotle elucidates this in the *Poetics* by discussing tragedy, but his conclusions can be extended to stories in general. A tragic drama is, he says, an "imitation of an action that is serious, complete (*teleias*) and of a certain magnitude" (1449b25). Later he reformulates: "tragedy is an imitation of an action that is complete and whole (*holês*: 1450b25)." And a "whole" is that which has a "beginning, middle and end." A good tragedy, therefore, must have a unified plot or story (*muthos*). Plot, "the arrangement of the incidents" (1450a5), is an "imitation of the action" (1450a4) and the animating principle or the *psyche* (1450a37) of tragedy as such. Without a unified narrative or plot, a drama is no more than a string of episodes. It is not only a bad or formless piece of work but also a lifeless one. For it is not whole, and life comes in wholes.

To take the measure of a human being is to take stock of her character as a whole. The answer to the question "Is she really generous?" is not found in the report of any single action she performs or a list of such actions. Instead, it requires a story, with a beginning, middle, and end, that knits together the salient events remembered from the past and makes a projection into the future.

A story is a narrative synthesis, not a proof or argument that aspires to certainty. This is one reason why moral philosophers like Kant or Mill, who insist that ethics must achieve the same kind of certainty as the (mathematized) sciences, reject character as the locus of moral worth: it cannot be grasped cleanly. A virtue- or character-based ethics like Aristotle's supplies no rules or algorithms and so it is locked into a level of informality and precariousness. This may be disappointing to some but it shouldn't be. For such is the nature of our lives. Aristotle makes this point when he discusses the level of "precision" (*akribeia*) that ethics, as a philosophical study, can be expected to attain:

> One should not seek for the same level of precision in all subjects. . . . Now, [ethics] studies what is fine and just, a subject that contains a great deal of divergence and disagreement.[18] As a result, it has seemed to some that it is a matter of convention rather than of nature. And what is good also has a great deal of this sort of divergence on account of good things sometimes leading to damaging consequences. For example, some men have been destroyed because of their wealth, while others because of their courage. . . . In general, it is a mark of a well educated man to seek for the level of precision that is appropriate to each kind of subject being studied, and this is determined by the nature of the object being studied. For it is the same sort of mistake to demand merely persuasive arguments from a mathematician as it to demand rigorous demonstrations from one who studies [ethics]. (1094b12–27)[19]

To expect ethical argumentation to achieve the clarity and certainty of mathematical demonstrations is deeply wrong-headed. For the nature of the subject, namely our lives in their practical inflection, is too complex, riddled with contingencies, and subject to interruptions to be suited for such treatment. In response, some thinkers, often called "relativists," believe that moral values are neither objective nor objectively knowable, but instead are simply matters of convention. But relativism is as wrong-headed as a mathematized or algorithmic conception of ethics. Moral virtue is "by nature" and so it is objectively determinable. As a result, moral knowledge is possible. It is not, however, akin to mathematical demonstration. Instead it emerges from the actual experiences of the moral life. And this, as the next section discusses, is "practical wisdom."

Today's ethicists and moral philosophers are engaged in an enterprise Aristotle would barely recognize. They line up and trade arguments, puzzles, and problems about abortion and euthanasia and human rights and saving the elephants. They rarely step back and take stock of life as a whole. They don't tell stories and so they lose sight of life as it is actually lived by real people in the world.

V.6: Smart Moral People Are Better than Dumb Moral People.

Aristotle's *Nicomachean Ethics* begins by establishing that there is a highest good, which is *eudaimonia* or happiness. The next step connects happiness to the human function, which is rational activity. In turn, this generates the definition of happiness as activity of the *psyche* according to excellence. Because there are two forms of rational activity, loosely categorized as "obeying" and "conceiving," there are two forms of excellence or virtue: the moral and the intellectual. To define the former, Aristotle says this: "Virtue is a characteristic (*hexis*) involving choice, consisting in observing the mean relative to us, a mean which has been determined by the sort of reasoning which a man of practical wisdom (*phronimos*) would use to determine it" (1106b36–1107a2).

Moral virtue is a "characteristic." Like our characters it abides and is something we "have." (The Greek *echein,* "to have," is the root of *hexis.* Also, note that "habit" derives from the Latin *habitus*, which is formed from *habere*, "to have.") Furthermore, it involves choice. For only insofar as one's actions are chosen can they be evaluated morally. If, for example, I am constrained to perform an act against my will or do it inadvertently I cannot be held morally responsible for it.

The crux, however, of Aristotle's definition of virtue is contained in the notion of the moral "mean." To explain, he compares it with the arithmetical mean. Both are in between the extremes of "too much" and "too little." The arithmetical mean can be determined by a mechanical decision procedure, or an algorithm. If 2 is one extreme and 10 the other, then the mean is computed by adding them together and dividing by 2. The answer is 6. This procedure is invariant and generates the right answer every time. The moral mean, by contrast, is "relative to us." This does not imply that Aristotle is a "relativist" of the sort mentioned above (<V.5). Instead, it shows that the moral mean is always situated within a particular human context in abstraction, from which it cannot be determined. To return to the example of generosity: assume Bob, who is rich, wants to be generous toward his friend Sue, who is poor. The question is, how should he do so? If he gives her too much Sue may feel belittled by it and then stubbornly refuse the assistance she actually requires. If he gives too little, the amount may not meet her needs. Bob must hit the mean and give just the right amount. But what this is depends upon, is relative to, the situation, which in turn is determined by Sue's circumstances and character. Bob is part of the context as well. If he is exceedingly rich and gives Sue a pittance then he's cheap. But if he were poor and the pittance he gave her were a significant chunk of his income then he would be generous. Someone truly virtuous gives the right amount and he does so for the right reasons, in the right way, and at the right time.

Aristotle analyzes a series of moral virtues, including courage, self-control, generosity, magnificence, gentleness, friendliness, wittiness, and magnanimity, in just such terms. Courage, for instance, is the mean between fear and confidence. If someone feels too much fear in situations that do not merit it, he is a coward. If he feels too little fear in situations that should be genuinely terrifying, he is reckless. "A man is courageous who endures and fears what he should, as he should and when he should, and does so for the right reason, and he is bold in a similar fashion. For a courageous man feels and acts in a way that is worthy and as *logos* would have it" (1115b17–20).

Courage is fearing the right things in the right way and for the right reason but when it comes to explicating what is "right" Aristotle only says that it is somehow determined by *logos* and is what the courageous or virtuous man establishes it to be. Such a definition, a critic might interject, is useless and perhaps even vacuous or circular. On the one hand, this objection is reasonable. Aristotle does not stipulate rules or solve dilemmas or give advice about how to be courageous. Instead, his *Ethics* is closer to a phenomenology of virtue, a letting be seen of what shows itself. And what shows itself to us in ordinary moral experience is that some people actually do get things right. When they do it is because they have hit the mean. The courageous man is afraid, but (virtuously) endures in the face of what is rightly fearful. And the generous man gives in the right way, at the right time, and so on. The question of what is right remains open until someone virtuous actually enters into and illuminates the mean governing a particular situation.

To reiterate: ethics cannot attain the level of precision properly demanded of mathematics. Even if it cannot be determined algorithmically or in advance of the situation as it is actually constituted by particular human beings, knowledge of what is "right" is available, for the mean is "determined by the sort of reasoning which a man of practical wisdom (*phronimos*) would use to determine it." Practical wisdom is one of the five virtues of thought (or intellectual virtues). Like the other four ("science," "intuition," "wisdom," and "craft"), it is a mode of "truthing" (<IV.7). It is unique because in uncovering its truth, in hitting upon the moral mean, it bridges the intellectual and the moral sides of our lives. To explain, Aristotle offers this distinction. There is one part of the rational *psyche*, ". . . by which we theorize (*theôroumen*) those sorts of beings whose principles cannot be other than they are, and there is one by which [we theorize] those whose principles can" (1139a6–8).

In studying the stars the astronomer "theorizes" eternal objects whose motions are necessarily invariable. Similar is the mathematician who studies the formal realities of geometry. In such disciplines the "theorizer" actualizes one side of the rational capacity, which Aristotle here calls the "scientific" (*epistêmonikon*: 1139a12). This capacity, when actualized in an excellent fashion, results in the intellectual virtues of "science," "wisdom," and "intuition" (none of which is discussed here). But human reason can do more than apprehend what is changeless and eternal. It can also "theorize" what is contingent; what is changeable and not locked into the vise of necessity. This is "the calculative" (*logistikon:* 1139a12) side of *logos*, and its function is to deliberate, as I do in trying to figure out how much money I ought to give Sue. If I do this excellently, I have practical wisdom. As Aristotle puts it, "it seems to be characteristic of the *phronimos,* the man of practical wisdom, to be able to deliberate in a fine manner about what is good and advantageous" (1140a25–27). Those with practical wisdom, "a practical, rational characteristic that 'truths' the human good, . . . are able to theorize what is good both for themselves and for human beings" (1140b9).

Because it is inextricably located within a context constituted by actual human beings, practical wisdom must not only comprehend universals—such as "adultery is wrong"—but "it must also recognize particulars; for it is practical and action (*praxis*) is always particularized" (1141b15–16). The *phronimos* accurately sizes up and then navigates effectively through the particulars of a situation. This notion of a "truthing" or knowledge whose object is particular seems nearly oxymoronic. After all, in the developmental scheme presented in *Metaphysics* I.1, knowledge emerges and is differentiated from experience precisely on the grounds that it apprehends "universals" (980b16). Practical wisdom, however, complicates this scheme for it is an ability to be sensitive to, to sniff out, to see the "ultimate particular" (*to eschaton*: 1142a26). As the metaphors suggest, it is like perception, which is of particulars and is also a kind of truthing. The *phronimos* sees, rather than demonstrates or proves, what is best to do in a given situation.

The *phronimos*, however, does more than just "see." As Aristotle puts it, "it is not possible to be a *phronimos* without moral virtue" (1144b32). Practical wisdom thus requires and implies virtuous action. If you know that you should give Sue twenty dollars but fail to do so then you don't really have it. For even though it is an intellectual virtue and thus does the work of truthing, practical wisdom is inseparable from moral virtue, which is a "characteristic" or disposition to act with an eye toward the moral mean. It bridges the moral and intellectual sides of our lives. Aristotle explains how it does so: "virtue makes the mark at which one aims correct, but practical wisdom the means towards that aim" (1144a8). A decent human being tries to do what is best but may well fail. Trying your hardest to be good to Sue you may give her too much money and thereby damage both her life and yours. In order to get it right, you have to be more than just decent and well-intentioned; you have to be smart and your *logos* has to do a good job.

These remarks generate an important distinction. There is "natural" virtue, which belongs to those who are decent and thus have the disposition or consistent desire to do what is best, and there is "strict" or "authoritative" (*kuria*: 1144b16) virtue. The latter is achieved only by those who are both decent and smart because "it is clear from what has been said that it is not possible to be good in the authoritative sense without practical wisdom" (1144a30–31). In this regard, recall Aristotle's citation of Hesiod. "The man is all-best who himself works out every problem." Second best is he who actualizes the "obeying" side and thus "follows one who speaks well." He is disposed to act in the right way but cannot think through the particulars as well as the first. Aristotle proposes a similar ranking. Someone decent whose moral virtue is "natural" aims for the mean but may not be smart enough to determine the right steps needed in order to achieve it. He is certainly better than the vicious man who does not even try to be good.[20] But moral virtue in the most authoritative sense is found only in someone who not only aims for and tries to do what is good but knows what to do in order to achieve it. "For moral virtue determines the end and practical wisdom makes us do what leads to the attainment of that end (*ta pros to telos*: 1145a5)." Translated into political terms, it becomes clear who should be in charge: "we say that the fine ruler is good and has practical wisdom, while the fine citizen need not be practically wise" (*Politics* 1277a14–16).

To clarify further: it is possible for a bad guy to be "clever" and able to deliberate well about how to achieve his goals. But "cleverness" (*Nicomachean Ethics* 1144a24) is just a component of practical wisdom, and not equivalent to it. For practical wisdom requires moral virtue. It is thus something like virtuous street smarts, an ability to navigate the particulars well in the effort to achieve a worthy goal.

Aristotle is no egalitarian: he does not believe that all human beings, even virtuous ones, are morally equal. As such, his views conflict with some that we hold dear. Consider what Kant has to say: "neither science nor philosophy is needed in order to know what one must do to be honest and good, and even wise and virtuous. . . . The most extraordinary thing is that ordinary understanding . . . may have just as good a hope of hitting the mark as that which any philosopher may promise himself."[21] For Kant, morality essentially requires a free act of the will and when it comes to this smart people have no advantage whatsoever. As a result, moral worth is an achievement in principle available to all human beings. Even though human beings have different strengths and weaknesses and so can be ranked in a variety of ways, when it comes to being moral all men are in fact "created equal."

Kant's moral theory is the culmination of a long tradition of Christian ethics. In this view, God the Father created the earth and all its creatures. From the beginning human beings arrived on a level field for all are children of God. God lovingly gave his only son to humanity and thereby posed for human beings their single greatest challenge; namely, to be open to His love. As Saint Augustine expressed in great detail in his *Confessions*, what is required above all is a "conversion" (from *vertere*, "to turn"). Human beings must, to save their souls, turn away from the temporal world and toward God and doing so is ultimately the core of the best attainable life here on earth. What is required, therefore, is a good will, a good heart, not a strong intellect. Augustine himself was a great thinker but reasoning alone proved incapable of fueling his own conversion. For that he had to open his heart to God's love, to "turn," and this finally was an act of the will. One cannot reason one's way onto the path toward God.

The *Gospel of Matthew* expresses the same point: "truly I say to you, unless you turn and become like children, you will never enter the kingdom of heaven" (XVIII.3). What is required is not street smarts but a pure openness, like that of a child, to the love of God. Augustine nods to this notion by reporting that it was by hearing a child's voice that he was finally led to his own conversion. All people are potentially childlike. Hence, all are eligible to enter the kingdom of heaven.

When this view was philosophically developed in the seventeenth century, John Locke claimed that natural law "teaches all mankind, who will but consult it, that being all equal and independent, no one ought to harm another in his life, health, liberty or possessions; for men being all the workmanship of one omnipotent and infinitely wise maker . . . there cannot be supposed any such subordination among us, that may authorize us to destroy one another."[22]

Aristotle would find these views ludicrous. For him, children are not yet fully rational and are, at best, potential adults, and so cannot possibly guide us to salvation. Similarly, being smart is better than being dumb and so "authoritative" is superior to "natural" virtue. Those with practical wisdom should run the show.

Aristotle's ranking of lives does not stop with his distinction between the *phronimos* and those with merely natural virtue. It would be absurd, he says, if someone were to construe practical wisdom as "the most serious" of all forms of knowledge. This would be true "only if human being were the best of all things in the world" (1141a20–22) and it is not. The heavenly bodies, for example, are composed of a material that "is more divine than and prior to" the four elements found on earth. Because in knowing (as in perceiving and even as in eating) the *psyche* becomes identical with its object (<IV.3, IV.5), one who knows the heavenly bodies thereby achieves a higher form of knowledge and simply is higher than one who knows human affairs. "Theoretical wisdom" is thus superior to "practical wisdom." But in trying to determine what this is and what its relationship to the altogether human virtue of the *phronimos* is we enter into the notorious problem that haunts readers of the *Nicomachean Ethics*. Is its ending, with its extraordinary praise of the theoretical life, consistent with what preceded it? How, if at all, is the divine life of thought connected to ordinary human, to moral, life? What finally is the relationship between theory and practice?

V.7: Lack-of-Leisure Is for the Sake of Leisure.

In Book X.7 of the *Nicomachean Ethics*, Aristotle says that if happiness is activity according to excellence, it is reasonable to assume that "complete (*teleia*) happiness" is the actualization of the "supreme" virtue, which in turn is the work of what is best in us, namely "mind" (1177a17–20). He describes a life spent in such work as "theoretical" and argues that it is the best available to human beings (1177a17–20). Most strikingly, he says this: "Such a life would be superior to a human life. For it is not as a human being that a man would live it but insofar as something divine belongs to him. This differs from the composite to the same degree that the actualization of [the mind] differs from the other virtue" (1177b26–29).

The merely human life is spent interacting with fellow human beings and is thus conditioned by our "composite" or bodily nature. Then there is the divine life of the mind. Unlike the ranking between those who are naturally virtuous and those who, because they have practical wisdom, are virtuous in the "strict" sense, this one cannot as easily be construed in developmental terms. A child may start on the path of virtue by simply obeying his elders and then mature to the point where he figures out what he is doing and why. This progression represents the most natural of all motions or changes; namely, the organic development of an animal as it proceeds toward its *telos*. But when it comes to the theoretical life, the ascent seems to culminate in a leap, one that echoes *On the Psyche* III.5, where in apparent departure from his otherwise thoroughly naturalistic account of the *psyche* (understood as the form of an organic body potentially having life) the active mind is said to be eternal, separate, and immortal.

Just as Aristotle's description of active mind embarrasses some of his contemporary readers, so too do his remarks in the *Nicomachean Ethics* X.7–8 about the theoretical life upset a reader like Martha Nussbaum. By her lights they are "at odds with the general anthropocentrism of [his] ethical method. . . . In the other books of the [*Ethics*], activities according to the excellences of character are explicitly said to be valuable or choice worthy for their own sake. It is part of the definition of excellent activity, indeed, that it be chosen for its own sake."[23] In Book X, by contrast, such activities are downgraded as merely human. For Nussbaum this represents a betrayal of what is best about the *Ethics,* namely its meticulous fidelity to and generosity toward the virtues of ordinary human life. After all, Aristotle esteems, at least to some degree, even a decent life of habitually performed activities.[24] But in Book X such activity pales in comparison with the divine life of the mind. In fact, Aristotle seems to treat moral virtue condescendingly by calling it "the other virtue" and "secondary" (1178a9–10). He explains why:

> For we engage in just and courageous actions, and all the rest that are morally virtuous, in interaction with one another. In keeping our agreements and in providing services to one another and in all such actions, as well as in our emotions, we observe what is appropriate in each case. And all of these appear to be human. Some of these seem to emerge from our bodily natures, and the virtue of character seems in many ways to be intertwined with our emotions . . . moral virtues are bound up with the emotions and thus concern our composite nature. And the virtues of the composite are human. Thus, the life lived according to these virtues and the happiness attainable within them is also human. By contrast, the virtue of the mind is separate. (1178a10–22)

Nussbaum is so upset by these remarks that she finally judges these sections of the *Ethics* to be "incompatible" with the rest of the book.[25] Aristotle, however, is aware that his remarks are potentially upsetting for he imagines and then rebuts a critic: "One should not heed those who recommend that a human being should only think (*phronein*) about human things or say that a mortal should think mortal thoughts alone. Instead, to the extent that it is possible one ought to be immortal and do everything with an eye towards living according to what is best within ourselves. . . . And for a human being this is a life lived according to mind and it is this that is especially human. Therefore, such a life will be happiest of all" (1177b31–1178a8).[26]

The most fully human life is one spent in the effort to become immortal, to be human. For the work of the mind is somehow "separate" from our bodies and emotions and all that pervades our temporal existence. As such, the praise it receives here seems, just as Nussbaum thinks, to abandon the anthropocentric and thoroughly human virtues Aristotle has apparently championed throughout the *Nicomachean Ethics.*

This, the notorious dilemma, can be resolved. Human beings regularly "separate" themselves from themselves. Indeed, the desire as well as the capacity to leap beyond the temporal, bodily confines of our own mortality is woven into the very fabric of being human. And it is not confined to the hyper-intellectual urge to "theorize." In fact, what appears to be an unprecedented and disturbing leap into the divine at the end of the *Ethics* is actually in keeping with and a culmination of what has been described throughout the treatise.

To elaborate, first consider a theme Aristotle takes up with surprisingly frequency: leisure (<II.5). Apparently innocuous, it actually offers a clue as to how the divine, the eternal, the extraordinary enters into even the most mundane of human lives.

"It seems that happiness is in leisure. For we endure the lack-of-leisure in order that we may enjoy leisure" (1177b4–5). A single Greek word is translated here as "we endure lack-of-leisure: *ascholoumetha.* More common translations include "being busy," "we accept trouble," "we busy ourselves," all of which obscure the fact that the Greek verb is formed by the "alpha-privative" and *scholazein*, "to be at leisure."[27] This linguistic point is significant because it suggests that "being busy" is a deprivation: it is the absence of leisure, which in turn is the genuinely positive or prior condition.

This reverses the order to which we are more accustomed. For us, leisure is an afterthought that follows the serious business of work or industry, and its best benefit is that it helps us to return to the office refreshed. The Greek words *ascholazein* and *scholazein,* by contrast, take "busyness" down a notch.

First and foremost, leisure is free time during which, unconstrained by external demands, we do just what we want. For healthy, normal people, such time is not idled away in doing nothing. Instead, it is occupied by activities chosen for their own sake. For many people, perhaps most, these become times of play, of *paidia* (a word derived from *pais*, "child"). In play, we aim to achieve no tangible benefit; we're just having fun. Strikingly, play is the subject of Book X.6 of the *Nicomachean Ethics.*

Aristotle begins this chapter by reminding the reader that happiness is an activity chosen for the sake of itself, and that no benefit or product results from it. This is why he must address the "pleasures of play" (1177b9), for it too is chosen precisely for itself. Aristotle, however, quickly dismisses play as unbecoming for a serious man and thus hardly a candidate for the best form of life or happiness. He associates it with powerful rulers who can afford to buy entertainment for themselves, and identifies it as a species of bodily pleasure. In fact, he argues, it would be absurd and childish if the *telos* of all our hard work and suffering were for the sake of play (*paidia*). Consequently, he agrees with Anacharsis, who said, "play in order that you might be serious" (1176b33).

Given this dismissal it is all the more striking that Aristotle bothers to discuss play at all. He does so because the player plays without an eye toward external reward and so her activity is at least isomorphic with genuine happiness. But even more important, because it occurs during and so is a manifestation of leisure it testifies to a fundamental human possibility: that of escaping the confines of temporality.

Play absorbs the player, for she is fully concentrated on the action at hand (<II.5). In an athletic competition, for example, she plays on a court or field cordoned off from the rest of the world. Oblivious to anything going on beyond the limits of the play space she is untroubled by the past and does not worry about the responsibilities that would drive her toward the future. As a result, as far as is humanly possible she is immersed in the present and separated from the "busyness," the *ascholia,* the temporal flow of daily life. What play thereby affords is a taste of eternity, and so a touch of the divine. Far from being some sort of mystical state, this is no more than a description of the spatial and temporal phenomenon of playing. The player still has a body, is still in the city, but because she is so fully immersed in her play, is simultaneously removed as well.[28]

To elaborate, recall the earlier discussion of pleasure (<III.5). Like happiness and play it is enjoyed for itself and so Aristotle also includes a discussion of it in Book X of the *Nicomachean Ethics.* Its basic structural feature is that it is experienced as a whole. Unlike a process (*kinesis*) such as building a house, which requires a series of steps each of which is incomplete in itself and which culminate in a product that terminates the process, pleasure, like seeing, is a self-contained activity that is "complete at every moment" (1174b3–4). If building a house is a change or motion that must take place "in time" (1174a19), pleasure, again like seeing, is an undivided *energeia* that "is something whole and is in the moment." All absorbing, pleasure takes us out of the flow, is not "in time" (1174b8–9). This does not mean that the temporal duration of a pleasurable experience cannot be measured, for of course it can. From inside the experience, however, Aristotle

is certainly right. For if I am really feeling pleasure, I do not look at the clock at all and so am unaware of the passage of time. Each moment of the massage, in which I'm lost, is complete.

Like pleasure, play is all absorbing. Fully actualized, the athlete loses touch with the passage of time. While the duration of a game can be measured in hours and minutes, and so while the athlete does not literally leap out of the flow of time, her actions are so concentrated, so thoroughly engaged in only for the sake of themselves, that it is experienced this way.

Even if Aristotle is dismissive of play it nonetheless is critical insofar as it signals an opening into leisure. And leisure is a necessary condition of theoretical activity; of philosophy itself. In fact, Aristotle claims that "those forms of knowledge that aimed for neither pleasure nor the necessities of life were discovered first of all in those places where they had leisure" (*Metaphysics* 981b21–23). His example is the priestly caste in Egypt where, he believes, the mathematical arts originated. Leisure is required in order for men first to feel and then to respond the wonder they experience at the world. "For it is on account of wonder that human beings both now and at the beginning began to philosophize" (982b12). Only when free from responsibility and distraction can someone afford to be open to and amazed by the world, which beckons us with its beauty, order, and promise of intelligibility.

An etymological fact that today is more than curious: the root of the English word "school" is *scholê*, "leisure." On the one hand, this should now make thorough sense from an Aristotelian perspective. From our own, however, it is preposterous, for schools have become vocational training grounds, corporate incubators, institutions where *ascholia* rules. There is no time left for leisure, for wonder, for the pleasure of thought.[29] Even our play spaces, our "gyms," have been taken away from us. They have become workout centers whose inhabitants pressure themselves to achieve specific goals. Strapped to machines and measuring devices, they industriously seek to lose weight, elevate heart rates, increase muscle mass and longevity. Now it's all work, all the time. Even our children have been subjected to this sort of deprivation, for they now too are chained to "play dates," an oxymoronic phrase if ever there was one.

To sum up: in ordinary and mundane moments of pleasure or play, in times of leisure, it is possible to escape the temporal and touch however briefly upon the eternal. At the conclusion of the *Nicomachean Ethics*, when he describes theoretical activity as divine, Aristotle is thus not hawking supernatural pap. Instead, and as usual, his feet are planted firmly on the ground.

V.8: *Theôria* Is Not "Contemplation."

This section focuses on a single linguistic point that reinforces the conclusions of the previous section. The Greek word *theôria* is usually, but misleadingly, translated as "contemplation." This term dates back to the Latin *contemplare,* which captures with etymological precision the Greek *theôrein*: the base meaning of both is "to look at or gaze upon." But "contemplate" in English sounds archaic and highfalutin, and is a word that can even carry spiritual overtones. This is unfortunate, for its meaning in Aristotle's Greek is actually quite mundane and is used throughout his writings. In *Ethics* X.7–8 the life spent in *theôria* is described as "divine" and so the temptation to use "contemplation" is strong. But it should be resisted.[30]

Even though Aristotle regularly uses *theôrein* to name the very activity in which he is engaged, he says next to nothing explicitly about *theôria.* As Trond Eriksen puts it, he "has no clear-cut conception of *theôria.*"[31] Nonetheless, he does provide clues. Most important, it is regularly characterized as the actualization of knowledge.[32] Recall, for example, that the *psyche* is defined as the "actuality" (*entelecheia*) of a natural body potentially having life (*On the Psyche* 412a27–28). "Actuality," however, has two senses, and the example of knowing is invoked in order to illustrate. The first sense is having but not using knowledge (*epistêmê*: 412a10); the second is *theôrein* (412a10–11), which means using or being "actively working with" (*energein*: 412a26) the knowledge one has.[33] So, for instance, I "have" knowledge of arithmetic, but I'm not solving a problem right now.[34] When actually doing a computation, say by adding 369 and 1215, I am engaged in *theôrein;* I am, to risk a word that sounds a bit odd, "theorizing."

Unfortunately this description of *theôrein is* ambiguous for it does not clarify what it means to use or activate knowledge of arithmetic. Is this really best exemplified, as just suggested, by the task of adding 369 and 1215? Or is theorizing more like gazing at a truth, such as 7 + 5 = 12, that we already know and that is immediately recognizable? The latter is supported by a statement found in the *Metaphysics*: "this 'A' that the man knowing his letters theorizes is an 'A' " (1087a20). Richard Kraut, along with most commentators, endorses this understanding of *theôria,* which he describes as "an activity that goes on whenever one brings certain truths to mind. . . . The teacher who is preparing lectures . . . is consciously considering truths that he has already come to understand, and so he is contemplating." He continues: "anyone who is actively reflecting on any proposition, whatever its content, may be loosely said to be engaged in *theoria* with respect to that proposition."[35]

Kraut's "loosely" and his ambiguous phrase "actively reflecting on" are apt, for the matter remains unclear. The notion that "looking at" the true sentence, 7 + 5 = 12, best captures the act of "using" knowledge of arithmetic doesn't quite ring true, for a more obvious example would be working through and solving the equation 369 + 1215 = X. Nonetheless, another remark Aristotle makes in the *Nicomachean Ethics* seems to support the 7 + 5 = 12 example. Arguing that the theoretical life is the most pleasant, he says that it is "reasonable that the way of life of those who know is more pleasant than of those who seek" (1177a26–27). This leads Kraut to assert that *theoria* "is not the activity of searching for the truth within some field, but rather a process of reflection on a system of truths already discovered."[36] Again, he does not explain what "reflection" means.

Another approach toward clarifying what *theoria* as actualization of knowledge means is suggested by this statement: "For this [theoretical] activity is supreme since mind is supreme of that which is in us, and of knowable objects, those of mind are supreme" (1177a19–21). This description might apply to necessary, eternal, and divine substances such as the stars.[37] In other words, to quote Kraut again, "the *theoria* Aristotle is talking about in X.7–8 . . . is the activation of theoretical wisdom." It is "exalted," he says, and represents "the activity of the understanding one has achieved when one has acquired *sophia*, theoretical wisdom; that is, the virtue described in *Nicomachean Ethics* VI.7, which is associated with thinkers like Anaxagoras and Thales who know extraordinary, amazing, difficult and divine things."[38] Andrea Nightingale (and most commentators) agree: "Aristotle," she says, "tends to associate *theoria* with supreme knowledge of the highest things."[39] As Amelie Rorty puts it, "the conditions for something's being contemplated is that it be necessary, unchanging, eternal."[40]

This conception of *theoria* might also be supported by the description of the motionless mover in the *Metaphysics*. In order to cause the eternal rotation of the heavenly bodies it must itself be eternal as well as ceaselessly "being in actuality" (1072b8). Its "mode of activity" (1072b14), in which it is permanently and continuously engaged, is like the best and the most pleasurable that we experience, albeit for a short time only. And this is thinking. It is not, however, just any sort of thinking. Instead, it is a "thinking that with respect to itself is of an intelligible object that is best with respect to itself; and maximalized thinking is of that which is maximally best" (1072b18–19). It engages in "*theoria,* which is the most pleasant and best" (1072b24) form of activity.

This passage reiterates the connection between *theoria* and actualization, and also seems to "exalt" it in precisely the way Kraut, Nightingale, and Rorty recommend. It is the activity of "the divine" (1072b25), as it thinks the maximally intelligible, the highest or "best" (1074b34) object, which is eventually described simply as "itself" (1074b33). Hence, the divine is famously called the "thinking of thinking" (1074b34).

This sketch sheds only a bit of light on what *theoria* is—it is what the divine mind does as it thinks itself—but it does suggest an answer to the question posed above: is *theôrein* understood as the actualization of one's knowledge of arithmetic, better exemplified in the "contemplation" of the sentence 7 + 5 = 12, or in the working through of the equation 369 + 1215 = X? Because motion or change is "the actualization of what is potentially, insofar as it is potentially" (*Physics* 201a12), and because the eternally actualized divine partakes in no bit of potentiality, it cannot move or change. As a result, it cannot change from a state of not knowing the answer to 369 + 1215 to knowing it. It must know it immediately. The divine mind thus seems to "contemplate" the solution to even the most complex arithmetic problems as easily as we see that 7 + 5 = 12.

As inviting as the above is, it isn't the whole story. For the exalted view of *theoria* as an immediate and maximally actualized apprehension of the highest intelligible object (that is necessary and eternal) is complicated by a passage cited earlier (<IV.7): "Let there be two aspects of the *psyche* that have reason. One is that by which we theorize those sorts of beings whose principles cannot be otherwise. The other is that by which [we theorize] those which can" (1139a6–8).

The second use of "theorize" (*theôroumen*) is implicit but unmistakable. Practical reason is a capacity to apprehend, to see accurately, to *theorize* a contingent state of affairs. (It is described as kind of perception at 1143b5 and elsewhere.) For this reason, a commentator like Rorty is mistaken when she says that to be "contemplated" an object must "be necessary, unchanging, eternal." She ignores the implicit use of the verb *theôrein*, which clearly suggests that there is some sort of "theorizing" of the contingent.

In this vein, consider how Aristotle begins his treatment of practical wisdom: "let us consider practical wisdom in the following way: by theorizing those whom we say are practically wise" (1140a24–25). A bit later he mentions the famous Athenian statesman Pericles: "We believe that Pericles and men like him are men of practical wisdom because they are able to theorize what is good both for themselves and for human beings" (1140b8–10).

Two senses of *theôrein* are at work in these passages. The first expresses the activity of the author and reader of the *Nicomachean Ethics* themselves:

we must "theorize," take a good look at, those men we call practically wise. The second expresses the activity at which Pericles excelled: in exercising practical wisdom he was able to theorize, to see, what was good. As Gabriel Richardson Lear puts it, such cognitive activity "is a sort of contemplation in action."[41] Pericles was able to navigate effectively through the particular circumstances that confronted him, and to do so with moral virtue. Clearly, in neither of these two cases is *theôrein* limited to "contemplation" understood as an immediate recognition of eternal and immutable substances. For this reason, Rorty is again mistaken in saying "that men like Pericles are thought to possess practical wisdom because they have contemplative understanding of what is good." For her, Pericles engages in *theôria* only because he contemplates the species "Humanity."[42] The passage, however, invites a wider, more mundane conception of theorizing.

Finally, consider this passage from Aristotle's discussion of "moral weakness" in the *Nicomachean Ethics*: "We talk about knowing in two ways: for both the one who has but is not using his knowledge and the one who is using it are said to know. There is a difference between someone who has knowledge of what he ought not to do but is not theorizing it and someone who theorizes it" (1146b31–34).

Aristotle concludes that the person who is "theorizing," fully actualizing, his knowledge that he should not do X, will not do X. Moral weakness, whereby one knows what he should do but fails to do it, "does not seem to occur in the presence of knowledge in the strict (*kuriôs*) sense" (1147b15–16), for such knowledge has become part of the knower; it has "grown into him" (1147a22). By contrast, the person who merely "has" a bit of moral knowledge and so can utter the sentence "I know I should not do X," but who, when overcome by desire, is unable to actualize it fully, might well do X. He is "not theorizing." Again, this sense of the word is (to use Kraut's word) neither "exalted" nor captured well by the English "contemplation."

Kraut and Nightingale would respond to the above by correctly noting that Aristotle regularly uses critical terms in both a narrow or technical and a broad sense. For example, he states that "if it is necessary to speak precisely and not just to use words," then *epistêmê* is restricted to knowledge whose objects exist "by necessity" (1139b19); in other words, it is "demonstrative science." By contrast, at the beginning of the *Nicomachean Ethics* he mentions medicine, navigation, generalship, and economics, all of which he later describes as kinds of "knowledge" (1094a18.)[43] In a similar fashion, in *Posterior Analytics* II.19 "mind" is limited to apprehension of the first principles (*archai*) of demonstrative science, whereas in *On the Psyche* it is characterized broadly as "that by which the *psyche* thinks (*phronei*) and judges" (429a23).

Nightingale maintains that this same pattern applies to his use of *theôrein.* "Aristotle often uses the verb *theôrein* to signify 'seeing' or 'observing' in the most general sense, and occasionally use the noun *theôria* to identify any sort of observation or investigation." Kraut agrees: "*Theoria* . . . does not always designate the activity in which one exercises theoretical wisdom. One can be said to be engaged in *theoria* whenever one closely observes or studies something—whatever that something is." Nonetheless, both he and Nightingale insist that the *theôria* Aristotle is talking about in X.7–8 is not the study of just any objects or truths. It is the "activation of theoretical wisdom."[44] It is *theôria* in the narrow or "exalted," sense, and for them the word "contemplation" fits it well.

These commentators have discounted the possible philosophical connection between Aristotle's ubiquitous use of inflections of the verb *theôrein,* whose meanings are quite mundane, and its appearance as a noun, where its meaning will sometimes, but not always, be more "exalted." If this connection can be established, then even the theoretical activity described in *Nicomachean Ethics* X.7–8 may not be as radically separate from ordinary forms of thinking and knowing as commentators tend to believe.[45] Most important, there is a philosophical basis underlying this connection. What differentiates the intellectual work of a Pericles from the "divine" thinker described in X.7–8 is not the nature of the activity itself—both are theoretical—but the nature of the object studied. To explain, turn to the *Metaphysics.*

Aristotle states that physics is a form of "theoretical" knowledge (*theoretikê epistêmê*: 1025b26). It is so because it is neither a practical (*praktikê*) nor a productive (*poiêtikê*) form of knowledge (or of "thought," *dianoia*: 1025b25). In turn, this is because of the "kind of being that it happens to be about"; in other words, its object. Productive knowledge is about "things produced," and these have their *archê,* their first principle or origin, in the producer. The object of practical knowledge is "things done," and their origin is in the rational choice of the doer. By contrast, the object of physics is natural beings whose origin of change and rest is in themselves (*Physics* 192b12), not in an external human agent. Without here explaining why, Aristotle assumes that there are only these three forms of knowledge. (He does the same at *Topics* 145a15.)[46] Therefore, he concludes, physics must be theoretical.

Three features of knowledge in general emerge from this succinct argument:

(1) Knowledge has an "about something" structure. The subject has an object; for example, physics studies that kind of being that has the origin of motion and rest in itself (and as Aristotle goes on to explain, is not separable from matter). This structure characterizes all three forms of knowledge. Indeed, it even characterizes "metaphysics." Rather than "circumscribing" (*Metaphysics* 1025b8) some specific kind of being, it is "about being simply, i.e., qua being." Similarly, at *Topics* 145a14 Aristotle characterizes all three kinds of knowledge as being "relative to something"; namely, their objects.

(2) As a consequence of (1), while the three adjectives—"theoretical," "practical," and "productive"—literally modify the noun *dianoia* at 1025b26 (or *epistêmê* at *Topics* 145a15), they are actually better construed as modifying the object of the three forms of knowledge. "Practical" in the phrase "practical knowledge" describes a kind of being; the rationally chosen actions of human beings. "Productive" describes another kind: things that are produced by human beings. Similarly, "theoretical" also names a kind of being. This one is illustrated by the three examples of mathematics, physics, and theology (1026a20), all of which have objects that are independent of human intention and so "cannot hold otherwise" or are "necessary."

(3) An important consequence of (2), unstated in this passage but frequent elsewhere, is that the goals of the three forms of knowledge are different. When it comes to practical knowledge, Aristotle says this: "The present inquiry is not for the sake of theory (*theôria*) as are the others. For we investigate not in order that we might know what virtue is, but in order that we might become good, since otherwise there would be no benefit to it" (1103b26–29).

The goal of theoretical knowledge "is the truth, while of practical [knowledge] it is action" (*ergon*: *Metaphysics* 993b20–21). The goal of productive knowledge, or, as it is officially designated in the *Nicomachean Ethics*, "art" (*technê*: 1140a10), "is something other than the producing" (1140b6); it is the well-made object. Aristotle takes pains to differentiate this from practical knowledge.

> When it comes to the arts and the virtues the situation is not similar. For the things that come to be from the arts contain their merit in themselves. It is sufficient if they come to be having this quality. By contrast, the things that come from the virtues are not done justly or moderately if they are of this quality, but only if the one doing is in a particular condition: first, if he knows what he is doing; second, if he rationally chooses

> the action; third, if he acts from a firm disposition that's hard to budge. (1105a26–33)

The product of an art speaks for itself and so it doesn't matter if the producer is a bad guy. By contrast, when it comes to practical knowledge, the action does not speak for itself. Simply performing a good deed does not make someone good. For that, one must have a virtuous character.

What connects practical and productive knowledge is the region of being they look at or study: namely, that which is constituted by human agency and is therefore contingent. As a result, those who possess these forms of knowledge can alter the object about which they know. After all, the student of ethics is, in essence, studying himself (qua political being), and the student of productive knowledge may be able to write better tragedies after reading the *Poetics*. By contrast, the objects of mathematics, physics, and theology either have their origin of motion and rest in themselves, and so cannot be altered by human intervention, or are immutable. The only change such knowledge can effect, therefore, is in the knower, not in the object. For this reason such knowledge "alone seems to be liked because of itself" (1177b1), rather than for any external benefit it might bring.

Two other attributes distinguish the various forms of knowledge: their precision and their rank. To cite a crucial passage once again: "In general, it is a mark of a well educated man to seek the level of precision that is appropriate to each kind of subject being studied, and this is determined by the nature of the object being studied. For it is the same sort of mistake to demand merely persuasive arguments from a mathematician as it to demand rigorous demonstrations from ethics" (1094b23–27).

Because of the nature of its object, namely abstract magnitudes, mathematics can achieve a high level of precision. Ethics, by contrast, is about human beings in their capacity to persuade and be persuaded. Here there are variation and contingency from which the study cannot abstract. Hence, only a rather low level of precision is possible.

When Aristotle discusses the intellectual virtues in the *Nicomachean Ethics*, he insists that "practical wisdom" should be ranked lower than wisdom, which studies the "most honorable things." It would be absurd, he says, if someone were to construe practical wisdom as "the most serious" of all forms of knowledge. This it would be "only if human being were the best of all things in the world" (1141a20–22), which it is not. The heavenly bodies, for example, are composed of a material more divine than and prior to the four elements of the sub-lunar world.

To sum up: despite the fact that they are ranked differently, attain different levels of precision, and even have different goals, the theoretical, practical, and productive forms of knowledge share a basic feature: *they are all theoretical.* They are a looking at, a cognitive apprehension of, some region of the world. They are a taking up of different kinds of beings that present themselves to the discerning mind. Ericksen is therefore quite right in saying that *theoria* need not be "tied to special objects."[47] To put this point imagistically, Pericles and the theoretical man described at the end of the *Nicomachean Ethics* are both active "lookers." One is looking straight ahead at the affairs of fellow citizens, while the other may be looking upward at the stars, but both are hard at work looking. To put this point linguistically, the fact that Aristotle uses inflections of the verb *theôrein* throughout his corpus, regardless of whether the treatise is theoretical, productive, or practical, is meaningful, for it reflects the fact that the cognitive activity at work throughout all his treatises is theoretical.

Theorizing is a pervasive human activity. Aristotle suggests as much when he famously begins the *Metaphysics* with the line "all human beings by nature strive to know," and then immediately offers as evidence for this the fact that "human beings enjoy the senses for their own sake, and the sense of sight above all the other senses. . . . This is because the sense of sight makes us know things and reveals many distinctions" (980a22–26). Recalling the original meaning of *theôrein* as "to look at," we might venture that human being is by nature theoretical. We are cognitive animals who look at the world, work hard to see it as it is, and then talk about it. This holds true whether what we are looking at is our fellow human beings, or the stars. In this regard consider the following passage: "For it belongs to the same capacity both to see the true and to see what is like the true, and at the same time humans have a sufficient natural disposition with respect to the true and hit upon the truth more often than not" (*Rhetoric* 1355a7–10).

We can see things for what they really are. Furthermore, as discussed above (<IV.6), because ordinary language "symbolizes" those "mental affections" that are "likenesses" of beings in the world, it is capable of generating a truthful *logos,* a "theory," about the world. As such, we are theoretical by nature whether we "truth" a practical situation or the stars. For these reasons, then, the "divine" *theoria* praised at the end of the *Nicomachean Ethics* is anything but special. It is the fundamental activity of being human, albeit undertaken at the highest possible level.

This link between the exalted and mundane senses of *theôrein* can be discovered even in the description of the motionless mover whose *theôria* is "the thinking of thinking." "Since its actualization is pleasure, its mode of being, which it engages in forever, is like that which is best for us during a short time. (For us this would be impossible.) And on account of this wakefulness, perception, thinking are most pleasurable, and hopes and memories are as well" (*Metaphysics* 1072b14–18).

The active pleasure of the divine is like what we experience, if only temporarily, when we are awake, perceiving, and thinking. Furthermore, remember this about pleasure: rather than being a *kinesis* or process (like building or learning) whose end result is distinct from it, it is more like an *energeia* such as seeing, which "seems to be complete at every moment and it lacks nothing that, coming to be later, will complete its form." The experience of pleasure is therefore "not in time" (1174b8–17). Such timelessness, however, is nothing supernatural. It is, instead, an intrinsic feature of our lived experience that occurs when we are immersed in hard work (or even play). Therefore, when at the conclusion of the *Nicomachean Ethics* Aristotle praises the theoretical life as divine, he does not transform it into some sort of otherworldly achievement, for whether we are grappling with a complex equation, trying to figure out how to help a friend, studying the stars or Being as Being, or simply contemplating the fact that 7 + 5 = 12, we are engaged in *theoria*. And immersed in this activity that completes our natures, we are separated from the petty pace of daily time and briefly touch upon the eternal.

Three critical moments in Aristotle's work threaten to wreck havoc with his otherwise thorough naturalism. In *On the Psyche,* after having treated the *psyche* as "life-force" and the actuality of an organism, Aristotle seems to lapse into metaphysical dualism or supernatural fancy when he says of active mind that it is separate, immortal, and eternal. Second, after the sober conceptual work of the central "ontological" section of the *Metaphysics*—whose subjects include substance, form, and essence—he may seem to leap toward the heavens when he theologizes and runs rapturously to a god that is separate, completely actual, and eternal. Finally, the same pattern obtains in the *Nicomachean Ethics.* After meticulously articulating the practical or human virtues, he again seems to jump out of his skin by praising the divine life of theory and bidding farewell to the world of bodies, emotions, contracts, friendship, courage, generosity, and cities.

These notorious passages have produced a considerable measure of "separation anxiety" in those tough-minded readers who feel uncomfortable in the presence of the divine. Therapy, however, is available to them if they only appreciate the fact that above all else Aristotle's thinking is coherent and his picture of the cosmos is consistent. He takes his bearings from being-on-the-earth; his perspective is anthropocentric, and so when he looks at the heavens he sees the sun moving from right to left. He begins with the phenomena, with what shows itself through naked-eye perception and in ordinary language, and then, animated by the conviction that the world makes sense, he reasons his way upward from the earth and its inhabitants to the sky.

The decisive marker of this ascent is *energeia.* The *Metaphysics* begins by studying beings with form and matter that change by actualizing the potential as potential, and culminates in a Being completely actual and therefore changeless. *On the Psyche* begins with eating and perceiving. In both activities what is potentially identical becomes actually identical. So too when it comes to thinking with the decisive implication that active mind is entirely separated from potentiality. The early chapters of the *Nicomachean Ethics* treat the moral, habitual, and distinctly human virtues but conclude with a divine life of pure theory in which the most basic human capacity is fully actualized. In each case, earlier stages are characterized by imperfection and oscillation between actuality and potentiality—in other words, by motion or change—and the drive to ascend is fueled by a teleology that allows for and even demands completion. *Energeia*, always the key, becomes progressively concentrated until, at the end stage, when the *telos* has been reached, it is pure. God, active mind, and the divine life of theory are the ultimate consequences of Aristotle's essential conviction, one that is itself born from the phenomena: that the world, from bottom to top, is a cosmos, an intelligible, finite, closed, and hierarchically ordered whole.

Chapter Six

Enough Is Enough.

Unbridled growth threatens the world. The Amazon jungle is going up in smoke as farmers clear land to raise ever more cattle to satisfy the endless demand for beef. In the suburbs of every major city it's known as "sprawl." The slums of the mega-cities, "where one-third of the world's 3 billion urban dwellers are already crammed in" and whose populations are projected to "double to 2 billion people within 30 years," relentlessly expand as the villages, which not too long ago were self-sustaining, are now being progressively drained.[1] Densely populated India is running low on water.

The hyperexpansion of population, industrialized agriculture, and the incessant consumption of natural resources are only the more palpable manifestations of a culture founded upon growth without limit. Others are more abstract. The nation-state, for example, long construed as a limited and self-contained political community with its own local culture and language, has been challenged by the forces of globalization. National borders are increasingly porous or even, from an economic point of view, irrelevant. More abstract yet: we live in an age in which a fundamental criterion of success has become growth itself. An economy that is not expanding is counted as a failure, and a standard typically used to assess the success of a society is the average life span, a strictly quantitative measure whose only version of "better" is "more." So too in the hospitals, as the doctors, equipped with ever more powerful machines, always push harder to keep the elderly alive longer, even when the quality of their lives is so severely diminished that they must be institutionalized. The medical imperative is unequivocal: more life, longer and longer. The dream of immortality inches closer toward realization.

Alive forever, but for what? Bereft of any measure of the quality of a human life, and certainly having no conception of a *telos,* the engineers cannot tell us when enough is enough. As a consequence they are left only with what the Greeks called *pleonexia,* the desire to have more and more.[2] Some of us fear that the outcome of this logic will be catastrophic.

In the age of globalization the Aristotelian ranking of the finite as superior to the infinite has been reversed (<II.8). Today expansion—of capital, markets, technology, life, stuff, and power—is all the rage and of this there is no limit. The universe of modern physics, wherein infinite space replaced the limited world of Aristotelian place (<I.4), has infiltrated the lives of us all.

There is no end in sight.

One force that has been galvanized in radical protest against the relentless and homogenizing sweep of globalization is fundamentalist religion. People are flocking to synagogues, churches, temples, and mosques in order to root themselves in a community and a tradition, to feel as if they do belong somewhere and that their lives do have meaning. For meaning requires an intelligible purpose, a *telos,* which the inexorable spread of globalization, with its single imperative of growth, cannot provide. Such fundamentalist reactions, however, are tinged with desperation, for they require and even celebrate a shutting down of reason. And this is equally as catastrophic as is the glorification of technical reason that is intrinsic to modernity.

As a resource for philosophical criticism, Aristotle's conception of the *polis*—the "city," the state, the self-sufficient political community—begs for retrieval. In the concluding chapter of this book, then, the topic is his treatise the *Politics*.[3] Like the other topics discussed in this book, however, his political philosophy is hopelessly out of date. Still, even if there is no hope of actually applying his theory in order to ameliorate, contain, or reverse the globalizing forces that threaten to swamp us all, it is nonetheless possible to think with him as he conceives of a good city, one that occupies its proper place in the natural world. But why bother? If his political philosophy is predicated upon an outdated teleological biology and cosmology and so cannot possibly be implemented at this late date, then why should anyone other than a historian or antiquarian study it? Even worse, when poverty, disease, and environmental degradation are causing great suffering around the globe is it not irresponsible to engage in such flights of scholastic "theorizing?" Perhaps entering into Aristotle's cozy little cosmos is nothing more than an escape into a phenomenological fantasy. Why, then, study his thought at all? Aristotle himself proposes an answer to this question at the end of this chapter.

VI.1: The Best City Needs the Best Life.

In Book VII of the *Politics,* Aristotle sketches what he takes to be the best possible (or ideal) city, the one, as he puts it, that exists "according to prayer" (1325b36).[4] He begins his discussion with this: "The one about to engage in the appropriate inquiry into the best form of government (*politeia*) must first distinguish the most choiceworthy life. For if this is unclear, so too must the best form of government be unclear" (1323a14–16).

To engage in political philosophy, one must determine the best conceivable "form of government" or "regime" (*politeia*), a task which in turn requires a conception of the best human life. With these remarks Aristotle sets himself at odds with most contemporary thinkers. Consider, for example, what John Rawls has to say. "Once the principles of justice are chosen. . . . there is no need to set up the account of the good so as to force unanimity on all the standards of rational choice. In fact, it would contradict the freedom of choice that justice as fairness assures to individuals and groups within the framework of just institutions. . . . Individuals find their good in different ways. . . . This variety in the conceptions of the good is itself a good thing."[5]

Rawls insists that it is possible to determine the best, the most just, form of government without having a prior conception of what counts as the best human life. In fact, any such conception of the Good would impede the construction of a truly just society, for what is of ultimate import to Rawls is the freedom of individuals to pursue whatever version of the good life that they choose. Indeed, the notion that the primary task of the government is to protect individual liberty is the core tenet of modern liberalism.

Aristotle is no liberal. When, for example, he says that "by inculcating [good] habits in the citizens lawmakers make [the citizens] good," he acknowledges that in the name of virtue it is legitimate to subordinate the autonomy of citizens to political regulation (<V.4). "Autonomy" is derived from the Greek words for "law" (*nomos*) and "self" (*autos*) and means "the giving of a law to oneself." In Aristotle's view citizens should obey laws that they did not give to themselves but that nonetheless make them better.[6] Freedom takes a back seat to excellence.

Because the laws of a good city should make the citizens good, what being good is must be understood before attempting to comprehend the ideal city. To do this, Aristotle reverts to the sort of virtues, both moral and intellectual, articulated in the *Nicomachean Ethics*:[7]

> Concerning one distinction, no one would disagree. There are three kinds of goods: external, those of the body, and those of the *psyche*. To be "blessed" one must have them all. For no one would say that the blessed man has no share of courage or moderation or of justice or practical wisdom, but is afraid of flies buzzing around, cannot restrain himself at all when it comes to extreme desires to eat or drink, or would kill his dearest friends for a dime. Similarly when it comes to thinking, no one would count as blessed a foolish man or one as ignorant as a child or a madman. (*Politics* 1323a24–34)

As usual, Aristotle is exceptionally confident: "no one would disagree," he says, that the most choiceworthy life is a virtuous one.[8] As obvious as he takes his assertion to be, he nonetheless observes a strange and disturbing feature of it. "Even though everyone would grant what has just been said, they differ on how much and what is preeminent. For they think that any amount of virtue is adequate, while of wealth, money, power, fame, and all of such things they seek an unlimited excess" (1323a34–38).

Even if "everyone" would agree with him that the best life is one lived in virtue, most people don't actually live this way. Instead, they become preoccupied with goods like money, power, and fame. Once this occurs they become implicated in an all-consuming and never-ending quest. For just as each of these goods is potentially unlimited, so too is the desire for them: "the nature of desire is unlimited," Aristotle says, "and it is towards the satisfaction of desire that most people live" (1267b4). If money is the object of my greatest desire and I have a million dollars, there is no reason not to seek a billion. Money itself can never inform me when enough is enough. If I have power in my city, I may well seek power over yours. And if I should conquer the world there would always be Mount Olympus left to storm.

It's "easy" to make arguments to show that the pursuit of goods like money, power, and fame are self-defeating and so cannot make someone genuinely happy. Aristotle offers this one:

> We will say to them that it is easy to come to a conclusion about these things through the facts. We observe that they do not acquire and then guard the virtues by means of the externals, but the externals by means of the virtues. Furthermore, when it comes to living happily, whether in pleasure or in human virtue or in both, greater preeminence belongs to those who are well equipped with the things concerning character and thought, and

> who are moderate concerning the possession of external goods, than to those who possess more money than is useful, but less virtue. (1323a39–b6)

Simply put, money can't be the highest good for it must be spent in order to take on value, and it can be spent well or badly. What confers value to money (or power or fame) is not the money itself, but how it is used. And how it is used depends on a good of the *psyche*; namely, the quality of one's character, or virtue (which the passage above illustrates with moderation). As a result, the happiest life consists in virtue rather than the acquisition of money, power, or fame.

"Everyone" agrees with the argument. Surely no rational person would choose to be a billionaire without knowing whether any strings were attached. If you could become rich but only if your beloved were to fall deathly ill, you might hesitate to choose the money. Arguments of this sort are "easy" to make. But such principles are not easy to live by. For goods like money, power, and fame are unlimited and thus they have the power to become addictive; there is always more of them to be had and so people always want more. The reasonable goal of attaining virtue is easily lost.

This failure, which is an essential feature of ordinary human life, is actually a version of the theory and practice split. On a conceptual level, "everyone" would agree that the best life requires virtue. In practice, however, money, power, and fame are intoxicants. Even though they understand the reasons why they shouldn't, most people disregard the argument showing that such goods require a virtue of the *psyche* in order to be used well.[9] Differently stated, Aristotle seems to imply that most people suffer from "moral weakness" (*akrasia*), the condition wherein someone knows he should not do something bad, but does it anyway because he is overpowered by a passion or desire. (See *Nicomachean Ethics* 1145b11–14, 1150b27–28, and 1151a20–22.)

It is precisely this potentially devastating conundrum that Aristotle's conception of the ideal city aims to address and, in its own indirect way, ameliorate.

VI.2: The Practical Life Is Not the Best.

The first task in conceiving the ideal city is to comprehend the best possible human life. In *Politics,* Book VII.2, Aristotle begins by narrowing the candidates to two:

> Among those who agree that the best life is most choiceworthy there is dispute whether the political and practical life is choiceworthy, or whether the life whose ties to all external matters have been dissolved—namely, the theoretical life, which some people say is the only life for a philosopher—is more choiceworthy. For it is nearly the case that the most honor-loving of men, both of the past and of now, seem to choose these two lives when it comes to excellence. The two I mean are the political and the philosophical. (1324a25–32)

Aristotle inherits the view that there are two forms of an excellent life, the theoretical (or philosophical) and the practical (or political), from a Greek tradition that was already centuries old when he wrote the *Politics.*[10] The historical antecedents are not the issue here and so we can simply let the notion of there being two forms of excellent life stand as an assumption and proceed to the examination of which is superior. Of course, we already know the answer: *Nicomachean Ethics* Book X.7–8 argues that the theoretical life is divine and thereby superior to one spent merely in human or political (or practical) affairs. In what follows, Aristotle approaches this point from a different angle. He shows what it would mean to count the practical-political life as the best available to human beings.

> Some think that only the practical and political life is fitting for a man. . . . Some think in this way, others say that the despotic and tyrannical way of governance is the only happy one. For some this is the definition of the laws and the form of government, namely how to rule over one's neighbors. Thus while in most regimes most laws are, so to speak, random, in those cases where they do aim at some one thing all aim for power (*kratein*). For example, in Sparta and Crete education and most of the laws have been devised with an eye to war. Furthermore, among all those nations, such as the Scythians, the Persians, the Thracians, and the Celts, which are capable of wanting more (*dunamenois pleonektein*), such power has been honored. (1324a39–1324b11)

The mention of tyranny here is abrupt, but it foreshadows the argument Aristotle later develops: if the political or practical life were elevated to the rank of the best life then tyranny would emerge as the best *politeia.*[11] For if political activity were the sole horizon of human existence, as it would be if the practical life were determined to be best, then the form of government continually seeking to expand itself would follow suit. In other words, if there were no life superior to the political, nor a reality beyond the human or practical, then ceaseless expansion would be the logical consequence. Aristotle cites Sparta and Crete as examples.[12] Both regimes are orderly and their laws are crafted deliberately, a fact distinguishing them from other cities whose laws are fashioned in a more or less random manner. But these regimes are devoted only to preparation for war. Because they are well disciplined, they "are capable of wanting more" (*pleonexia*); they have the wherewithal to expand. Such cities have, however, no purpose other than expansion.

Ranking the practical above the theoretical life logically implies that cities like Sparta and Crete are the best sorts of regime. But this they are not for, to get ahead of the argument, they have no *telos* other than expansion and therefore war. For them, as Heraclitus put it, "war is the father of all things,"[13] and so they violate the precept "war is for the sake of peace" (*Politics* 1333a35), a phrase that goes to the heart of Aristotle's political thought and is discussed shortly (>VI.6). Because they are not the best regimes, it follows that the practical life is not superior to the theoretical one.

Aristotle begins the argument that reveals the limitations of cities like Sparta: "It would be absurd if what is despotic and not despotic did not exist by nature. Therefore, if this is the case, there must be no attempt to rule over everybody, but only those who are fit to be ruled. This is analogous to the fact that one ought not to hunt human beings for food or sacrifice, but ought to hunt only that which is suited to this, namely those wild animals that are edible" (1324b36–41).

This argument is densely packed with presuppositions. Its key phrase is "by nature" and its key concept is that of natural superiority or rank ordering. Just as some animals are fit to be eaten, some human beings are by nature fit to be ruled. This implies that not all human beings are fit to be ruled. In turn, this implies that in its unlimited expansion and quest to dominate all, the tyrannical or globalizing regime is blind to the natural heterogeneity of a human population and thus acts in a manner contrary to nature.

Even if this argument is designed to criticize tyrannical or expansionist regimes, its presupposition is disturbing. For Aristotle, here reveals a willingness to defend slavery. There are some human beings, he asserts, who are "fit to be ruled." We turn next to his argument on behalf of natural slavery in *Politics* I.

VI.3: Natural Slavery Is Justified.

Aristotle's justification of natural slavery occurs in the context of his discussion of the nature of the *polis,* the city itself. "Since we see that every city is a community and every community is constituted for the sake of some good (for everybody does everything for the sake of what seems good), it is clear that all communities aim for some good. And the most authoritative of all communities, which embraces all the others, aims for the most authoritative of all goods. This is what is called the city and the political community" (1252a1–6).

This passage puts us on familiar teleological ground. Human communities are natural and so aim at some good. The largest and most important of all communities is the *polis*, and it is the *telos* of the following sub-communities from which it emerges:

1. The family is the primal human community and is composed of male and female, "those who cannot exist without each other" (1252a26). The *telos* of this community is reproduction, the most basic requirement of the species.

2. The household is composed of both the family as well as masters (those naturally suited to rule) and slaves (those naturally suited to be ruled). Its *telos* is one step beyond reproduction: namely, "survival" (1252a31).

3. The village is a combination of several households. Its *telos* goes beyond daily or even short-term survival (1252a17). The village looks forward to its long-range enhancement.

4. The city is formed from a number of villages. "It comes to be for the sake of living, but is for the sake of living well. Therefore, if the prior communities are by nature, so too is every city by nature, for it is their *telos*, and nature is *telos* (1252b27–32).

The city develops organically from smaller sub-communities, each of which emerges in order to fulfill a human need. Initially, in the family and household, humans gather together simply to survive and then maintain themselves. Ultimately, however, we enter into political communities because we need and desire to flourish. The city provides us with the conditions in which we can strive not merely for the preservation of life, but for the attainment of the good life. Being a citizen, then, is an essential feature of human nature. Or, as Aristotle puts it, "apparently the city is among those beings that are by nature, and human being is by nature a political animal" (1253a4). He elaborates in the following (<II.6):

> Why a human being is more of a political animal than any bee or other gregarious animal is clear. For nature, as we say, does nothing in vain, and alone among the animals human beings have rational speech (*logos*). While voice signifies pleasure and pain, and so belongs to the other animals . . . rational speech is for the purpose of clarifying what is advantageous and what is harmful, and hence what is just or unjust. For this is unique to human beings in comparison with the other animals: they alone have a perception of good and bad and justice and injustice, and so on. When a community shares in these it produces a household and a city. (1253a7–18)

Just as wings do for an eagle, *logos* characterizes our species, a notion prominent in the *Nicomachean Ethics* (<V.1–2). Because "nature does nothing in vain" this attribute must play some role in fulfilling our organic possibilities. Its purpose—more accurately, one of its purposes, because the *logos apophantikos* (<IV.7) is for the sake of articulating the truth—is to articulate and thus make possible the sharing of values, and hence the political community itself.

Aristotle continues: "The city is by nature prior to the household and to each one of us as individuals" (1253a19). "Prior" here is not meant historically because families and households came into being before cities did. Instead, the word suggests that being a citizen is more basic to the human species, closer to its *telos*, than being an individual. As always, this sort of teleological reasoning has normative implications. In this case, if people fail to be actively political—if, for example, they conceive of themselves as isolated individuals rather than citizens and so fail to identify their interests with those of the city—they distort human nature and thereby fall short. As Aristotle later puts it, someone estranged from the city is "either a beast or a god" (1253a29). Gods are self-sufficient and so have no need for cities. Nor are beasts political; they have no *logos*. Only humans make cities and in doing so we actualize our nature.

(The description of someone apolitical as either "a beast or a god" should set off an alarm. In the *Nicomachean Ethics* Book X.7–8, Aristotle claims that the theoretical life is "most divine" and hence superior to the merely human or practical. Somehow, then, the philosopher stands both outside the city as "divine," and inside of it as well; for he or she is, after all, a human being [>VI.7].)

Central to Aristotle's conception of the household, which is a basic element in the development of the city, is slavery, an institution prevalent in Ancient Greece. (Athens, for example, probably had a total population of about 300,000, of which only 30,000 were adult male citizens, and 150,000 were slaves.)[14] A slave is a human being who has been reduced to the status of a thing, an animate piece of property or tool. How could a thinker as sophisticated and generous, and as apparently humane, as Aristotle defend a practice that to us is thoroughly repugnant?

The first point to note is that Aristotle does not defend or justify all forms of slavery, only that which he calls "natural." In ancient Greek warfare, if one city conquered another it would often kill the men and enslave the women and children. Such was the actual institution of "legal" or "conventional" slavery. It was the result of the imposition of political and military force and was indifferent to the qualities of the people enslaved. By contrast, the defining feature of the natural slave is precisely his unique quality. He is by nature constituted to receive orders and so is benefited by being subordinated to a master. "For being able to use thought to see ahead is characteristic of one who rules and is master by nature, while being able to labor with the body is characteristic of the one who is ruled and is by nature a slave. In this way, the interests of both master and slave are served" (1252a31–33).

The rational capacity of a natural slave is so limited that he does not have the foresight to make decisions for himself. He needs someone to think for him, which is precisely what the master does; and in doing so he benefits the slave.

Aristotle justifies the distinction between natural ruler and slave by appealing to nature itself:

> It is apparent that it is by nature and advantageous for the body to be ruled by the *psyche*, and for the emotional part to be ruled by what has mind and by the rational part, while it is harmful for their relationship to be equal or reversed. This holds true for both human beings and the rest of the animals. For tame animals are better in their nature than wild ones, and it is better for all of these to be ruled by human beings. . . . Furthermore, the male relates to the female as better does to the worse, and the ruler does so to the ruled. And so it must go for all of

> humankind. Therefore, those who are as different [from other human beings] as the soul is from the body or humans from beasts—and if using the body is their proper work (*ergon*), and if this is the best that can come from them, then this is the condition they are in—are slaves by nature. . . . For someone is a slave by nature who is capable of belonging to another . . . and who participates in reason only to the extent of perceiving it, but does not have it. . . . That some are free and others slaves by nature, and that for these slavery is both advantageous and just, is evident. (1254b5–1255a3)

The ruler–ruled relationship exists throughout nature and as a concept emerges directly from Aristotelian teleology. Most elemental is the case of the *psyche* and the body. A healthy adult is able to exert a significant measure of rational control over his appetites and passions. Indeed, the *telos* of the human species is to exercise its unique function, namely rational activity (<V.1–2). Those who cannot do this well fall short of the *telos* and so are deficient. Because the *psyche* of the natural slave is unable to rule his body he stands to be benefited from the reception of orders from a master. To reiterate, being benefited in this fashion is an essential criterion of the natural slave. If a person is not benefited, as of course the overwhelming majority of the human race would not be, there is no justification for enslaving him.

The passage just cited also pronounces that "the male relates to the female as better does to the worse." And this message only becomes more extreme: "For the male is by nature better fit to lead than the female, unless he is somehow defective and contrary to nature" (1259b2–3). Aristotle summarizes: "The free man rules the slave, the male the female and the man the child. Parts of the *psyche* belong to each but they belong differently. For the slave does not at all have the part that deliberates. The female does have it but not in an authoritative way (*akuron*). The child has it but it is incomplete (*ateles*)" (1260a9–14).

There are fundamental and natural distinctions that exist within the human population and it is both just and reasonable for political institutions to acknowledge them. A natural slave is unable to deliberate for himself; hence, it is justifiable and beneficial for a master not only to give him orders but to own him. A woman is able to deliberate but not as well or authoritatively as a man. Hence, it is reasonable for a woman to take orders from her man. Alternatively, it would be contrary to nature to enslave women, as do the "barbarians" (those who do not speak Greek); for "by nature the female is distinguished from the slave" (1252b1). Her place is in the home. Finally, because a child is at best a potential adult, he should be subordinated to the discipline imposed by an actual adult.

The awful sting of Aristotle's defense of natural slavery can be significantly mitigated by realizing that it provides, covertly but also quite powerfully, a critique of the institution as it actually existed in Ancient Greece. Jonathan Lear has noted that as "the first political thinker to realize that slavery needed a defense," Aristotle initiated the process of challenging it.[15] Wayne Ambler makes the point more forcefully by arguing that Aristotle's teleologically based defense of natural slavery functions as a critique of slavery as actually practiced in the Greek world. As mentioned, a standard Greek practice was to conquer a city, kill the men, and indiscriminately take the women and children as slaves. Therefore, as Ambler puts it, "Aristotle's natural master and natural slave establish standards which deny rather than establish the naturalness of actual slavery."[16] This contention is reinforced by the following passage: "There is both advantage and affection between the master and the slave when both are worthy of these designations by nature. When master-slave are not determined in this way, when the relationship exists by convention and has been instituted by force, the opposite is the case" (1255b13–15).

To be properly counted as natural, a slave not only must be objectively benefited by his master, but also must feel some affection for him. By contrast, in the conventional practices of actual Greek cities, which Aristotle implies are unjust, slaves were those conquered in war and no doubt rarely felt affection for their masters. If affection is a necessary condition of being a natural slave, then such beings are certainly miniscule in number. In fact, it is even possible that Aristotle intends to define the natural slave out of existence. After all, the rational capacity of the putative natural slave seems to be so limited as to preclude any sort of deliberation about the future. But surely all human beings, except those whose brains are damaged, can do that.

Consider the implication of the following statement: "Slaves by nature are those who differ to the same extent that the *psyche* differs from the body, and a human being differs from a beast" (1254b16–18). On the basis of this analogy a natural slave is not a real human being at all. At the very least, given Aristotle's criteria the number of natural slaves in any given population would have to be extremely small; so small, that he himself wonders (at 1254a17) whether one (*tis*) actually exists.[17]

VI.4: A Woman's Place Is in the Home.

Even if Aristotle's defense of natural slavery can be transformed into a critique of the Greek institution of slavery, his position is still far from agreeable. Because his conception of the *polis* takes its bearings from nature, which is teleologically and thus hierarchically ordered, his conception of the citizenry is analogously stratified. By his lights, it is not the case that people, simply by virtue of being human, are politically or morally equal. So, for example, because of their natures, those who do the hard work of mechanical labor and craft do not even deserve to be citizens of the best city (1278a10–25.) "The citizens should not live a vulgar or a merchant's way of life, for this sort of way of life is ignoble and contrary to virtue" (1328b38). Even more drastic is his assertion that farmers should be slaves (1330a24).

Aristotelian stratification of the virtues corresponds to his rank ordering of human natures.

> It is necessary to suppose that when it comes to the moral virtues, the situation is similar. All human beings must have a share in them but not in the same way. Instead, each can attain virtue in a manner proportionate to their function. Therefore, the man who rules must have complete moral virtue . . . while each of the others has as much virtue as falls to him. Thus it is apparent that moral virtue belongs to all who have been discussed, but that the moderation, justice and courage of a woman is not the same as that of a man. (1260a14–22)

This passage suggests what could be called a "topological virtue-ethics." Human beings naturally occupy a place (*topos*) in the city, which in turn determines their virtues. Recall that "place" is the foundational concept of Aristotle's physics (<I.4). Defined as the first unmoved limit "of the containing body" (*Physics* 211b10), "place" answers the question "Where is it?" and as he puts it "everyone assumes that things that are are somewhere. For what is not is nowhere" (208a29–30). When the notion of place is transferred to the practical or political world, however, it gives rise to a sentiment as anachronistic as it is disturbing: everyone should "know their place." Because of his nature, a man is fit to rule, so he belongs in the seat of power. Because of her nature, a woman's place and her corresponding virtue are in the home. Because her job is to run the household rather than

to speak in the assembly or argue with philosophers her motto should be "silence is golden" (1260a30).[18] Those whose intellects are lacking belong in the fields where the work is backbreaking.

To pigeonhole a person into a specific place and insist that he or she needs to stay there for his or her own good seems perverse. Even if such a procedure were remotely fair, it hardly seems plausible, for it would require a competent judge of human natures who could accurately determine in what place someone properly fits. As a result, and at a minimum, Aristotle's view is terribly dangerous and subject to misuse. Consider the following transcription of an e-mail received by the author of this book after he had given a lecture on Aristotle's *Politics* that covered some of the issues discussed in this section.

> I would like to add something you said about Aristotle on women and slavery. He was basically right about women being less intelligent. This has been born out by IQ tests, which show women to not have the very high IQ levels of men. The bell curve is the same for men and women, but women have fewer at the very top and bottom, so it is unlikely that there will ever be a female Shakespeare (or philosopher Queen?).
>
> Regarding slavery, most blacks would qualify for the status of natural slaves. Their brains are 8 cubic inches smaller than whites and Asians, and they naturally have a more emotional temperament. IQ is strongly associated with brain size, so consistent with this is the fact that the black has IQs about 20 points lower than whites and Asians. We know all of these because the basic differences between the races are present at birth. Given the condition of the black communities, many would benefit by having their lives directed by whites. If you want more info on the biology of race, see "Race, evolution and behavior," by P. Rushton.[19]

Such a message, which takes itself to be Aristotelian in spirit, is chilling but may not be entirely off the mark. For Aristotle himself seems subject to the charge of racism. Engaging in a bit of geographical determinism, he asserts that people from the cold climes of Northern Europe are filled with "spirit" (*thumos*: 1327b24) but lack thought and art. As a result, they are difficult to subdue militarily but at the same time do a poor job of ruling over their neighbors. At the other extreme, Asians are quite capable of thought and art but lack spirit and so they are slavish. "But the Greek race, just as it is in the middle geographically participates in both extremes. For the Greeks are spirited but also thoughtful. As a result, they remain free and are best at governing themselves and ruling over others" (1227b29–32). It is possible, therefore, that when Aristotle quotes Euripides (*Iphigenia in Aulis,* 1400–01), he does so approvingly: "it is fitting for Greeks to rule barbarians" (1252b8).

Anyone who even vaguely remembers the twentieth century should tremble when they hear such talk of natural rulers and those fit to be ruled. Racial or "topological" politics, putatively based on natural distinctions, can have vicious consequences of staggering proportions. It might thus be wise to jettison not only the notion of the political place, but perhaps even to banish the natural altogether when it comes to politics. Karl Popper, a fierce critic of both Plato and Aristotle, certainly thought so: "the more we try to return to the heroic age of tribalism, the more surely do we arrive at the Inquisition, at the Secret Police, and at a romanticized gangsterism. . . . There is no return to a harmonious state of nature. If we turn back, then we must go back the whole way—we must return to the beasts."[20]

Modern liberal democratic theory of the sort championed by Popper began with a critique of Aristotle. Recall that Hobbes, one of its founders, found Aristotle's *Politics* "repugnant to government" (< Introduction). For Hobbes, the state was an artifice, not an organic outgrowth of human nature. "For by art is created that great Leviathan, called a commonwealth, or state, which is but an artificial man, though of greater stature and strength than the natural, for whose protection and defence it was intended."[21] The state is constructed in order to protect human beings from their natural urges; in other words, to remove them from the state of nature in which all are at war with one another and to transfer them into a state where peace and security become possible. As this notion develops, especially in Locke, it gives rise to a conception of government whose primary purpose is to protect the lives, property, and liberty of its citizens. As such, the modern liberal state is, from the perspective of Aristotelian virtue, far less ambitious than what is proposed in the *Politics.* For Aristotle, we are animals whose very being requires the *polis,* itself an organic development of human nature, for our virtue, completion, and happiness.

In the Aristotelian *polis,* "what the law does not order it forbids" (*Nicomachean Ethics* 1138a7; <V.4). In other words, citizens are permitted to do only what the laws, crafted by the good lawmaker with an eye toward the inculcation of salutary habits, tell them to do. The modern or "liberal" thinker flips this: citizens are free to do whatever the law does not forbid as long as their actions do not harm or infringe upon the rights of other

citizens. As Locke puts it, there is "liberty to follow my own will in all things, where the rule prescribes not."[22] They are especially free, as Rawls makes clear, to determine what qualifies in their own mind as a good place or a decent life. In the liberal state citizens are liberated from topological constraints.

Remember, however, the context in which Aristotle invokes the naturalness of the human hierarchy: he is trying to show what's wrong with an expansionist regime like Sparta. It has no purpose except to get bigger and it does so by means of the warfare by which it enslaves all who are conquered regardless of what kind of people they are. In their own way, then, such regimes are egalitarian: they consider all people, except themselves, equally subject to being dominated. In fact, if the Spartans were honest with themselves, they would have to admit that, given their own principles, they are not intrinsically superior to those they have conquered. If a city stronger than their own happened to come on the scene and defeat them, they would have no rational basis on which to object. (See 1333b20 for a version of this argument.) All are equal insofar as all are equally implicated in the oscillations of a continual power struggle. Aristotle's topological stratification renders this sort of thinking incoherent. All men are not created equal. Therefore, it is wrong to attempt to subdue everyone who stands in the way.

Of course, egalitarianism can cut the other way. Kant and other moralists maintain that all human beings are morally equal and thus everyone deserves to be treated with dignity and to be respected for their capacity to act autonomously. This view also provides a conceptual impediment to expansionism or tyranny by insisting that it is wrong to tyrannize anyone, anywhere, ever.

However anachronistic and distasteful the phrase "a woman's place is in the home" may be, it brings into sharp focus the placelessness of our own age. (The Greek word, *atopos*, literally "out of place," also means "strange" and "absurd"). In the age of globalization, a woman's place is not in the home. She has no place. No one does. Place is a limit, which these days is unacceptable. Instead, we demand the freedom to choose the kind of life that we want. We take ourselves to be free to choose our jobs, homes, sexual partners, genders, and whether we will have children. Just as the scientific revolution transformed physics, and so an infinite universe replaced the closed world of the Aristotelian cosmos, so too in the practical sphere have human beings moved from being topologically bound to having unlimited possibilities; to being free.

The question remains, however, of whether limitless freedom can actually nourish a human life. Today millions of people around the globe are voting with their feet by flocking to fundamentalist religion and thereby voluntarily placing upon themselves under the yokes of tradition. Muslim women in France often choose, despite the opposition of the secular state, to wear the veil. Orthodox Jewish women in the United States, despite the freedom to walk the streets half-naked, choose to wear long skirts. They voluntarily, often enthusiastically, place themselves into traditional communities (even if their parents actually abandoned such communities long ago). They welcome, sometimes fanatically, constraints.

Such fundamentalism is an extreme reaction to a technologizing, globalizing mono-culture that is sweeping the world. It is fueled by a desperate energy that requires and then even celebrates the shutting down of reason. As such, it too risks having catastrophic consequences. What is needed today is not an abandonment of reason, but a revitalization, a humanization of it. And for this task Aristotle offers a great resource. Thoroughly theoretical, he thinks the world from bottom to top, and he consistently does so in terms that are in accord with the phenomena, with the way the world appears to us down here on earth.

There is a second way to mitigate the apparently oppressive, sexist, or racist implications of Aristotle's topological political philosophy and that is to note that despite his elitism he does speak favorably of democracy, a regime in which the many rule or have power. To begin his analysis, he first divides regimes into three broad types based upon where political "authority" (*to kurion*: 1279a27) is concentrated: in one man, in a few, or in the many. Each of these three is divided again into a "correct" and a "deviant" version. The former is characterized by a single feature: the governing body rules with an eye to the common good. In deviant regimes, the ruling body rules with an eye toward its own "special" (*idion*) interests. The three correct regimes emerging from this typology are "kingship," "aristocracy" (which literally means "rule of the best"), and a word impossible to translate usefully into English, *politeia*. The three incorrect regimes are "tyranny," "oligarchy," and "democracy." Aristotle's terminology is potentially misleading here, for he defines "democracy" as "rule with an eye to the advantage of the poor" and so classifies it as "deviant." But his description of the *politeia* includes democratic features, principally political participation of the "many," and because it is a "correct" regime it operates for the sake of the common good. About the very notion of "majority rule" Aristotle has something positive to say.

> Even though no single individual among the many is excellent, it is nonetheless possible that they become superior when they come together, not as individuals, but as a conglomerate. . . . For each one of those who belong to the many has a part of virtue and of practical wisdom, and when they come together they become, just like a single human being, with many feet and hands, and having many senses. And it is thus with regard to their characters and their intelligence. Therefore, the many often judge the works of music and poetry better. Some appreciate a certain part, and all of them all of the parts. (1281b1–10)

Because the judgments of "the many" can have some merit Aristotle assigns them a significant, even if limited, role to play in the *politeia*: they can take responsibility for deliberating and judging (1281b31): in our lingo, participating in the legislative process and serving on juries. Including the many in politics is analogous to mixing an impure with a pure substance, a process that "makes the whole more useful than the small amount of the impure" (1281b32). The many must be kept away from some governmental tasks, and so Aristotle is hardly a radical democrat. Furthermore, as mentioned above, he is selective about who should be allowed citizenship. Certainly women, farmers, mechanics, and those involved in backbreaking physical labor are excluded. Nonetheless, he is not entirely exclusionary, for he does say that "nothing prevents the multitude from being at some point better than the few and wealthy; not as individuals but taken together" (1283b33). Finally, "what is many is more incorruptible; like a greater amount of water, the multitude is more incorruptible than the few. The judgment of a single person is necessarily corrupted when he is dominated by anger or some other passion, whereas it is hard for all to become angry and err at the same time" (1286a31–35).

In *Politics* IV.11, Aristotle sketches what he takes to be the best regime that is realistically attainable. Not surprisingly, it is characterized according to the notion of the "mean": "If virtue is a mean (*mesotêta*), the life in the middle (*meson*) is necessarily the best. . . . And in all cities there are three parts of the city: the excessively well-off, the excessively poor, and the third group, those in the middle (*hoi mesoi*) of these. Since it has been agreed that what is moderate and in the middle is best, it is apparent that in the possession of goods of fortune what is in the middle is best of all" (1295b1–5).

Those who are excessively wealthy, beautiful, or strong are likely to be violently arrogant or "hybristic" (*hubristai*: 1295b9), while those on the opposite extreme tend toward vice. But those in the middle—not too rich, not too poor, not too beautiful but not ugly, strong enough—are best able to fulfill the dualistic function of a citizen: both to rule, that is, to participate actively in shaping a city's policies, and to be ruled; namely, to submit to and obey the laws. Differently stated, "a city wishes to be composed of equals and those who are most similar to one another, and this belongs especially to those in the middle" (1295b25–26). In sum, Aristotle approvingly quotes Phocylides: "many things are best for those in the middle. In the city I would willingly be a man in the middle" (1295b35).

A similar line of reasoning leads Aristotle to recommend that the best attainable city have a substantial middle class. This provision is stabilizing primarily because if a majority of citizens are poor, factionalism ensues, while those who own property have a stake in the future of the community and hence work hard for its benefit. (See 1296a1.)

The best attainable regime is a mixture of democracy, which empowers the multitude, and oligarchy, in which the wealthy few rule. Aristotle again uses the term *politeia,* sometimes translated here as the "polity," to name it. Like the oligarchy, officials are elected rather than chosen by lot. But like the democracy, no level of wealth or property is required in order to run for office. (See *Politics* IV.9.)

One last stab: "democracy" as the rule of the poor is the best of the three deviant regimes. As such, it is the best of the worst (1289b3). At this point, it is nearly impossible not to quote the line attributed to Churchill: "democracy is the worst form of government except for all those others that have been tried from time to time."

VI.5: Small, but Not Too Small, Is Beautiful.

To review: in order to determine the best city, Aristotle must first determine the best life, and for this there are two candidates: the practical and the theoretical. It cannot be the former. If it were, then the horizon of human endeavor would be identified with the political realm, and as a result a regime like Sparta, which seeks only to extend itself, could be counted as best. And this it is not because in its unbridled expansionism Sparta enslaves those who are not natural slaves. Human beings occupy appropriately different places in a reasonable political order, and expansionism violates this natural stratification by treating all who stand in its way as equally worth subjugating. With the practical life thereby eliminated, the theoretical takes the prize.

Even though the supremacy of the theoretical life was a foregone conclusion—it was already established in *Nicomachean Ethics* X.7–8—Aristotle himself raises doubts about its guiding the conception of the best city here in the *Politics*. Engaged in the study of stars, animals, being as being, and so on, the theoretical man, or "the philosopher," hardly seems to *do* much of anything; and one who does nothing cannot qualify as best or most happy. After all, happiness as *eudaimonia* is excellent activity and thus seems equivalent to "good acting" (*eupragia*: 1325a22). Aristotle poses the dilemma in stark terms: "Which is the more choiceworthy life, that of engaging in political activity and sharing in the life of the city, or is it rather the life of the stranger (*ho xenikos*) whose ties to the political community have been dissolved?" (1324a14–17).

Gazing at stars and plants, the theoretical man is *xenikos,* "alien," "strange," "foreign"; he is disengaged, separated from the life of his fellow citizens. It is therefore hard to see how such an apparently apolitical being could possibly function as a guide to political theory. There are other problems as well. First, theory requires leisure, whereas "the actualization of the practical virtues is found in political and military activities, and the doing of these seems to lack leisure" (*ascholoi*: *Nicomachean Ethics* 1177b8). The practical man takes responsibility for his family and fellow citizens. Because he is fully engaged in the lives of others, his own life is continually subject to distraction and interruption by their needs. To put the point imagistically, the practical man is bound to a "horizontal" plane, to the human level above which the demands of others like himself prevent him from rising. The theoretical life, by contrast, is leisurely and free from interruption; the philosopher can concentrate on any thought that seems appealing and go as far with it as he is able. If he has the time, he can even think the stars. To reiterate the dilemma: it hardly seems plausible that this sort of "vertical" life, one that is detached, irresponsible, alienated, or *xenikos*, could be of much use as a guide to political theory.

Another objection: *theoria* is not technical knowledge and so its results are not directly applicable. Aristotle's *Politics* is not a "political science" whose findings can be implemented in order to manipulate, improve, or control the *polis* or its citizens. His version of political theory, indeed of his *theoria* in general, issues no rules or algorithms or any sort of engineering. In this sense, it is useless (<II.9) and so once again seems unpromising as a guide to political life and theory.

Finally, recall the distinction forged in *Metaphysics* I.1 between "experience" and "knowledge": the latter can give a *logos* of universals, while the former is no more than a coagulation of particular memories. Nonetheless, the person who has it "may have more success than those who have a *logos* without experience. This is because experience is of particulars, while knowledge is of universals, and action and processes are all particularized" (981a14–17). An expert in physics can explain how an internal combustion engine works far better than an uneducated mechanic. But in needing to have your car fixed, you'd go to the guy who has worked on it in the past rather than to the scientist who understands its underlying theory.

Aristotle anticipates the objection that the theoretical life he champions is utterly impractical, and then counters it by claiming that his critics misunderstand the nature of "praxis."

"But the practical life need not be in relationship to other human beings (*pros heterous*), as some think it must, nor should only those kinds of thoughts (*dianoias*) that come to be for action and for the sake of what results be counted as practical. But much more [practical] are those thoughts that are 'auto-telic' (*autoteleis*) and the kinds of *theoria* that are for the sake of themselves. For the *telos* is good practice (*eupraxia*), so that [*theoria*] is some sort of practice (*praxis*)" (1325b16–21).

There are two senses of *praxis*. The first refers only to political or ethical activity that is *pros heterous*, "toward other human beings"; in other words, that is essentially social. The second is far more broad and refers to all forms of activity, of actualizing a potentiality, from metabolic functioning to *theoria*. Even if it is not directly political, even if it is divine, separate, and *xenikos,* theoretical work can nonetheless be counted as "practical" in this sense. Aristotle goes even further, however: *theoria*, he says, is "much more" (*polu mallon*) practical than political activity. This is true because it is "autotelic" (*autoteleis*); it is for the sake of itself and so contains its *telos* within itself. These words should trigger two recollections. First, at the outset of the *Nicomachean Ethics* the "highest good" is described in precisely these terms. It is a *telos* that we desire "on account of itself" (1094a19). Second, there is the most important distinction discussed in this book: an *energeia* is an actualization that has no *telos* apart from itself; by contrast, a *kinesis* is a process that issues in an external product or result (<III.4). Thinking is an example of the former, house building of the latter. Because its activity is contained within itself, rather than being deposited in something outside itself, *energeia* in general is "more practical" or more active than a *kinesis.*

To sum up: a critic might object that the theoretical cannot be the best life, for happiness is *eupragia*, and a life devoted to *theoria* seems to do nothing at all. It cannot function as a guide to politics because looking at the stars, studying plants, and so on require leisure and are not "practical," while the busy life of the city is nothing but. Aristotle retorts: this objection misconceives what *praxis* is, for it wrongly restricts it to social interaction. It fails to comprehend that theoretical activity can be "much more" practical than those thoughts and actions to which we typically ascribe this label. This failure is all too familiar, for most people regularly assume that what is human is most real and best. Recall an earlier point: even if they can be persuaded in an abstract sense that true happiness cannot be attained through the acquisition of such infinitely expandable goods as money, power, and fame, but only through virtue—and there are, Aristotle says, "easy" arguments available to make this case—most people pursue them nonetheless and lose sight of virtue altogether. Their doing so is parallel to the mistaken belief that *praxis* is limited to moral and political interaction, for money, power, and fame are goods whose value is socially constructed. In their actions and desires, therefore, most people lose sight of the fact that "human being is not the best thing in the world" (*Nicomachean Ethics* 1141a22).

Differently stated, most people are "anthropocentrists" in the sense of believing that "everything has a value or is good only in relation to human beings."[23] Aristotle himself certainly does not share this view, although he too is a kind of anthropocentrist. He studies the world but does so from a human perspective. He is a geocentrist for whom the stars are above. From this vantage point, rooted on the earth and taking its bearings from the way the world appears to us, he sees that natural beings and their goodness exist quite independently of us. There is a world out there, intelligible and open for inspection, ready to be theorized.

Despite such arguments, the assertion that the divine, alienated, or *xenikos* life of *theoria* is best of all, and so both can and should guide political theory, is still tough to swallow. Aristotle makes it because he discovers a startling analogy between the best city and the theoretical life. Both are "self-contained." Just as *theoria,* the study of the world, does not require a product or an external application in order to complete itself, just as it is desirable for its own sake, so does the best city not need to look beyond its own borders for political satisfaction. Opposed to the self-aggrandizing globalization of Sparta and Crete, the best city stays resolutely "local," a word derived from the Latin *locus,* which like the Greek *topos* means "place." And just as the theoretical life should not be deemed impractical because it is not devoted to social interaction, so too should the best, the thoroughly localized city not be faulted for lacking political energy because it does not seek to expand or conquer its neighbors. "It is not necessary that cities that have been established with respect to themselves (*tas kath' hautas*) and have chosen to live in this way be inactive (*apraktein*). For it is possible that [being active] occurs in regard to its parts" (1325b23–26).

A self-contained, non-aggressive city is an organic whole consisting of dynamically interacting parts. As such, it can be every bit as active, even more so, than a city that devotes its energy to expansion beyond its borders. It can be more like an *energeia* than a *kinesis.* Aristotle strikingly employs a metaphysical phrase to explain: cities can be "with respect to themselves" (*kath' hautas*). In other words, a city can be like a substance.[24] Recall that the category of substance is characterized by having the highest degree of ontological independence; it does not depend on any other category for its being. By contrast, a quality (such as green) depends on there being a substance (such as tree) of which it is predicated. In an analogous fashion, a substance-like city can aspire to self-sufficiency and remain content to stay within its political and economic limits. "A single city, the one which governs in manifest fineness, could be happy with respect to itself (*kath' heautên*), if it is possible for a city to live by itself (*kath' heautên*) using decent laws. Its form of government (*politeia*) would not be directed towards war or domination of its enemies" (1325a1–4).

Expansionist or globalizing regimes reflect ontological confusion: they wrongly elevate the category of quantity over that of substance, and thus the infinite over the finite.[25] As a consequence they are doomed to catastrophe. By contrast, the ideal city, resolutely local, affirms its own limitations. It is an organic whole whose parts are properly organized. As in a healthy organism, that which is fit to rule will issue commands, while that suited to be ruled will obey. Those who are capable of putting free time to good use will be given leisure.

To go even further, the best city emulates not only a substance but both the cosmos and god as well. "For many communities are with respect to each other in their political parts. And in a similar vein this condition can be achieved by a single human being. For [if this were not so] then god could not be in a leisurely and fine condition nor could the whole cosmos (*kosmos*), because they have no external actions in addition to those that belong to themselves" (1325b23–30).

The argument seems to be this: if a community or an individual could not be "itself with respect to itself" or a substantial whole in which one part rules another, then god, understood as a maximally actualized being, could not be "itself with respect to itself" either. But god certainly is this. Therefore, it is possible for an individual or a city also to be in this condition, namely limited, localized, well-functioning, and happy. The same argument applies to the cosmos. Because nothing is beyond it, it can only be active with respect to itself. Because the world is characterized by this consummate level of ontological self-sufficiency, so too can (and should) a city aspire to political self-sufficiency rather than the expansion of its power. The same holds on the level of the individual. Believing that greater and greater amounts of money or fame constitute happiness is fundamental self-deception. Instead, the best goal is to become substance-like, like god or even the world itself.[26] The best life is one that stays at home and works hard to develop character and virtue rather than one that continually tries to gain the spotlight.

As if he understands that these descriptions might sound fanciful, Aristotle turns next to concrete descriptions of the sort of city he has in mind. Above all else, it knows when enough is enough. So, for example, it vigilantly monitors its own population, making sure there are neither too many citizens nor too few. A city must not be excessively populous, because it should be ruled by law, and this becomes unmanageable if it gets too big. Furthermore, "procreation must be limited" because "too many people will lead to more poverty, which in turn leads to instability (1265b12).[27] Nor must a city be too small, for like a work of art it must be beautiful and fine, qualities it cannot achieve if it is does not have sufficient magnitude. In general, a city does not become great "by number," which is of course without limit and hence unable to generate a meaningful *telos,* but by its "capacity" (*dunamis*: 1326a12).

Not surprisingly, Aristotle offers the following comparison: "as is the case with animals, plants and tools, for a city there is a certain proper measure (*metron*). For each of these will not achieve its own potentiality if it is too small or too big" (1326b35–38). A ship only a few inches wide or ten miles long is not really a ship. Similarly, living beings are big enough when they have matured and attained their proper form. More specifically, a city is big enough when it is self-sufficient and, most important, able to provide the conditions that allow the citizens, or at least some of them, to achieve their excellence, to live "in leisure and freely and with moderation" (1326b31). A city is big enough when some of its citizens have the free time to theorize.

One final way to make this point: a good city must be of such a size as to allow a "synoptic" view of itself; it must be "easily seen as a whole" (*eusunopton*: 1327a2). Again, this word suggests a comparison with a basic metaphysical concept: "form" translates the Greek *eidos*, which itself derives from the verb "to see." A "form" is what shape a being has and thus what it looks like. Most literally, then, the *eidos* is the "look" of a thing as a whole. A properly scaled city should be form-like. Its boundaries must give it shape by limiting it to a specific place; not too big, not too small, but just what it takes to be easily seen as a whole.

That such views are hopelessly outdated is obvious from one comment Aristotle makes. In order best to distribute the responsibilities for judging and ruling, "citizens must recognize one another and know what sort of person each other is" (1326b15). His ideal city now sounds like a small town in which gossip flows freely and keeps the citizens well informed of each other's characters and actions. Of course, such towns have virtually disappeared and the local, so prized by Aristotle, is long gone. Globalization has become the fundamental fuel of political and economic life, the Web is worldwide, and political boundaries are increasingly irrelevant. Nonetheless, as the next two sections argue, even at this late date Aristotle's political theory still has much to teach.

VI.6: War Is for the Sake of Peace.

There is much in Aristotle's *Politics* to dislike, even to fear, and a thinker like Popper dislikes it mightily. And yet, give Aristotle at least this much credit: his worldview, so thoroughly teleological, makes it possible for him to declare that "war is for the sake of peace." In his city, the military exists only to protect the citizens from foreign invasion and to allow them to pursue the *telos* of human existence, which is excellence, without the brutal distractions of war (1333b40).

The statement "war is for the sake of peace" is coupled with another: "lack of leisure (*ascholia*) is for the sake of leisure (*scholê*)" (1333a35). Both teleological precepts speak to the heart of human *energeia*, for peace and leisure are necessary for genuine flourishing. For only when time is free, when external constraints do not impinge, can we most fully pursue our most natural aspirations. Aristotle knows what these are, for his is a teleological view of nature. "All human beings by nature strive to know." We are completed in thinking, in *theoria,* an autotelic act desirable for itself.

Even if Aristotle's views are anachronistic and include the inferiority of women and natural slavery, even if Karl Popper, scarred as he was by the horrors of the twentieth century, hated his teleologically drenched "naturalistic" politics, this at least must be granted: Aristotle's theoretical philosophy discloses a coherent worldview in which peace is superior to war. It is unlikely that our present understanding of the universe does as well.

VI.7: Philosophy Cures.

Quite unlike John Rawls, Aristotle affirms a fundamental symmetry between an individual citizen and the city. Both share the same *telos* and are governed by the principle "for as has been said many times, the *telos* of war is peace, and of lack-of-leisure leisure" (1334a15–16). An individual requires leisure in order to live well; most important, in order to engage in *theoria*. Analogously, a good city should aim to maintain the peace in order that its best citizens can be free from the least leisurely of all activities, namely war. In order for a city to achieve this goal it must itself be virtuous. The citizens must be law-abiding, show moderation, and be just. When the city is attacked they must be courageous enough to put on their armor and hold to their posts in order to defend it. When there is peace they must be sufficiently patient in order to engage in political deliberation, and be well enough disciplined to resist those who urge the city to attack its neighbors or expand its borders. Distressingly, however, it is during peace that the trouble begins. In a brief statement that has terribly sobering consequences, Aristotle says this: "For war forces men to be just and moderate, while the enjoyment of good fortune and peaceful leisure makes them more violently arrogant (*hubristas*)" (1334a25–28).

As intrinsically desirable as both may be, peace and leisure are nearly impossible to sustain, for most men cannot tolerate them.[28] Especially those who are high-spirited and ambitious are restless. They lack the ability to amuse themselves and the self-discipline required to use free time well. Unconstrained by external commands, they don't know what to do with themselves and so are ill at ease. With too much time on their hands, they get bored. They start pointless fights and do stupid things. That this regularly occurs is yet another expression of the conundrum that Aristotle locates at the heart of ordinary human life: most people mistake the source of their own happiness even when "easy" arguments are available to show that they are being wrongheaded. They devote their best energy to the pursuit of wealth, power, or fame and thereby misconstrue the very meaning of their own lives. They are incapable of appreciating the gift of leisure and so they disturb the peace. In fact, most young men are far better behaved when they are in uniform. Military discipline forces them to act moderately and to take heed of the common good rather than simply indulging their own violent impulses or seeking their own pleasures.

A bit of evidence that Aristotle is right: happen upon a group of unemployed young men hanging out on the street with too much free time on their hands, and if they are not wearing a uniform, either military or athletic, trouble is almost sure to arrive soon.

War is for the sake of peace, but most men can't tolerate peace. They get bored easily, and free time puts them ill at ease. But therapy is available. These restless, potentially violent men who have strong, selfish desires "should seek no cure except for philosophy" (1267a12).

In studying the world the philosopher is *xenikos,* alienated, strange. Thinking about the stars or plants or the motionless mover he separates himself from the ordinary doings of his fellow citizens. In this one sense he is almost like a criminal. But for this very reason philosophy can be used to cure a certain kind of criminality. For the philosopher teaches, or at least shows, how to separate oneself well. By teaching that the "human being is not the best thing in the world," he exhibits a healthy indifference to ordinary affairs. Most people become restless or violent if no one tells them what to do. Not the philosopher. He does not need external constraint to keep him in line because the world is ever present as a source of wonder and amazement. "For it is on account of wondering and being amazed (*thaumazein*) that human beings both now and at first began to philosophize. At first, they were amazed and wondered about those oddities that were staring them in the face, and then little by little they progressed and became puzzled by greater questions; for example, about the changing attributes of the moon and the sun and stars, and about the becoming of the whole" (*Metaphysics* 982b12–17).

The world is wonder-ful, beautiful, intelligible, nourishing, and welcoming. For those who use their intellects, it promises rewards greater than money, power, or fame. Philosophy, the theorizing of the world, can thus satisfy even the most restless of souls. As such, it can "cure" those "hybristic" criminals whose powerful desires propel them to the dangerous margins of the city. For the philosopher too is marginalized. Preferring leisure to being-busy, and therefore opting out of the realms of politics and war, of power and fame, he is *xenikos.* But his alienation is simultaneously a completion. For thinking is separating and he thinks the world. In doing so the philosopher is a paradigm of how to enjoy peace and use leisure well. He is a reminder that the too familiar urge to succeed in the city rather than to pursue excellence is wrongheaded. The philosopher exhibits a *telos* for human activity, without which there would be nothing for humans to want but more of the same; without which it would be impossible to say when enough is enough. This is his contribution, however indirect, to the well-being of the city. For he teaches the rest of us to prize the city as a place; a place wherein the world, which is much bigger than ourselves, should be studied rather than conquered.

Epilogue

The story's over. It began with the stars and ended on earth, where a philosopher living in a peaceful, moderately sized city has the leisure to study the world. Finite and purposive, just like us, Aristotle's world stands before our eyes, ready to be studied. It is neither the infinitesimally small universe of the particle physicist nor the impossibly vast one of the contemporary astronomer. It is, instead, our niche, our place, and it remains the center of human life.

Even today, when the computers are zipping at unimaginable speed and the impulse is always to make them faster yet, this world must not be denigrated. For it is at risk of being overwhelmed by forces unleashed through the application of the mathematized science to whose authority we have become mindlessly accustomed to defer. The bombs waiting to be exploded and the vast amounts of carbon being pumped into the atmosphere are only the most egregious examples. In our age, an age of crisis, Aristotle offers a great philosophical resource, for the world he illuminates so brilliantly is humanly scaled and inhabitable. And it is the one in which we actually find meaning in our lives. For this very reason it is both easy and common for today's intellectual to hold Aristotle in contempt. But this would be a terrible mistake. As Tom Stoppard's character Bernard reminds us, "a great philosopher is an urgent need." And the job of the philosopher, unlike that of the contemporary scientist, is to understand who and where we are. Bereft of such understanding, we will become careless with what nourishes us best. Regardless of how powerful our technologies become, such carelessness will be catastrophic.

Of course, Bernard is something of a fool. And so are we who, like him, "prefer" Aristotle at this late date. Indeed, it may seem that the logic of this book requires us to embrace illusions: the sun orbits the earth, stars and species are eternal, organisms are purposively structured, and ordinary language is ontologically informative. In fact, however, these are truths;

truths about the world as it is experienced within the limits of a human time frame. Even though he was mistaken about the death of Ezra Chater, Bernard is not wrong about everything. Perhaps the lesson of *Arcadia,* then, is that a willingness to be foolish is a risk worth taking.

Notes

Notes to the Prologue

1. This is a reference to the fifty-five planetary spheres that Aristotle, working with the astronomical theories of Eudoxus and Callippus, identifies at *Metaphysics* 1074a1–15. See Ross (1970), vol. II for an extensive commentary on Aristotle's calculations. All citations from *Arcadia* come from Stoppard (1993).

2. Stoppard offers a parallel complication when he has the anti-romantic Hannah also quote Byron (II.7). Unlike Bernard's recitation of "She Walks in Beauty," her lines are taken from "Darkness," in which the landscape depicted is so bleak that it may have inspired Cormac McCarthy's *The Road.* He also has Hannah, who early in the play boasts that "I don't dance" (I.2), end the play by dancing, even if "rather awkwardly."

3. See Crandell (1993), especially chapters 3 and 9, for a thorough discussion of these issues.

4. The translation of Descartes (1980) is by D. Cress.

5. The twin-earth was imagined by Hilary Putnam, the two spheres by Max Black.

Notes to the Introduction

1. McKibben (2010).
2. Wilson (2006), 17.
3. Koyré (1968), 29.
4. See Roochnik (2004), 4–6, for an earlier version of this section.
5. Husserl (1970), 270, 290, 295.
6. These remarks come in the "Appendix" to part I of Spinoza's *Ethics.*
7. Dawkins (1989), 21.
8. Dawkins (1996), 5.
9. Koyré (1968), 2.

10. Quotations are from Bacon's *New Organon.*

11. Descartes *Discourse on Method,* part Six.

12. Descartes *Discourse on Method,* part One.

13. Hobbes, *Leviathan,* chapter 46.11.

14. The phrase "save the phenomena," or *salvare phenomena,* was important throughout the history of astronomy. See Koyré (1992) for a thorough discussion. As Kosman (2000) shows, the sense in which Aristotelian theory "saves the phenomena" is quite different from what became standard for the astronomers. "According to Simplicius, Plato thought that a central question of astronomical science was this: 'what hypotheses using uniform circular and regular motion can save the planetary phenomena?' " As the tradition developed, the phrase became "emblematic of a view according to which astronomical theories are designed merely to reproduce mathematically the appearances as observed" (36).

15. See Barnes (1980) for a thorough discussion of the notion of the "reputable belief."

16. See Owen (1975) for a discussion of this issue.

17. See Aristotle's *On the Heavens* 306a5 and *On Generation and Corruption* 325a13 for criticisms of Parmenides. Also see Nussbaum (1986), 247 and Feyerabend (1978) for general discussions of Aristotle's "phenomenology."

18. See Owen (1975), Barnes (1980), and Nussbaum (1986, 244–45) for commentaries.

19. Johnson (2005), 4.

20. Protagoras fragment B1. The issue of whether Aristotle is or is not a Protagorean relativist is raised by Wians (1992) in his criticism of Nussbaum (1986).

21. Broackes (1999), 75.

22. The quotations are from "Meditation One" of Descartes's *Meditations on First Philosophy.* The phrase "hyperbolic doubt" can be found in "Meditation Six."

23. Bacon, *New Organon.*

24. Dawkins (1996), xv.

25. Nussbaum (1986), 261.

26. Heidegger (1962), 58.

27. See Brogan (2006).

28. Netz (2001), 225.

29. See Roochnik (2004), 179–81.

30. The citation comes from "An Historical Sketch" that precedes *The Origin of the Species.*

31. Rosen (2002), 59 and 71.

32. Rémi Brague's masterful *The Wisdom of the World* (2003) should be read carefully in order to understand the historical background to the issues discussed in the Introduction. His is a thorough study of the very concept of the "world," especially in its relationship to ethics.

Notes to Chapter One

1. That this is being summoned as evidence is signaled by the *gar* at 268a11. For a brief introduction to the Pythagoreans, see Roochnik (2004), 28–30. Some of the material in this chapter appeared in an earlier form in Roochnik (2006), 134–36.

2. See Leggatt (1995), 172 for a list.

3. See Hesiod's *Theogony* 125–30 and Plato's *Symposium* 202a–e.

4. Leggatt (1995), 173 notes that this reasoning "falls down in the case of, e.g., French, which for 'both' says '*tous (les) deux*,' literally 'all (the) two.' "

5. As Barnes (1980, 491) puts it, "*phainesthai* in Greek may be either (a) non-veridical ("he seems to be alive (but maybe he isn't)"), or (b) veridical ("he is evidently guilty"). This distinction coincides, by and large, with the syntactical distinction between *phainesthai* + infinitive and *phainesthai* + participle." In the passage cited here, *phainetai* is followed by the participle.

6. See Owen (1975), 114 and Nussbaum (1986), 244. See Cooper (1988) and Wians (1992) for critiques of Nussbaum on this issue.

7. The above reinforces Nussbaum's contention that Aristotelian "anthropocentrism need not imply relativism" (1986, 242). Even if truth only appears "inside the circle of appearances," even if his method is phenomenological, Aristotle does not think the human attempt to know and articulate the world as it really is in itself is compromised.

8. This is why Leggatt (1995) translates *pan* at 268a13 as "the whole cosmos."

9. The example comes from Plato's *Theaetetus* 201e–204e, which likely influenced Aristotle as well.

10. The citation is found in Koyré (1958), 41.

11. Nussbaum (1986), 257.

12. Lang (1998), 70.

13. Translations come from Treddenick (1976, 1996).

14. At *Physics* 189b29, Aristotle says that it is a "great puzzle" whether the principles are two or three, but at *Metaphysics* 1069b33 he says that "the principles are three": first is form, second is privation, and third is the matter.

15. Aristotle's demand that stories have a unified plot may sound outdated. Many modernist and postmodernist conceptions of fiction would surely call it into question. But such an objection can be suppressed for the moment, and storytelling should be taken here in its most elementary sense. A story begins with "once upon a time" and then spins its tale until it is over.

16. See Sacks (1987).

17. Lang (1998), 172. Aristotle's discussion of "place" and "void" in his *Physics* is long, technical, and difficult. Fortunately, it is not required to examine the issue in detail here. Lang is a good guide to these matters and has significantly

informed this section of my own work. I quote her in what follows by putting page numbers in parentheses.

18. It is difficult to render forms of the Greek participle, *on*, into English. Literally, it means "being," and so *ta onta*, the neuter plural used as a substantive, means "beings" or "things that are."

19. In other words, "where" is one of the questions the answer to which is a category. See, for examples, *Categories* 1b26 and 2a1, as well as *Metaphysics* 1017a26.

20. Lang (1998), 71 describes the quotation from Hesiod as a "punctuation mark" that ends the argument.

21. Koyré (1973), 15.

22. The passage is from appendix I, section III of Hume's *An Enquiry Concerning the Principles of Morals.*

23. Leggat (1995) translates *timioteran* (*On the Heavens* 269b16) as "more noble." Guthrie (1986) renders it as "higher." Such translations obscure the root of the word: *timê* means "honor," and honor is conferred by someone.

24. Bacon, *New Organon.*

25. Leggat (1995), 181.

26. Leggat (1995), 184

27. With these words, Ford, a great believer in progress, meant almost the opposite of what Aristotle believes. For him, human beings should forget the past and live in the present with an eye to the future.

28. See Canto IV of the *Inferno.*

29. Richard Rorty, *Consequences of Pragmatism* (Minneapolis: University of Minnesota Press, 1983), xix. The quote from Hegel comes from the *Introduction to the History of Philosophy.*

30. Daniel Dennett, *Breaking the Spell: Religion as a Natural Phenomenon* (New York: Viking, 2006); Richard Dawkins, *The God Delusion* (New York: Houghton Mifflin, 2006).

31. The quote comes from Leon Wieseltier, "The God Genome," *New York Times,* February 19, 2006. It is a hostile review with which I am sympathetic. I do not discuss these books themselves because, from my perspective, they add nothing to Spinoza.

Notes to Chapter Two

1. See the chapter titled "Nature Does Nothing in Vain" in Lennox (2001), 205–24 for a discussion of this phrase as well as a thorough catalog of its appearances in Aristotle's corpus.

2. See Ross (1970), 116. Also see LaBarge (2006), 23 for an alternative interpretation of *empeiria.*

3. The Greek for "why" here is *dioti*, which is a contraction of *dia touto hoti*, literally, "on account of this that" or "for this reason that." See Johnson (2005), 40–63 for a general introduction to the notion of an Aristotelian cause.

4. See Roochnik (2004), 180–84 for an earlier discussion of this theme.

5. Sedley (1991), 180, argues that Aristotle is in fact this sort of anthropocentrist. Johnson (2005, 231–37) rebuts, effectively I think, and also takes up a famous passage in the *Politics* (1256b6–26) that is often used, wrongly he thinks, to support Sedley's version of anthropocentrism.

6. That Aristotle says this about rain runs the risk of being inconsistent with the earlier example of rain as purposeless. Also remember (<I.7) that Aristotle is himself aware of the cyclical changes in climate that occur in the expanse of geological time.

7. This is from the footnote to the first paragraph of the "Historical Sketch" that opens Darwin's *The Origin of the Species.*

8. Gallop (1996) discusses a line from *On Divination Through Sleep*: "nature is daemonic but not divine" (463b14–15). He takes this to mean that "the daemonic [is] the appearance without the reality of intelligent design" (45). In other words, nature often seems, but isn't, purposive when chance is at work. So, for example, there may be no purpose for a lunar eclipse (*Metaphysics* 1044b12).

9. In quoting Dawkins (1996), I simply put the page number in parentheses.

10. Paley (1972), 2, 3 and 14.

11. Michael Behe, "Design for Living," *New York Times*, February 7, 2005.

12. Gotthelf (1987), 229.

13. The Greek translated as "artifice" here is *techne* and is the root of our words "technical" and "technology." Its meaning here is narrower than when it is used in *Metaphysics* I.1, where it was rendered as "knowledge."

14. See Roochnik (2009) for a thorough discussion of *theoria.*

15. This phrase is borrowed from section 14 of Nietzsche's *The Birth of Tragedy,* where it is used to described Socrates.

16. Berkeley uses an argument something like this near the end of the first of his *Three Dialogues Between Hylas and Philonous.* Philonous says, "I am content to put the whole upon this issue. . . . It is not as great a contradiction to talk of conceiving a thing which is unconceived?"

17. Dawkins (1989), 19.

18. Dawkins (1989), 22.

19. Two works that should be consulted in this context are Huizinga (1955) and Pieper (1963).

20. It is important to note that Aristotle rarely indulges in any sort of global teleology. Instead, his paradigmatic case of purposiveness is a part of an animal contributing to the well-being of the whole. Nonetheless, he is not immune to the temptation:

> Plants exist for the sake of animals and the other animals for the sake of human beings. Tame animals are useful and provide nourishment and if not all wild animals at least most of them provide nourishment and other kinds of assistance in that they supply clothing and other tools. If nature makes nothing incomplete (*ateles*) or in vain, then it is necessary that nature has made all the animals for the sake of men" (*Politics* 1256b16–22).

Because it seems to suggest a "universal teleology"—and so to be "anthropocentric" in Sedley's sense of a "position that the entire contents of the natural world . . . exist and function primarily for the benefit of man"—because, in other words, it seems to stand at odds with Aristotle's typically more modest stance, this passage has generated much controversy. Johnson, however, has effectively rebutted the notion that it does in fact imply such a globalizing teleological view. To cite just one of his arguments: "it is true that humans and other animals benefit from plants and other animals, but we can no more infer from this that they function primarily for our benefit, than we can infer that humans function primarily for the sake of mosquitoes, since they benefit from biting us." That human beings benefit mosquitoes is an "incidental" rather than an "intrinsic" feature of the former, and so plays no role in a scientific account of human being. In a similar fashion, "it is clear that we can use horses for entertainment, transportation. . . . and so forth." But none of these "benefits to human who use horses. . . . plays into the scientific account of what a horse is." They are, instead, incidental as opposed to intrinsic ends; for the horse the latter include "its own survival, reproduction, and pleasure. These are active states of its intrinsic capacities." See Johnson (2005), 136.

21. See Roochnik (2004), 166–67, 183–85.

22. Koyré (1968), viii.

23. The thesis of Burtt (1955) is that "modern physical science" is essentially Pythagorean.

24. Cited in Koyré (1968), 45–46.

25. Koyré (1968), 45–46.

26. It is, however, actual in the sense that "the infinite is in actuality (*entelecheia*) as we say the day is actual or the contest is actual." A day is composed of many hours. To say that "today is Thursday" is thus to speak somewhat ambiguously. It may be Thursday, but more accurately it is 11:17 A.M. In other words, only a limited chunk of time can be actual, not a full day. Today will include 4:00 p.m. but it is not 4:00 P.M. right now. It will be 4:00 P.M. later and so it is potentially 4 P.M. now. To reiterate, the infinite is in potentiality.

27. Apostle (1979), 269.

28. Johnson (2005) flirts with ideas like this. See, for example, the "conclusion" to his book.

Notes to Chapter Three

1. Owens (1978), 1–4 explains this problem thoroughly. He also provides a historical overview of the various responses to it.

2. Briefly, to paraphrase the argument that being is not a genus (*Metaphysics* 998b22–27): if it were, then it would be impossible to differentiate species. To explain, consider a normal genus: animal. If the species man is defined as a "rational animal," then rationality differentiates man from other species. For this to work, "both genus and differentia must be principles of and not analysable into the species." Therefore "rationality cannot be an animal or a man. For, if animality were in rationality, then 'animal' in 'rational animal' would be superfluous." Because each "difference of any genus must be" (*Metaphysics* 998b24), if Being were a genus, and X a differentia, "since X must be a being, the genus 'being' would be a predicate of its differentia . . . and this cannot be so" (Apostle [1979], 276).

3. Hence in *Exodus* III.14 God gives his name simply as "I am."

4. Owens (1978), 149–53 argues on behalf of "entity" as a translation for *ousia.*

5. "Really real" translates *ontôs on,* a familiar Platonic phrase. *Ontôs* is the adverbial form of "to be."

6. See Locke's *Essay* III.6.

7. Goodwin (1893), 11.

8. See Halper (2005), 229–44 for a thorough treatment of the relationship between form, individual, and universal in the *Metaphysics.*

9. Furth (1988), 68.

10. Locke's *Essay* II.23.

11. Would that things were so simple. See Crivelli (2004), 100–07, "Existential Assertions Concerning Simple Items," for a real scholar's treatment of this subject.

12. There are two accounts of pleasure given in the *Nicomachean Ethics,* in Books VII and X. They may not be the same. For a thorough discussion of this possible discrepancy, see Pakaluk (2004), 286–308. Some material in this section appeared in an earlier form in Roochnik (2009).

13. Goodwin (1893), 14.

14. The *pros hen* locution is used to describe the relationship of the other categories to substance: "Being is said in many ways, but towards one" (*Metaphysics* 1003b33).

15. Hume's *Inquiry,* section II.

16. "Bishops Must Stand Firmly on the Side of Life, Against the Culture of Death—Encouraging Those Who Defend It," Pope John Paul II, "Ad limina address of the Holy Father to US Bishops of California, Nevada and Hawaii," October 2, 1998, http://www.wf-f.org/JPII-Bishops-Life-Issues.html.

17. The Greek *kalon* has meanings that span the aesthetic and the moral. It can be thus be translated as "beautiful" or "good." Perhaps best of all, because it preserves the ambiguity, is "fine."

18. A challenge to this reading can be marshaled by citing *On the Psyche* III.4–5, which might seem to promise an immortal and separable "soul" and hence some protection from death. I address this possibility in the second half of this book.

19. Epicurus, "The Letter of Menoecus."

20. This is the central theme of Nussbaum (1986).

Notes to Chapter Four

1. Some of the material in this chapter overlaps with that found in Roochnik (2004), 185–98.

2. A superb philosophical account of nutrition, which is entirely Aristotelian in spirit, is found in Kass (1994), 1–44.

3. Sorabji (1992), 209 disagrees and says that "the eye-jelly . . . takes on colour patches." Seeing on this account is "literally a taking on of colour."

4. Broackes (1999), 75.

5. This material comes from Galileo's essay "Corpuscularianism" in *The Assayer*.

6. John Locke, *An Essay Concerning Human Understanding* (book II, chapter 8).

7. In his *Treatise on Human Nature* (book I, part IV, section 4), Hume states, "The fundamental principle of [modern] philosophy is the opinion concerning colors, sounds, tastes, smells, heat and cold, which it asserts to be nothing but impressions in the mind, derived from the operation of external objects and without any resemblance to the qualities of the objects."

8. All page numbers from Gilbert (2006) are given in parentheses.

9. Burnyeat (1992), 19–20.

10. Everson (1997) is a useful book that has assisted me in the writing of this section.

11. Ibid., 14.

12. Ibid., 20

13. The contemporary version of this story tells us that the human ear has the material components to detect sound waves ranging approximately between 20 and 20,000 hertz. Because its ear is configured differently, a cat can detect frequencies as low as approximately 45 Hz and as high as 85,000 Hz.

14. Burnyeat (1992), 21.

15. Burnyeat (1992), 22. Because Aristotle cannot possibly "explain life from the bottom up"—in other words, he does not have a thoroughly materialist or mechanical explanation of life functions—Burnyeat thinks his "philosophy of mind" should be "junked" (26).

16. Shawn (2007), 70.

17. Lear (1990), 101–15 offers a useful account of Aristotelian perception.

18. See also *Parts of Animals* 647a14–24.

19. Commenting on this passage, Sorabji (2006) reports that "the phrase [common-sense] (*koinê aisthêsis*) is used only three times in Aristotle, at *PA* 686a27, *DA* 425a27, and here" (75).

20. Everson (1997), 176.

21. Ibid., 152.

22. Schofield (1992), 257.

23. Ferrarin (2006), 103 and 110.

24. Schofield (1992), 251.

25. Ferrarin (2006), 101.

26. Ibid., 105.

27. Of course, this begs the question of "where" the intelligible objects are.

28. Brentano (1992), 313.

29. Wilkes (1992), 124.

30. Ferrarin (2006), 105–06.

31. Kahn (1992), 361–62.

32. See Roochnik (2004), 186–87 for an earlier version of this section.

33. Modrak (2001) is comprehensive explication of the few lines from *On Interpretation* that were cited above.

34. The Greek preposition *kata* literally means "down towards."

35. See Crivelli (2004), 4–5 and 46–62. He characterizes certain "composite objects" as "states of affairs" that are themselves, not just the language about them, true or false.

36. The translation is from Ackrill (1968).

37. The quotations are from Heidegger (1962), 56–57.

38. As Ross (1970) reports in his note to this line, there are some problems with the text.

39. There is actually a third category: the "productive" (*poiêtikê*: EN1139a28), which here is subsumed under the practical.

40. It is possible that the metaphor may refer not to a "door" as something to walk through, but as a target for an archer. No one could miss that. The saying is listing in Leutsch's *Corpus Paroemiographorum Graeocrum,* vol. II, 678.

Notes to Chapter Five

1. Aristotle wrote three treatises on ethics: the *Nicomachean Ethics*, *Magna Moralia,* and *Eudemian Ethics.* Only the first is discussed in this book.

2. The official conclusion of the *Nicomachean Ethics* actually comes in X.9, which consists of the transition from this work to the *Politics.* Nussbaum (1986) uses the phrase "notorious" to describe the problem.

3. Because the *monê* at 1177b1 renders the meaning of the sentence somewhat ambiguous, Irwin (1999) offers two translations: "study seems to be liked because of itself alone" and "it is the only virtue" liked because of itself. His translation of *theôria* as "study" is, as will be discussed extensively below, a good choice.

4. At 1107a11, Aristotle does assert that adultery, theft, and murder are just plain wrong.

5. There is some overlap between this section and Roochnik (2004), 199–210.

6. *Agron* is a pun, for it is composed of the alpha-privative and *ergon.*

7. Pakaluk (2005), 77.

8. This is true only according to Aristotle's own zoology. Our knowledge of animal brains may lead to quite different conclusions.

9. Gilbert (2006), 31 insists that happiness is "emotional. . . . a feeling, an experience, a subjective state" that has "no objective referent in the physical world." Williams (1985), 34 does a good job explaining why "happiness" is problematic for Aristotle: "It makes sense now to say that you are happy one day, unhappy another, but *eudaimonia* was a matter of the shape of one's whole life. I shall use the expression 'well-being' for such a state." Also see *Nicomachean Ethics* 1099b20–25 for a discussion of the relationship between *eudaimonia* and chance.

10. Aristotle restricts real friendship to those who are virtuous. See *Nicomachean Ethics* 1156b7–12.

11. Quoted in Ostwald (1999), who himself is quoting Lattimore's translation.

12. As will be seen shortly, "practical wisdom" or *phronêsis* will complicate this story.

13. On habit, also see *Politics* 1332b1–10.

14. See Kant's *Foundations of the Metaphysics of Morals* (Second Section).

15. Recall this passage from the *Metaphysics*: "Everything is ordered in some way; water-animals and birds and plants. But these do not lack a relationship of one to the other. Instead, there is a relationship. For everything is related towards one (*pros hen*). It is like a household (*oikia*) in which the freemen are least able to act in a random fashion" (1075a16–25). Freedom here requires the taking on of responsibilities, which is a form of constraint.

16. See *Politics* 1331b42.

17. This is the overarching theme of Nussbaum (1986).

18. Aristotle actually says *politikê*, which here can be treated as synonymous with "ethics."

19. The last sentence cheats. Aristotle doesn't say "ethics." Instead he uses "rhetoric" as his example. But the point would apply to ethics as well.

20. See Roochnik (2007) for a discussion of Aristotle on "vice."

21. Kant, *Foundations of the Metaphysics of Morals* (First Section).

22. John Locke, *Second Treatise of Government* (chapter 2).

23. Nussbaum (1986), 373 and 375.

24. She takes this to be one way in which Aristotle differs sharply from Plato, who regularly condemned a life of habitually performed virtues.

25. Nussbaum (1986), 374.

26. Aristotle may be referring to Euripides (*Fragment* 1040) in this passage.

27. In order: Ostwald (1999), Irwin (1985), Broadie and Rowe (2002). Sachs (2002) comes closest when he translates it as "we engage in unleisured pursuits."

28. See Huizinga (1955) for a thorough discussion of play.

29. See Pieper (1963) for a thorough discussion of leisure.

30. Roochnik (2009) covers this material in detail. Irwin's (1985) translation of *theoria* as "study" also should be kept in mind throughout this chapter.

31. Eriksen (1976), 89.

32. Ibid., 82–84 cites the following passages to support it: *Nicomachean Ethics* 1146b30, 1153a22, *Metaphysics* 1048a34, 1072b24, *Physics* 255a33–b5, *On the Psyche* 412a9–22, *Generation of Animals* 735a9. He also reviews Burnet's, Düring's, and Stenzel's discussions of this issue.

33. The distinction between "having" and "using" knowledge was first suggested by Plato in the "aviary" image of the *Theaetetus* (196d–199c).

34. The "right now" reflects the phrase *êdê theôrôn* at 417a28–29.

35. Kraut (1989), 73.

36. Kraut (1989), 73. In a similar vein, Rorty (1992), 386 describes *theôria* as a "single act of mind" as opposed to an explanation or a demonstration. For a useful corrective, see Guthrie (1971), 396–98.

37. As Eriksen (1976), 87 notes, *theôria* was traditionally associated with astronomy.

38. Kraut (1989), 16 and 73. "Theoretical wisdom" translates the Greek *sophia*. The "theoretical" is typically added by translators in order to distinguish it from *phronêsis*, "practical wisdom."

39. Nightingale (2004), 238.

40. Rorty (1992), 379.

41. Richardson Lear (2004), 4.

42. Rorty (1992), 377.

43. Another example is from *Metaphysics* 1026a22: "the theoretical forms of knowledge are more choiceworthy than the other forms of knowledge (*epistêmôn*)."

44. Nightingale (2004), 6 and Kraut (1989), 16.

45. A computer search will quickly supply the evidence that inflections of *theôrein* are ubiquitous and often mundane. Two somewhat random examples: the "magnificent" man is able to "theorize" (*theôrêsai*) what is "appropriate" to give (*Nicomachean Ethics* 1122a35); and in *Parts of Animals* Aristotle asks whether the student of anatomy should begin with what is common in a genus and then "later theorize (*theôrêteon*) the particulars" (639b5).

46. In this passage, *theôrêtikê*, *praktikê*, and *poiêtikê* each unmistakably modifies *epistêmê* at 145a5.

47. Eriksen (1976), 86.

Notes to Chapter Six

1. "The Challenge of Slums," *The Boston Globe*, October 6, 2003.

2. *Pleonexia* is, for example, a prominent theme in Plato's *Gorgias*, where it is associated with the fictional character of Callicles.

3. There is a bit of overlap between this chapter and pages 214–24 of Roochnik (2004).

4. An earlier version of this section appears in Roochnik (2008).

5. Rawls (1971), 447–48.

6. Compare John Locke, *Second Treatise of Government* (chapter IV). Miller (1995) would challenge this assertion.

7. He actually refers to what he calls "the exoteric discourses" (1323a22), which, whatever exactly they were, articulate basic ethical principles. See Lord (1985), 19 for a discussion.

8. Full-blown blessedness, he adds, requires good fortune as well, and this Aristotle alludes to under the category of "external" goods, ones that are out of the agent's control.

9. Recall that although he operates from a thoroughly non-Aristotelian perspective, Gilbert (2006) also argues that most people are thoroughly misguided in their own pursuit of happiness.

10. See Nightingale (2004) for a discussion of the historical background of the theory–practice distinction.

11. This argument can be read differently; namely, as distinguishing between political and tyrannical. So, for example, Miller (1995) says, "Aristotle sympathetically discusses the political way of life, distinguishing it from the tyrannical, which involves the performance of unjust acts of excessive possession towards one's neighbors. . . . Aristotle's discussion is somewhat inconclusive because he does not explicitly answer the question he has posed as to whether the best life is political and or philosophical" (215–16). Kraut (1997, 62) says that Aristotle "does not decisively draw a conclusion about which is better." Reeve (1998, xlvi) describes him as "cagey, dialectically balancing the claims on the political life against the philosophical, but not giving decisive precedence to either." Solmsen (1964, 196) put the point strongly by saying that "we have to accept the oscillations of Aristotle's argument and the ambiguity of his conclusion; they are indicative of a deeper conflict between diverging tendencies and inclinations in his mind."

12. There is no need to discuss the historical accuracy of this description of Sparta and Crete. That there are expansionist regimes is a given.

13. Diels (1903), 74.

14. From Miller (1995), 4.

15. Lear (1988), 197.

16. Ambler (1987), 390.

17. I owe this observation to Ambler (1987), 395, who says, "I am not surprised that he asks not whether there are many such creatures but whether there is

any." There is, unfortunately, countervailing evidence concerning Aristotle's stance on institutional (non-natural) slavery. For he seems to take it for granted that slaves are a necessary component of the best city. See 1329a25–26 and 1330a25. Also, as Silvia Carli pointed out to me, Aristotle even suggests that freedom should be held out as "a reward for all slaves" (1330a33), which is a clear indication that they are not "natural."

18. This is actually a quote from Sophocles' *Ajax* (293). The actual Greek word is not "golden" but *kosmon*, "cosmos," which also means "ornament."

19. This e-mail was received on December 23, 2004, and has been transcribed verbatim and in its entirety. The "Rushton" referred to is Philippe Rushton, who has published widely on race, brain size, and intelligence.

20. Popper (1950), 195. This book is most famous for its critique of Plato, but in chapter 11 it attacks Aristotle, whose thought, according to Popper, "is entirely dominated by Plato's" (200).

21. Thomas Hobbes, *Leviathan* (46 and then 1).

22. John Locke, *Second Treatise of Government* (chapter IV.22).

23. Johnson (2005), 4.

24. In the *Metaphysics*, this phrase is said to refer to "the essence of a being (1022a26). See Roochnik (2010) for a thorough elaboration of this notion.

25. Silvia Carli suggests that this statement conflicts with the notion that both citizens and cities suffer from moral weakness, for here I state that they "wrongly" elevate the category of quantity over substance. In other words, they seem not to know better. Recall, however, that Aristotle is convinced that "everyone" would agree that the best life requires virtue. Therefore, the "confusion" I here attribute to cities is a component of the complex and conflicted condition that characterizes moral weakness. The arguments against expansionism are so "easy" to make that even regimes like Sparta and Crete would upon hearing them know they should change their ways, even if they don't.

26. Brague (2003) is masterful on cosmology as ethics.

27. Aristotle assumes that the poor will always be many: "the rich are everywhere few and the poor many" (1279b37–38).

28. As Kraut (1997, 144) rightly puts it, "Paradoxically, although war endangers our lives and freedom, peace and abundance pose greater threats."

Bibliography

Primary Texts

Categories, ed. Minio-Paluello. Oxford: Oxford University Press, 1966.
De Anima, ed. W. D. Ross. Oxford: Oxford University Press, 1963.
Generation of Animals, ed. A. L. Peck. Cambridge, MA: Loeb Classical Library, 1990.
Metaphysics, ed. W. D. Ross. Oxford: Oxford University Press, 1970.
Nicomachean Ethics, ed. I. Bywater. Oxford: Oxford University Press, 1962.
On Interpretation, ed. Minio-Paluello. Oxford: Oxford University Press, 1966.
On the Heavens I and II, ed. S. Leggatt. Warminster: Aris & Phillips.
Parts of Animals, ed. A. Peck. Cambridge, MA: Loeb Classical Library, 1998.
Physics, ed. W. D. Ross. Oxford: Oxford University Press, 1998.
Politica, ed. W. D. Ross. Oxford: Oxford University Press, 1988.
The Poetics, ed. S. H. Butcher. New York: Dover, 1951.
Topics, ed. E. Forster. Cambridge, MA: Loeb Classical Library, 1976.

Translations

Ackrill, J. L. 1968. *Aristotle's Categories and De Interpretatione.* Oxford: Oxford University Press.
Apostle, H. 1979. *Aristotle's Metaphysics.* Grinnell: Peripatetic Press.
Apostle, H. 1980. *Aristotle's Physics.* Grinnell: Peripatetic Press.
Butcher, S. 1961. *Aristotle's Theory of Poetry and Fine Art.* New York: Dover, 1961.
Broadie, S., and C. Rowe. 2002. *Aristotle: Nicomachean Ethics.* Oxford: Oxford University Press.
Freese, J. H. 1973. *The "Art" of Rhetoric.* Cambridge, MA: Loeb Classical Library.
Hamlyn, D. W. 1968. *Aristotle's De Anima: Books II and III.* Oxford: Clarendon Press.
Irwin, T. 1985. *Aristotle's Nicomachean Ethics.* Indianapolis: Hackett.
Lee, H. D. P. 1967. *Meteorologica.* Cambridge, MA: Loeb Classical Library.
Leggat, S. 1995. *Aristotle: On the Heavens* I & II. Warminster: Aris & Phillips.
Lord, C. 1985. *Aristotle: The Politics.* Chicago: University of Chicago Press.
Ostwald, M. 1999. *Aristotle: Nicomachean Ethics.* Englewood: Prentice Hall.
Sachs, J. 2002. *Aristotle's Nicomachean Ethics.* Newburyport: Focus Press.

Tredennick, H. 1976. *Aristotle: Posterior Analytics.* Cambridge, MA: Loeb Classical Library.
Tredennick, H. 1996. *Aristotle: Prior Analytics.* Cambridge, MA: Loeb Classical Library.

Secondary Sources Cited

Ackrill, J. 1968. *Aristotle's Categories and De Interpretatione.* Oxford: Clarendon.

Ambler, W. 1987. "Aristotle on Nature and Politics: The Case of Slavery." *Political Theory* 15: 390–410.

Barnes, J., ed. 1975. *Articles on Aristotle.* London: Duckworth.

Barnes, J. 1980. "Aristotle and the Method of Ethics." *Revue internationale de philosophie* 34: 490–511.

Brague, R. 2003. *The Wisdom of the World.* Chicago: University of Chicago Press.

Brentano, F. 1992. "*Nous Poieikos.*" In *Essays on Aristotle's De Anima*, edited by M. Nussbaum and A. Rorty, 313–341. Oxford: Clarendon Press.

Broackes, J. 1999. "Aristotle, Objectivity, and Perception." *Oxford Studies in Ancient Philosophy* 17: 57–114.

Brogan, W. 2006. *Heidegger and Aristotle.* Albany: State University of New York Press.

Burnyeat, M. 1992. "Is an Aristotelian Philosophy of Mind Still Credible?" In *Essays on Aristotle's De Anima*, edited by M. Nussbaum and A. Rorty. Oxford: Clarendon Press.

Burtt, E. A. 1955. *The Metaphysical Foundations of Modern Science.* New York: Doubleday.

Crandell, G. 1993. *Nature Pictorialized: The "View" in Landscape History.* Baltimore: Johns Hopkins.

Cooper, J. 1988. Review of *The Fragility of Goodness. Philosophical Review* 92: 543–564.

Crivelli, P. 2004. *Aristotle on Truth.* Cambridge: Cambridge University Press.

Dawkins, R. 1989. *The Selfish Gene.* Oxford: Oxford University Press.

Dawkins, R. 1996. *The Blind Watchmaker.* New York: Norton.

Descartes, R. 1980. *Discourse on Method and Meditations on First Philosophy.* Translated by D. Cress. Indianapolis: Hackett.

Diels, H. 1903. *Die Fragmente der Vorsokratiker.* Berlin: Weidmannsche.

Eriksen, T. 1976. *Bios Theoretikos: Notes on Aristotle's Nicomachean Ethics X.6–8.* Oslo: Universitetsforlaget.

Everson, S. 1997. *Aristotle on Perception* Oxford: Clarendon Press.

Ferrarin, A. 2006. "Aristotle on *Phantasia.*" *Proceedings of the Boston Area Colloquium in Ancient Philosophy.* Edited by J. Cleary and G. Gurtler, 89–112.

Feyerabend, P. 1978. "In Defense of Aristotle. In *Progress and Rationality in Science*, edited by G. Radnitsky and G. Andersson, 144–180. Boston: Reidel.

Furth, M. 1988. *Substance, Form and Psyche: An Aristotelian Metaphysics.* Cambridge: Cambridge University Press.

Gallop, D. 1996. *Aristotle On Sleep and Dreams.* Warminster: Aris and Phillips.

Gilbert, D. 2006. *Stumbling Towards Happiness.* New York: Knopf.

Gill, M. 1989. *Aristotle on Substance.* Princeton: Princeton University Press.

Gotthelf, A., and J. Lennox 1987. *Philosophical Issues in Aristotle's Biology.* Cambridge: Cambridge University Press.

Goodwin, W. 1893. *Syntax of the Moods and Tenses of the Greek Verb.* Boston: Ginn.

Guthrie, W. K. C. 1971. *History of Greek Philosophy Volume 6.* Cambridge: Cambridge University Press.

Halper, E. 2005. *One and Many in Aristotle's Metaphysics.* Las Vegas: Parmenides Press.

Heidegger, M. 1962. *Being and Time.* Translated by J. Macquarrie and E. Robinson. New York: Harper and Row.

Huizinga, J. 1955. *Homo Ludens: A Study of the Play-Element in Culture.* Boston: Beacon.

Husserl, E. 1970. *The Crisis of European Sciences and Transcendental Philosophy.* Translated by D. Carr. Evanston: Northwestern University Press.

Johnson, M. 2005. *Aristotle on Teleology.* Oxford: Oxford University Press.

Kahn, C. 1992. "Aristotle on Thinking." In *Essays on Aristotle's De Anima*, edited by M. Nussbaum and A. Rorty, 359–380. Oxford: Clarendon Press.

Kass, L. 1994. *The Hungry Soul.* New York: Free Press.

Kosman, A. 2000. "Saving the Phenomena: Realism and Instrumentalism in Aristotle's Theory of Science." In *Aristotle and Contemporary Science*, edited by Demetra Sfendoni-Mentzou. New York: Peter Lang Publishing.

Koyré, A. 1968. *From the Closed World to the Infinite Universe.* Baltimore: Johns Hopkins University Press.

Koyré, A. 1992. *The Astronomical Revolution: Copernicus, Kepler, Borelli.* New York: Dover.

Kraut, R. 1989. *Aristotle on the Human Good.* Princeton: Princeton University Press.

Kraut, R. 1997. *Aristotle: Politics Books VII and VIII.* Oxford: Clarendon Press.

Kraut, R. 2002. *Aristotle: Political Philosophy.* Oxford: Oxford University Press.

LaBarge, S. 2006. "Aristotle on *Empeiria.*" *Ancient Philosophy* 26: 23–44.

Lang, H. 1998. *The Order of Nature in Aristotle's Physics: Place and the Elements.* Cambridge: Cambridge University Press.

Lennox, J. 2001. *Aristotle's Philosophy of Biology.* Cambridge: Cambridge University Press.

Lear, J. 1988. *Aristotle: The Desire to Understand.* Cambridge: Cambridge University Press.

McKibben, Bill 2010. *Earth: Making a Life on a Tough New Planet.* New York: Henry Holt.

Miller, F. 1995. *Nature, Justice, and Rights in Aristotle's Politics.* Oxford: Oxford University Press.

Modrak, D. 2001. *Aristotle's Theory of Language and Meaning.* Cambridge: Cambridge University Press.

Netz. R. 2001. "On the Aristotelian Paragraph." *Proceedings of the Cambridge Philological Society* 47: 211–232.

Nightingale, A. 2004. *Spectacles of Truth: Theoria in its Cultural Context.* Cambridge: Cambridge University Press.

Nussbaum, M. 1986. *The Fragility of Goodness.* Cambridge: Cambridge University Press.

Nussbaum, M., and A. Rorty, eds. 1992. *Essays on Aristotle's De Anima.* Oxford: Clarendon Press.

Owen, G. 1975. "*Tithenai ta Phainomena.*" In *Articles on Aristotle*, edited by J. Barnes, 61–75. London: Duckworth.

Owens, J. 1978. *The Doctrine of Being in the Aristotelian 'Metaphysics.'* Toronto: Pontifical Institute of Medieval Studies.

Pakaluk, M. 2005. *Aristotle's Nicomachean Ethics.* Cambridge: Cambridge University Press.

Paley, W. 1972. *Natural Theology: Or, Evidences of the Existence and Attributes of the Deity, Collected from the Appearances of Nature.*" Houston: St. Thomas Press.

Pieper, J. 1963. *Leisure: The Basis of Culture.* New York: Random House.

Popper, K. 1950. *The Open Society and its Enemies.* Princeton: Princeton University Press.

Rawls, J. 1971. *A Theory of Justice.* Cambridge, MA: Harvard University Press.

Richardson Lear, G. 2004. *Happy Lives and the Highest Good: An Essay on Aristotle's Nicomachean Ethics.* Princeton: Princeton University Press.

Roochnik, D. 2004. *Retrieving the Ancients.* London: Blackwell.

Roochnik, D. 2006. "Aristotle's Commonsense Cosmology." In *Logos and Eros: Essays Honoring Stanley Rosen*, edited by N. Ranasinghe. South Bend: St. Augustine's Press.

Roochnik, D. 2007. "Aristotle's Account of the Vicious: A Forgivable Inconsistency." *History of Philosophy Quarterly* 24: 207–220.

Roochnik, D. 2008. "Aristotle's Defense of the Theoretical Life: Comments on *Politics* VII." *Review of Metaphysics* 61: 711–735.

Roochnik, D. 2009. "What is *Theoria? Nicomachean Ethics,* Book 10.7–8." *Classical Philology* 104: 69–81.

Roochnik, D. 2010. "Substantial City: Reflections on Aristotle's *Politics.*" *Polis* 27: 275–291.

Rorty, A. 1992: "The Place of Contemplation in Aristotle's *Nicomachean Ethics.*" In *Essays on Aristotle's De Anima*, edited by M. Nussbaum and A. Rorty, 377–394. Oxford: Clarendon Press.

Rosen, S. 2002. *The Elusiveness of the Ordinary.* New Haven: Yale University Press.

Sacks. O. 1987. *The Man Who Mistook His Wife for a Hat.* New York: Perennial Library.

Schofield, M. 1992. "Aristotle on the Imagination." In *Essays on Aristotle's De Anima*, edited by M. Nussbaum and A. Rorty, 102–119. Oxford: Clarendon Press.

Sedley, D. 1991. "Is Aristotle's Teleology Anthropocentric?" *Phronesis* 36: 179–196.

Shawn, A. 2007 *Wish I Could Be There.* New York: Viking.

Solmsen, F. 1964. "Leisure and Play in Aristotle's Ideal State." *Rheinisches Museum für Philologie* 107: 196.

Sorabji, R. 1992. "Intentionality and Physiological Processes: Aristotle's Theory of Sense Perception." In *Essays on Aristotle's De Anima*, edited by M. Nussbaum and A. Rorty, 195–225. Oxford: Clarendon Press.

Sorabji, R. 2006. *Aristotle on Memory.* Chicago: University of Chicago Press.

Stoppard, T. 2003. *Arcadia.* London: Faber and Faber.

Wians, W. 1992. "Saving Aristotle from Nussbaum's *Phainomena.*" In *Essays in Greek Philosophy,* vol. 5, edited by John P. Anton and Anthony Preus. Albany: State University of New York Press.

Williams, B. 1985. *Ethics and the Limits of Philosophy.* Cambridge: Harvard University Press.

Wilson, E. O. 2006. "Apocalypse Now." *The New Republic* 235 (September 4): 17–20.

Index

Ackrill, J. L., 227, 233, 234
actuality (*energeia* or *entelecheia*), 61–63, 67, 69, 71, 74, 100, 101, 103, 110, 113, 117, 118ff., 127, 133, 138–39, 142, 149, 154, 157–58, 176, 178–79, 185–87, 197, 209, 213, 224, as activity 29, 126–28; relation to pleasure 102–106; two senses of 116–17, 127, 178. See also *ergon*, form, matter, potentiality
Ambler, W., 200, 230, 234
anthropocentrism, anthropocentric, 3, 4, 7, 10, 20, 24, 38, 49, 174, 175, 186, 210, 221, 223, 224, 236
anthropomorphism, anthropomorphic, 3, 4, 8, 10, 13, 20, 29, 30, 36, 37, 63, 65, 75, 76, 88, 108, 135
Arcadia, xi, xiii, xiv, 218, 236
Bernard (character), xi–xiv, xvi, 4, 8, 13, 75, 77, 126, 217–18, 219
archê (beginning, first cause, first principle, origin: plural *archai*), 18, 21, 22, 24, 25, 27–29, 31, 36, 47, 57–59, 74, 75, 93; 99, 116, 129, 139, 166, 182–84
Arendt, H., 14–15
Aristotle: *Categories*, 85–86, 88–89, 90, 94, 222; *Generation of Animals*, 64, 71, 81, 105, 109, 129, 229; *Historia Animalium*, 29; *Metaphysics*, 8, 11, 20, 21–22, 42, 45–46, 67–68, 71, 74, 75, 77–78, 81–109, 115, 124, 127, 131, 145, 146, 149, 170, 177, 178, 179–80, 183, 185–87, 208–209, 215, 221, 222, 223, 225, 228, 229, 231; *Meteorology*, 39–40, 48; *Nicomachean Ethics*, 8, 8–11, 25–26, 29, 76, 93, 102–105, 112–13, 135, 142, 146, 149–87, 191, 193, 194, 197, 203, 207–10, 227–29; *On Divination Through Sleep*, 223; *On Dreams*, 129; *On Generation and Corruption*, 220; *On the Heavens*, 17–44, 72, 135, 140, 220–22; *On Interpretation*, 143–48; *On Memory*, 133, 134, 136–37; *On the Psyche*, 26, 64, 105, 112, 115–42, 149, 150, 151, 173, 178, 182, 186–87, 226, 227, 229; *On Respiration*, 45; *On Sense and Sensible Objects*, 124; *On Sleep*, 128; *Parts of Animals*, 125, 129, 227; *Physics*, 11, 19, 21, 23, 24, 27–28, 31–33, 37, 38, 45, 46–51, 56, 57–59, 61–62, 63, 65, 72, 73–74, 98–100, 134, 142, 147, 156, 180, 182, 201, 221, 229; *Poetics*, 28–29, 166, 184; *Politics*, 8, 29, 40, 45, 68–69, 70, 76, 105, 110, 111, 151, 171, 190–215, 223, 224, 228, 230–31;

Aristotle *(continued)*
Posterior Analytics, 25, 45, 47, 89, 93, 181; *Prior Analytics*, 25; *Rhetoric*, 21, 26, 115, 166, 185; *Topics*, 9, 18, 182, 183
atomism, 111–12
Augustine, 172

Bacon, 5, 8, 12–13, 20, 30, 34, 37, 38, 52, 88, 92, 220, 222
Barnes, J., 220, 221, 234, 235
Behe, M., 56, 223
being, 86–87, 146–47, 187, 211, as finite 74; subject of metaphysics 81–92, 183, 186. *See also* substance
Berkeley, 223
biology, xi, xiv, 4, 6, 13, 29, 44, 50–54, 58, 63, 64, 67, 81, 91, 109, 151, 190, 202, 234, 235. *See also* teleology, Intelligent Design
Black, M., 219
body, 31, 73, 87, 116–18, 125, contrasted with *psyche* 64, 70, 109, 192, 198; heavenly 43, 72, 85, 98, 100, 173, 178, 184
Boyle, 15
Brague, R., 220, 231, 234
Brentano, F., 14, 140, 227, 234
Broackes, P., 220, 226, 234
Brogan, W., 220, 234
Bruno, G., 24, 73–74
Burnyeat, M., 125–26, 226, 234
Burtt, E.A., 224, 234

Carli, S., 231
cause, 32, 100, 101, knowledge of 45–46, 82, 208–209; not infinite 75–76, 100; total of four 46–47; efficient 125; final cause: see *telos*; formal cause, *see* form
chance, 163–64
Churchill, 207
Cooper, J., 221, 234
Copernicus, 3, 34, 235
Copernican revolution, xvi
cosmos, xi–xii, xiv, 4, 5, 8, 18, 38, 57, 69, 73, 77, 105–107, 109, 135, 140, 153, 186, 187, 190, 204, 211, 221, 231, definition by Koyré 19, 34, 68; heterogenous 32, 63, 68, 190; homogenous 17, 63, 68, 69
Crivelli, P., 225, 227, 234

Dante, 41, 115, 117, 222
Darwin, xvi, 4, 15, 50, 52, 223
Darwinism, 53–54; compared with Intelligent Design, 55–56
Dawkins, R., 4, 13, 43, 51–56, 62–63, 65, 76, 121, 219, 220, 222, 223, 234
Democritus, 15, 27
Descartes, xiv–xv, 5, 7, 11, 12, 41, 147–48, 219, 220, 234
Donne, J., 2
doxa (opinion, belief), 9–10, 94, 135, 151, 153. See also *endoxa*

Empedocles, 15, 48–50, 56
endoxa (reputable opinions or beliefs), 9, 10, 18, 20, 30, 71, 82, 83, 84, 135, 148, 151, 153, 220
ergon (work), 104, 154, 156–58, 183, 199. *See also* actuality, virtue
Eriksen, T., 178, 229, 234
essence (*to ti ên einai*), 89–90, 95, 139, 141, 186. *See also* form, substance
Euclid, 36, 93
Eudemus, 140, 149
Eudoxus, 219
Euripides, 203, 229
Everson, S., 129, 130, 226, 227, 234

Ferrarin, A., 133, 134, 137, 141, 227, 234
Feyerabend, P., 220, 234

finite, 34, 69, 86, 93, 152, 187, 211, 217, prior to the infinite 71–77, 87, 135, 153, 190
form (or species, *eidos*), 40, 46, 47, 63, 64, 67–69, 77, 82, 88, 89–91, 98, 101, 105, 108, 112, 113, 116, 138, 186, 187, 212, as cause 60, 62, 60–67; as ontological integrity 47, 56; sensible 119–20, 125, 139. *See also* matter, *telos*
Furth, M., 91, 225, 234

Galileo, 3, 6, 7, 15, 71, 120–21, 128, 226
Genesis, 83–84, 106
Gilbert, D., 122–23, 131, 144, 226, 228, 230, 234
God (biblical), xiii, xiv–v, 7, 42, 44, 55, 68, 83, 84, 106–108, 172, 222, 225
god, generic vi, xi, xiv, 18–20, 43, 45, 48, 69, 76, 85, 98, 109, 135, 149, 186, 187, 197, 211–12; as Aristotelian, motionless mover 75, 84, 100–102, 105–106, 108, 137, 140, 141, 149, 179, 185
  as the ultimate Good, 84, 106–108, 108–109
Gospel of Matthew, 172

habit, 160–62, 163, 187, 191, 203. *See also* virtue
Halper, E., 225, 235
happiness (*eudaimonia*), xiv, 29, 75–76, 111–13, 122–23, 149, 153–58, 160, 167–68, 173–76, 203, 208–10, 212, 214, 228, 230, 234, definition 158; in relation to *makarios* 113, 164, 192. *See also* the highest good, virtue
Heidegger, 14, 77, 145, 147, 220, 227, 234, 235
Heraclitus, 230
Herodotus, 163
Hesiod, 18, 32–33, 159, 171, 221, 222
Hobbes, 8, 30, 203, 220
Homer, 29, 115
household (*oikia*) 68, 196–98, 201, 228, as metaphysical ecology 107–108
Huizinga, J., 223, 229, 235
Hume, 36–37, 67, 108, 222, 225, 226
Husserl, 2–3, 6–7, 13–15, 219, 235
hylomorphism, 90, 141. *See also* form, matter

infinite, 40, 70–77, 96, 109, 152, 192–93, 211. *See also* finite
Intelligent Design (ID), 52, 54–57, 106, 223

Johnson, M., 220, 223, 224, 231, 235
Jonas, H., 14

Kahn, C., 141, 227, 235
Kant, 163, 166, 171–72, 204, 228
Kass, L., 226, 235
kinêsis (change, motion, process), 9, 27, 31–38, 40, 61ff., 98, 100, 101, 103, 125–27, 176, 180, 183, 186, 209, 211, as locomotion 31, 35, 61, 99, 124
Kosman, A., 220, 235
Koyré, A., 2, 4–5, 34, 68, 73, 219–22, 224, 235
Kraut, R., 178–79, 181–82, 229, 230, 231

Lear, J., 200, 227, 230, 235
Leggat, 39, 221, 222, 233
leisure (*scholê*), 66–67, 78, 141, 149, 173–77, 208, 209, 211–15, 217, 229, 235, 236, as verb in Greek 175, 229; lack of (*ascholia*) 176, 177, 208, 213, 214
Leutsch, 227

Locke, xvi, 8, 89, 91–92, 97, 121–22, 124, 128, 147, 172, 203, 204, 225, 226, 228, 230, 231
logos (speech, language, reason), 14, 25, 26, 46, 47, 59–60, 78, 81, 83, 94, 142–48, 141, 155, 156, 158–59, 169–71, 185, 197, 208, relation to phenomena 43, 135–36; *logos apophantikos* 145, 156, 197; as *telos* of human beings 68–69

magnitude, 17, 22, 28, 31, 35, 72, 74, 128, 138, 166, 184, 212–13
mathematics, mathematical, xi, xii, 3, 15, 34, 78, 81, 82, 83, 142, 166–67, 169, 177, 183, 184, 220, as language of physics 6–8, 71, 74, 121; too precise for ethics 166–67, 169
matter, 28, 100–101, 119–20, 139, 183, 221, as material cause 46; correlate of form 90, 91, 98, 116, 125, 187. *See also* form, potentiality
McKibben, B., 1, 219, 235
mean, ethical, 168–69; political 206–207
medieval philosophy, 7, 34, 68, 106
Mill, J.S., 166
Miller, F., 230, 235
Modrak, D., 144, 227, 235
moral weakness (*akrasia*), 8–10, 181, 193, 231

nature, natural, xiii–xvi, 3, 4, 4–8, 11–13, 15, 16, 18–21, 21–24, 26–27, 30, 31–33, 35, 37–39, 41–45, 58, 73, 77, 79, 84, 85, 98, 104, 107, 109–12, 116–17, 121, 124, 138–41, 147, 152, 154, 156, 160–62, 166–67, 171–74, 178, 182, 184–86, 190, 192, 195, 196–200, 201–204, 207, 209, 210, 213, 222–24, 231, 234, 235, Aristotelian conception of xiv, 3, 47–49, 52, 61ff., 63, 68–70, 110; distinguished from artifice 57–58; modern conception or criticism of (*see also* mathematics) 5–6, 12–13, 15, 45, 71. *See also* form, teleology, *telos*
natural selection, xvi, 4, 7, 13, 15, 50, 51, 53, 54, 56. *See also* Darwin
Netz, R., 220, 235
Nietzsche, 223
Nightingale, A., 179, 181–82, 229, 230, 235
nous (mind, intellect), 93, 106, 108, 117, 149, active and passive 136–42, 174, 186, 187
Nussbaum, M., 13, 20, 24, 174–75, 220, 221, 226, 227, 228, 229, 234–36

ontological integrity, 4, 47, 51, 56–58, 87, 92, 97
ordinary experience, xvi, 9, 14, 20, 23, 30, 43, 53, 59, 63, 136, 147, 149. *See also* phenomena
Ostwald, M., 228, 229, 233

Paley, W., 52, 54–56, 223, 235
Parmenides, 9, 28, 220
Pericles, 180–82, 185
phainesthai (to appear, to seem), 20, 59, 87, 101, 145, 154, 160, 221, in *phantasia* 131, 132, 135
phaneron (apparent, evident), 42, 59, 65, 87, 99, 147, 152
phantasia (imagination), 73, 131–36, 140, 234, 236
phantasma (image), 129, 131–36, 144, in thought, 136–38, 141, 142
phenomena (*phainomena*), 8, 10, 14, 59, 97, 100, 133, 135, 235, 236

"saving the phenomena," 8, 74, 235
phenomenology, 14, 15; Aristotelian, 10, 20, 23, 24, 30, 36, 74, 76, 79, 134, 142, 169, 190, 220, 221
Philolaus, 71–72
Phocylides, 207
Pieper, J., 223, 229, 235
Plato, 19, 26, 203, 220, 221, 229, 230, 231
platonic, 225
Platonists, 71
pleasure, 102–106, 141–42, 149, 176, 185–86, 192, 197
polis (city), 69, 110, 151, 190, 191, 196, 197, 201, 203, 208, as substance 211
politics, political, 40, 69, 110, 151, 156, 163, 171, 184, 189–216
politeia (regime; best form of government), 191, 194–95, 204, 205–207, 211, 230
Pope John Paul II, 109, 113, 225
Popper, K., 203, 213, 231, 235
potentiality (or power, *dunamis*), 32, 44, 61–62, 63, 67–69, 71, 74, 76, 90, 100, 101, 106, 110, 116–19, 119 ff., 126–28, 138–40, 142, 164, 172, 173, 178, 180, 187, 200, 209, 212, 224. *See also* actuality
practical wisdom (*phronêsis*), 124, 146, 147, 167, 168, 169, 170–73, 180, 181, 184, 192, 206, 228, 229. See also *sophia*
primary and secondary qualities, xvi, 120–25, 128, 147
principle of non-contradiction (PNC), 59–60, 93–96
Protagoras, 10, 220
psyche (*psuchê*), 26, 27, 28, 40, 63, 64, 70, 118–44, 152, 158, 160, 164, 166, 168, 169, 173, 178, 180, 182, 186, 192, 193, 198–200, 234, as actuality 105, 109, 110, 192, 198; definition 115–18; higher than inanimate beings 13, 27, 64, 68, 87, 109, 116, 124, 198; participation in eternity 64, 112; relation to *logos* 146
as soul: 215, 226
Putnam, H., 219
Pythagorean, 18, 22, 71–72, 135, 221, 224

Richardson Lear, G., 181, 229, 236
Rosen, S., 15, 220, 236
Rorty, A., 179–81, 229, 234–36
Rorty, R., 42, 222
Ross, D., 219, 222, 227, 233
Rushton, P., 202, 231

Schofield, M., 133, 227, 236
Sedley, D., 223, 224, 236
sense perception (*aisthêsis*), xiv, 4, 11, 45, 68, 73, 83, 89, 102–104, 106, 119–31, 131–33, 144, 155, 236
common-sense (*koinê aisthêsis*), 129–30, 227
Simplicius, 220
Socrates, 8–10, 90, 135, 223
sophia ([theoretical] wisdom), 82–84, 108, 160, 170, 173, 179, 182, 184, 229
Sophocles, 231
Sorabji, R., 226, 227, 236
Spinoza, 3, 6, 8, 12, 13, 20, 30, 44, 45, 52, 92, 219, 222
Stoppard, T., (see also *Arcadia*) xi–xiv, 4, 44, 126, 217, 219, 236
substance (*ousia*), 67, 84–98, 100, 101, 108, 109, 113, 124, 139, 179, 181, 186, 206, 225, 231, 234, primary and secondary 88–89; as substratum (*hupokeimenon*) 86, 90, 91; three kinds of

substance *(continued)*
98; *psyche* as 115–16; city as 211–12
syllogism, 25, 37, 38
syllogistic, 25, 100, 140
to "syllogize," 37, 42, 99, 141

ta pragmata (things, beings) 37, 100, 143
technê (art, artifice), 46, 56, 58, 82, 89, 146, 151, 183, 223
technology, 77–78, 126, 141, 190, 217
teleios (complete, perfect), 21–22, 22, 28, 35, 44, 62, 71, 74–75, 102–103, 153, 159, 160, 164, 166, 173, pleasure 104–105
teleology, teleological, xvi, 3, 4, 12, 13, 45, 49–57, 55ff., 67–71, 85, 92, 110–11, 110, 123–24, 127, 133, 152, 155–57, 187, 190, 196, 197, 199, 200, 201, 213, 223–24, 235, 236, critique of 12, 62–64. See also *telos*
telos (end, purpose, final cause), 22, 26, 35–37, 44, 45, 47, 63, 67, 69, 71, 74, 78, 84, 102, 104, 109–11, 113, 117, 124, 126, 152, 155, 160, 166, 171, 173, 176, 187, 189–90, 195–97, 199, 209, 212, 213–15, as final cause 50, 61, 75–76; relation to form or formal cause 62. *See also* actuality, form, nature, teleology
auto-telic, 209
Theophrastus, 140
theôria (study, theorize: verb *theôrein*), 10, 59, 60, 72, 74, 76, 104, 117, 131, 148, 169, 175, 178–87, 190, 208–10, 212–14, 223, 228, 229. See also *energeia* and *telos*
theory, (theoretical: *theorêtikê*), 106, 149, 173, 179, 182, 205, 213, 229, and practice 155–56, 160, 182, 183, 193; as way of life 194–95, 207
the highest good, 151ff., 160, 191f., 209
thinking (*noêsis* or *noein*), 59, 74, 106, 137, 179, 180, 185, 209. See also *nous*
time, 24–25, 40, 53–54, 64–67, 72, 74, 87, 89, 91, 94–96, 98–99, 103–104, as cause of destruction 65, 134; difference from motion 98–100
topos (place), 31–35, 69, 73, 124, 138, 201–204, 210
atopos (out of place, absurd, strange), 69, 204
to "truth" (*alêtheuein*), 21, 97, 144–48, 169, 170, 185, 234, 235

Virgil, xiii, 41
virtue *(aretê*, also "excellence"), 75, 149, 158, 167–71, 174, 183, 187, 191–93, 194, 201, 206, 210, 213

whole, 18, 21–29, 60–62, 74, 130, 155, 165–67, 206, 210–12, 228, cosmos as a 107–108, 140, 187, 215, 221; definition of 21; organisms 56, 58, 116, 119, 210–11, 223; pleasure as a 103, 142, 176. See also *teleios*
Wians, W., 220, 221, 236